TWEN'
WITH
ALZHEIMER'S DISEASE

Lowell Beach Sykes

Twenty Years with Alzheimer's Disease

ISBN: 978-1-4357-0382-7

Published by Lulu.com

Printed in the United States of America by Lulu.com

Distributed by Lulu.com

Front cover picture: Barbara Jean Powell and Lowell Beach Sykes, on their wedding day, September 4, 1955, in University Methodist Church, Salina, Kansas. "… to have and to hold from this day forward, for better for worse, for richer for poorer, in sickness and in health, to love and to cherish, till death us do part, according to God's holy ordinance…" This was their solemn vow.

TABLE OF CONTENTS

DEDICATION

TO THE GLORY OF GOD

and in honor of my wife

BARBARA JEAN POWELL SYKES

whose illness is the focus of this account,

for our adult children

Lowell Beach Sykes, Jr. (Laddie and his wife Gina), Richmond, Virginia

Charles Powell Sykes (Powell and his wife Kathy), Burlington, North Carolina

Mary Elizabeth Sykes Marcum (Mary Beth and her husband, Alan), Cookeville, Tennessee

whose invariable love and support have lightened our load and brightened our path throughout this journey,

and for

All whose lives are touched by Alzheimer's Disease

ACKNOWLEDGEMENTS

If I should attempt to name all the people who have helped us since Barbara became ill, I would have a book-sized document on that subject alone. Obviously I cannot do that. But I do wish to mention some groups and individuals who have shown extraordinary care for us as we have walked this difficult road. Some appear more than once because they were members of different groups which have come to our aid.

Charlotte Powell Shaffer, Barbara's sister, of Bunker Hill, Kansas, who has shown continuous love and concern;

The whole **Rivermont Presbyterian Church** (now Rivermont Evangelical Presbyterian Church) family who have prayed for us; the countless numbers of this remarkable body of believers who have brought us meals, some repeatedly; the many volunteers who have sat with Barbara as long as she was well enough for that to be possible;

Pam Ruble, a member of Rivermont Presbyterian, who has extended all kinds of practical help throughout these years and has been and continues to be a loving and devoted friend to Barbara;

My co-pastors at Rivermont Presbyterian Church, **Wayne Meredith** and **John Mabray**, without whose help I would have had to retire much sooner than I did;

Many others of our Rivermont Presbyterian Church family who have assisted us in various outstanding ways: **Greg Alty, Eleanor Atkins, Mary** and **Bill Bell, Betty Lynn Blanks, Terry Bright, Gary Brizendine, Liz Broyles, Jessie** and (the late) **LeRoy Burrows, Lucy Cardwell, JoAnne Caylor, Angie Coleman, Steve Cropper, Lori Davy, Joey Day, Beth** and **Ken Dunn, Shirley Embrey, Wilma** and **Joe Ernsberger, Brigetta** and **Curtis Eshleman, Judy Fairfax, Jill Fees,** (the late) **Carroll Freeman, Lerlyne Garcia, Statham Gilliam,**

Caroline and **Chip Godine**, (the late) **Frank Gough**, **Kay** and (the late) **John Happell**, **Dorcas Harbin**, **Alyce** and **Lionel Harrison**, **Janice Hatton**, (the late) **Shirley Hobbs**, **Becky** and **Allan Howerton**, (the late) **Barbara King**, **Heidi Lang**, **Pam Langley**, **Jean** and **Pat Markham**, **Todd Matthews**, **Mary** and **Jim McCann**, **Joan Menge**, **Prue Miller**, **Mary Kathryn** and **Franklin Moomaw**, **Diane** and **Jim Morgan**, **Gail** and **Paul Mudrick**, **Mary Muller**, **Christy** and **Bert Murphy**, **Darin Nelson**, (the late) **Elaine North**, **Claudia** and **Tulane Patterson**, **Linda Paulson**, **Paula Petrey**, **LoisAnn** and **Ed Pfister**, **Lois Porter**, **Dolly** and **Bill Pugh**, **Adriana Ribeiro**, **Anna** and (the late) **Ed Schaefer**, **Marie Seiger**, **Robin Smith**, **Dot Spencer**, **Mary** and (the late) **Joe Spencer**, **Sandra** and **Jay Spencer**, **Barbara Steadman**, **Ruth** and **Doug Stinespring**, **Cindy** and **Dan Sweeney**, **Mary Jane** and (the late) **Raine Sydnor**, **Connie Thacker**, **Shirl** and **Cliff Thomas**, **Becky Tweedy**, **Kay** and **Vic Uotinen**, **Beth** and **Hermann Ulrich**, **June** and **Eric Vess**, **Mildred Vess**, **Liz** and **Scott Wade**, **Corinne Ware**, **Teresa** and **Jay White**, **Kathy** and **Fred Whitten**, **Lori Widmeyer**, **Jane** and **Bill Wingfield**, and **Dianne** and **Jim Wright**;

Other friends: **Pat Brockman**, **Sybil** and **John Brown**, **Jean** and (the late) **Peter Brumby**, **Sandra** and **David Norman**, **Frances** and **Andy Sale**, **Starke Sydnor** and (the late) **Willia Wilkes**;

Our physicians and dentists who have gone to amazing lengths in their thoughtful, compassionate and skillful treatment of Barbara: **Greg Alty**, **Octavio de Marchena**, **Bill Gayle**, **Bill Hobbs**, **Paul Mudrick**, **Dwight Oldham**, **Bo Sorenson**, (the late) **Raine Sydnor**, **Scott Wade**, **Miles Wallace**, and **David Wilson**; Drs. Alty and Wade, for a number of years now, have come to our house to take care of Barbara's medical needs. Dr. Sorenson and his assistant, **Teresa Cheverton**, started doing Barbara's dental work in our home November 16, 2007.

Our lawyers, members of Rivermont Church, who readily have given expert advice and painstakingly have drawn up many documents: (the late) **Carroll Freeman** and **Dan Sweeney**;

My Thursday Morning Prayer Group, Rivermont Churchmen all: **Chip Godine**, (the late) **Frank Gough**, **Jay Hutt**, **Jim Morgan**, **Bert Murphy**, **David Simms**, **Scott Wade**, and **Massie Ware** (not all of these were in the group the whole time);

Barbara's and my twice monthly evening prayer group, all Rivermont folks: **Susan** and **Chris Burch**, **Bonnie** and **Bob Hazen**, **Amber** and **David Hoke**, **Meg** and **Rodney Laughon**, **Jane Miller**, **Adriana** and **Paulo Ribeiro**, and **Beverly** and **Ben Rosenthal**;

Our "Four Couples' Dinner Group," Rivermont people all, which met regularly every few weeks in a restaurant for an evening meal: **Pam** and **Richard Ruble**, **Ruth** and **Doug Stinespring**, and **Shirl** and **Cliff Thomas**;

My First Monday Discussion Group: **Sonny Culverhouse**, **Bill Gayle**, **Max Guggenheimer** and **Ed Lovern**;

All our faithful and dedicated professional caregivers who previously have worked or presently do work part-time with skill, love and kindness in our home, especially: **Faye Hughey**, **Sherri Lindstrom**, **Lorene Payne**, **Barbara Richerson** and the support staff at **Generations Solutions, Inc.** Of these caregivers, Lorene has been with us in this capacity the longest – from 2000 to the present.

Wanda Eubank Murphy has come a half day, at first every other week and for the past several years every week, to keep our house clean while looking after Barbara since 1995.

Gary Brizendine, a member of Rivermont Church, cut our grass until he moved out of town; then **Mike Shirey** took over.

Glenn Murphy for years has come to "fix things" at our house.

Eileen Lass, a member of Rivermont Church, did the proofreading for this book and made some editorial suggestions.

All these wonderful people, both those named above and many unnamed, have, I believe, been used by God to help fulfill his providential care of Barbara and me. So, in a real sense, they have become the hands of God to us. This is also true of many whose names I have never known, such as those who have invented, made, and distributed the equipment that makes it possible for us to care for Barbara at home. Martin Luther, making this point, observed that when Christians look to their Heavenly Father and pray, "Give us this day our daily bread," some people are already at work in the bakeries. The Apostle Paul was persuaded, and so am I, "My God will supply every need of yours according to his riches in glory in Christ Jesus" (Philippians 4:19).

INTRODUCTION

My wife Barbara Jean Powell Sykes and our family have been dealing with her Alzheimer's Disease about twenty years now. For some time I had thought a written account of all this might be of value to our children and grandchildren. Therefore, I went back to my daily journals and extracted the story of Barbara's decline so far. Although Alzheimer's Disease eventually does draw most of the family's attention to itself by the havoc it creates, it does not occur in a vacuum. Family life keeps moving on. Therefore, I also included the context by highlighting some of what was going on alongside and around us during these years. In addition, I had obtained copies of Dr. Scott Wade's medical records on Barbara, and, of course, I had my own memories. I gave that volume to our children a couple of years ago. Several friends have suggested that much of our story might be helpful to people outside our own immediate family whose lives are touched by Alzheimer's Disease. Since not many have experienced Alzheimer's for so long, given that fewer have kept daily journals as the disease has progressed, and fewer still have been able to care for the disabled person at home the whole time, I have agreed that my account might make a helpful contribution. So I have prepared this updated edition, omitting much of the family detail, with such a prospect especially in mind.

The most important thing to know about Barbara and me is that we are Christians. That is, we believe that we and all people are rebels against our holy and merciful Creator. God's divine nature is holy love – love which yearns over sinners while at the same time refusing to condone their sin. God solved this "problem" by substituting himself for us sinners in the person of his eternal Son Jesus Christ. What good news, "the power of God for salvation to everyone who believes" (Romans 1:16)! This is the Gospel, the Good News, "that Christ died for our sins in accordance with the Scriptures, that he was buried, that he was raised on the third day in accordance with the Scriptures" (1 Corinthians 15:3b,4). Now God calls all people everywhere to renounce their war against their Creator, embrace Jesus Christ by faith, receive the forgiveness of their sins and, out of gratitude for such a great salvation, seek to live according to God's will as it is revealed in Scripture. At early ages Barbara and I consciously trusted Jesus Christ as our Savior and have sought to serve him as our Lord. This was and is the core commitment of our lives.

Barbara is from Kansas. I grew up on Long Island, New York. We met when we were freshmen at Wheaton College in Illinois. We married three years later, when we were twenty-one. Barbara became an elementary school teacher, I a Presbyterian minister. When Alzheimer's Disease slithered into our family, our boys were adults, married and living elsewhere; our daughter was a college student; Barbara was teaching second grade in a public school; and I was a pastor in a large church.

In their later years my parents Ruth Beach Sykes and L. Claude Sykes moved to Lynchburg, Virginia to be near us. At first they lived in a house, then at Westminster Canterbury, a local retirement facility which offers (when appropriate) first "independent living," then, "assisted living," and finally "bed care." While it was always a joy to have Mother and Dad nearby, and in the early years of Barbara's illness Mother was able to help me some with Barbara, as Mother and Dad got older and their needs increased so did my duties toward them. I am the oldest of five children. By the time Mother and Dad located here one of my brothers had already died, the other brother lived in New York, and my sisters lived in California and South Carolina respectively. In our story I tell of my parents' declining health and deaths, because it is not uncommon, when debilitating disease strikes in middle age, for a person to be caring for a sick spouse and at the same time to have added responsibilities for aging parents.

Since all our children live far away and we have no other blood relatives anywhere near, many people from our church family have become like actual family to us and supported and helped us in all kinds of practical ways. I do not know what we would have done without our brothers and sisters in Rivermont Presbyterian Church, Lynchburg, Virginia (now Rivermont Evangelical Presbyterian Church). They have been marvelous!

It will be important for people who read this whose own families are experiencing Alzheimer's to realize that, although there are many similarities shared by Alzheimer's patients, each person's descent is unique in both the length of time it lasts and in the order of diminishments that come. There are also extreme variations in whether or not the sick person develops hostility towards the caregiver. A major problem for some is "wandering" (walking away from home and getting lost), while others do not do this at all. Some Alzheimer's patients experience "the terrors," while others do not. Alzheimer's Disease seems to run in some families, but for others it apparently pops up out of the blue. Most of the time, the younger a person is when Alzheimer's symptoms begin to show, the faster it progresses. But this is not invariable. Seizures sometimes accompany Alzheimer's Disease, but not always.

Some may feel, by telling our story, I am implying that unless they do for their loved one what I am doing for mine, they are dropping the ball and shirking their responsibility. I mean no such thing. In our case, I believe God has called me to and equipped me for this task. But obviously there are other ways people can be faithful to marriage vows. Circumstances vary widely. For example, a lady whose husband had Alzheimer's Disease telephoned me on one occasion. She was sobbing, "I ought to be able to do for him what you are doing for your wife, but I simply cannot handle him at home any longer." I was familiar with their circumstances and replied, "Of course, you can't. He is twice as big as you. You are not physically capable of giving him what he needs now. I think the time has come for you to place him in a nursing home." And she did with good conscience. In another situation of which I am aware, quite early in the husband's Alzheimer's Disease, he, who had been a gentle soul, became extremely combative with his wife. When she would attempt to assist him in dressing which he could no longer do for himself, he interpreted that as a physical attack and would begin to hit, bite and kick her. She became afraid of him, and for good reason. She had no choice but to put him in an institution. So, I assure my readers I have no wish to add guilt to already breaking hearts. We do the best we can in our diverse situations.

Frankly, I hesitate to reveal some of the messy details of this account to the public. (In fact, I did give veto power to our children over all I have included in this edition. Although they made some helpful suggestions, they did not ask me to withhold one thing.) I am naturally a private person and am not inclined to divulge the inner workings of my own or my family's life to strangers. I rarely used personal illustrations in my sermons. So if it were not for the possibility that it might help others going through similar difficulties, believe me, I would not publicly uncover some of these embarrassing things about my wife's Alzheimer's behavior. I hate to think what I might have been like if I had been stricken with this disease! Let me assure you, I mean absolutely no disrespect to my dear Barbara. I hold her in highest honor and esteem. And I have taken care of her in her time of great trouble not only because I believe God has called me to do it, not only because of our marriage vows, but because I love her more than I can say. She is still "my sweetheart!" I would never want to do anything that might cause anyone to think less of her. I have asked myself the question, "If I were the one incapacitated with an awful disease that stole my brain and therefore radically altered my behavior, would I object if ugly details were shared in order to help others?" And I know my answer would be, "No, not if you think it might aid anyone else. Tell the whole, true story if there is a possibility that it could be of assistance to anyone." And I feel sure my Barbara's answer would be the same.

Although Alzheimer's Disease paves a path of inexorable descent into fog, darkness and oblivion, for those who know Christ, there are, on this way, recurring shafts of light and joy. And even this road of sorrow, disappointment and grief ultimately leads the Christian to his or her final home where "God himself will be with them as their God. He will wipe away every tear from their eyes, and death shall be no more, neither shall there be mourning, nor crying nor pain anymore, for the former things have passed away" (Revelation 21:3c-4).

In the words of Christian F. Gellert (1757, Tr. by J. D. Lang, 1826):

Jesus lives, and so shall I,
Death! Thy sting is gone forever!
He who for me deigned to die,
Lives, the bands of death to sever.
He shall raise me from the dust:
Jesus is my hope and trust.

Jesus lives and reigns supreme,
And his kingdom still remaining,
I shall also be with him,
Ever living, ever reigning.
God has promised; be it must:
Jesus is my hope and trust.

Jesus lives! I know full well
Naught from him my heart can sever:
Life nor death nor pow'rs of hell,
Joy or grief, henceforth forever.
None of all his saints is lost:
Jesus is my hope and trust.

Jesus lives and death is now
But my entrance into glory.
Courage, then, my soul, for thou
Hast a crown of life before thee;
Thou shalt find thy hopes were just:
Jesus is the Christian's trust.

Now "we walk by faith, not by sight" (2 Corinthians 5:7). So "straighten up and raise your heads, because your redemption is drawing near" (Luke 21:28). To God be the glory!

Lowell Beach Sykes

Lynchburg, Virginia

Advent* 2007

Advent is a season set aside by many Christians during weeks that include the four Sundays before Christmas. *Advent* means *coming*. Referring to the coming or arrival of Jesus Christ there is a threefold meaning for the term *advent*: (1) The *Advent* of Jesus in the flesh at Bethlehem; (2) the *Advent* of Jesus by his Word and Spirit here and now; and (3) the *Advent* of Jesus when he returns bodily in glory at the end of the world. In churches where *Advent* is kept the sermons on the four Sundays before Christmas usually focus on these themes. The emphases that permeate are thanksgiving for and trust in the promises of God – for those God has already accomplished, for what he is doing now, and a yearning for the fulfillment of those he will yet bring to fruition.

Advent occurs (in the northern hemisphere) during the shortest days of the year. In the darkness we hear God calling, "Be comforted! Don't be afraid!" "The people who walked in darkness have seen a great light; those who dwelt in a land of deep darkness, on them has light shined… For to us a child is born, to us a son is given; and the government shall be on his shoulder, and his name shall be called Wonderful Counselor, Mighty God, Everlasting Father, Prince of Peace. Of the increase of his government and of peace there will be no end, on the throne of David and over his kingdom, to establish it and to uphold it with justice and righteousness from this time forth and forevermore. The zeal of the LORD of hosts will do this" (Isaiah 9:2, 6, 7).

One of Barbara's favorite hymns:

Face to face with Christ my Savior,
Face to face – what will it be –
When with rapture I behold him,
Jesus Christ who died for me?

Only faintly now I see him,
With the darkened veil between,
But a blessed day is coming
When his glory shall be seen.

What rejoicing in his presence
When are banished grief and pain,
When the crooked ways are straightened
And the dark things shall be plain.

Face to face! O blissful moment!
Face to face – to see and know;
Face to face with my Redeemer,
Jesus Christ who loves me so.

Refrain*: Face to face I shall behold him,*
Far beyond the starry sky;
Face to face in all his glory,
I shall see him by and by!

(Carrie E. Breck)

Chapter One: 1988 - 1990, EARLY SIGNS

In 1988, when Barbara was only in her mid-fifties, I began to notice her memory slipping. This was neither constant nor consistent so was easy for me to ignore. If I thought about it at all, I figured she simply had too much on her mind. But it was not like her. She was the one in our family who never had misplaced anything, rarely had forgotten anything and seldom had made mistakes. She had been the detail person in and the organizer of our home. She had always had a high energy level. Usually she was busy. She rarely "sat around." She could multi-task and do it all exceptionally well. She was both quick and thorough. This was how she managed to do an outstanding job as wife, mother, housekeeper, cook, second grade teacher in a public school, Sunday school teacher, and friend.

On the July 4th weekend of 1989 Barbara went to a church conference at Montreat, North Carolina, with a group from our church. She rode with our friend Marie Seiger in Marie's car. The others had traveled earlier in the church van. Barbara and Marie stopped on the way for a meal. Barbara ate from a cold salad bar. Marie had something else to eat. Two days after they got to Montreat, Barbara became violently ill. (No one else at Montreat got sick.) Barbara became dehydrated (which was not unusual for her when she had diarrhea), and had to be hospitalized in Asheville. When Wayne Meredith, my co-pastor, telephoned me to inform me of Barbara's condition, he said there was absolutely no reason for me to come, they were hydrating Barbara at the hospital, she was going to be fine, that he would stay an extra day with Barbara and Marie, and come home with them in Marie's car. I talked with Barbara on the phone and she agreed with Wayne that there was truly no need for me to come. Wayne and Marie had to leave by 4:00 PM. So if the Asheville doctor did not think Barbara ought to leave by then, I would drive down to be with her. Barbara did get stable enough to make the trip in time and they drove home without incident. (Wayne told me later that Barbara, who normally had reacted to challenges by conquering them, had seemed unusually frightened, full of panic and helpless during this episode. He had never seen her like that before.)

After Barbara got home she was not well. She kept having diarrhea and was tired all the time. Although she had planned to go to Kansas for a visit with her family that summer, she did not feel well enough to make the trip. She also missed a visit to our son Powell and his wife Kathy in Hallsville, NC, and my niece's wedding in New York. Our family physician discovered Barbara had picked up shigella, a bacteria most often found in third-world countries. Since no one else had gotten sick in Montreat, we figured she must have picked it up from the cold salad bar on the way there. Our doctor treated Barbara appropriately and before long tests showed she was free of shigella.

But it took Barbara a long time to regain her strength. Although she continued to teach school and Sunday School and keep up her regular things at home, she was exhausted most of that year. We began eating out for supper a lot. Most days she was simply too tired to get a meal together. And it was during that time that it became obvious that Barbara was not always thinking clearly. I attributed it to tiredness and weakness as a result of the shigella and was not overly worried at first. But before long, Barbara herself became concerned about her memory problems.

In the spring of 1990 Barbara had a very painful infection in both ears. One ear developed spontaneous drainage and the other was lanced by our Ear, Nose and Throat physician. He treated her with a two week course of Erythromycin but it seemed to cause abdominal cramping and diarrhea that became fairly severe. All of this made her extremely tired and did not help her ability to think.

During the summer of 1990 Barbara took a course to keep up her teacher certification (the sort of thing she had always done easily and well). She had to write a paper and simply could not get it together. She knew she had to get it done, but seemed to have no idea how to go about it. This produced a lot of anxiety in her. So I basically wrote the paper for her. I had always typed Barbara's papers (since our college days), but had never written them. This was a desperation measure.

While Barbara was on a trip to be with her sister in Kansas in the summer of 1990 she became so ill with a stomach upset she had to see a doctor out there. He insisted she postpone her departure for home at least a few days. She followed his advice, and her delayed flight home worked out fine.

Around this time one evening I was reading in the living room and Barbara was writing the weekly checks (as she normally did) at the den table. She came into the living room and said, "I can't get the answer," which was a school room way of putting it. "What do you mean,?" I asked. Again, "I can't get the answer." I asked her to show me. She handed me the check record book. She had entered in a bank deposit. Although she knew this should not be subtracted as a check would be, she simply did not know what to do. My heart froze, although I did not give a sign of my concern to her. "Oh, you just add it in," I said casually. She responded positively and went back into the other room. She returned shortly, crying, "I still don't know how to do it." Here was a lady who had taught hundreds of children how to add, subtract, multiply and divide. And she was unable to add a number into the column. I said, "Here, I'll do it for you." And I added it for her. She was greatly relieved. She took it back into the den, wrote checks and subtracted their amounts from the column. I went over it later that evening and found she had done it correctly. But I knew something was dreadfully wrong. Needless to say, I took over the regular check writing.

Then Barbara got it in her head that the doctor she had gone to for years in Lynchburg was not doing her any good with her thinking problems. When I pointed out to her that she had not told him anything about her confusion, what I said did not make sense to her. She wanted to go to another doctor! So she went to Scott Wade, a new, young physician in town who was a member of our church. Her first appointment with him was August 14, 1990. After doing a physical examination and finding nothing amiss, and hearing Barbara's story from both of us, Scott wanted to do a few further tests to see if he could get to the bottom of her frequent stomach upsets. He also suggested that she have an MRI to make sure she had not had a stroke and did not have a brain tumor. His opinion was that her memory problems were probably related to her frequent stomach upsets of the past year that caused a general exhaustion and also to her trying to do too much. Because of her age (she was only 56 by then) and her one illness after another the previous year, Dr. Wade did not think she had Alzheimer's. He suggested if I could relieve her of some of her responsibilities at home this might help clear her thinking. So I started doing more at home and we ate out almost every weekday evening.

A couple of months later Barbara was quite confused about where she was supposed to be for her Sunday School class. Later that same week she could not get straight when she had to get her hair done in order for us to leave for Bristol, Tennessee to visit our daughter Mary Beth who was in college there.

The October 8, 1990 issue of *Christianity Today* contained an article by Dr. Robertson McQuilkin, former president of Columbia (SC) Bible College, "Living by Vows." (This was later expanded and published as a book under the title A Promise Kept by Tyndale House in 1998.) I wept as I read it. Dr. McQuilken's wife Muriel, ten years before, had started showing symptoms of what turned out to be Alzheimer's Disease. The article came out shortly after McQuilkin had resigned his position with the college in order to take care of his wife full-time. From then on this article was always in my mind. Of course, at that time I did not know Barbara had Alzheimer's, but I feared she might. And if she did, when the time came, I knew I would feel called by God to step up to the plate as McQuilkin had done.

Dr. Wade thought it might be wise for us to see a neurologist. I readily agreed it would be good to have a second opinion regarding Barbara's thinking problems. I spoke with my good friend Harold Riley, a neurologist, about seeing Barbara. He told me he was planning to retire within a year and so would not be able to take care of Barbara long-term if that should prove necessary. Therefore he recommended we see a younger colleague of his, Miles Wallace. We made an appointment to see Dr. Wallace.

During October 21-23, 1990 I preached at West Parish Congregational Church, Haverhill, Massachusetts. It was good to be with Eleanor and Jim Gustafson again. We had been close friends since Wheaton College days. Jim had been my best man and Ellie had been the organist for our wedding and I had been in theirs a couple of months earlier. Jim had become the pastor of West Parish Church when he had finished Fuller Seminary in 1959. His solid evangelical ministry had been blessed by God and the church had come alive. They had invited me to be their guest preacher for a series of renewal services. I was glad to be able to talk frankly with these dear old friends about whatever it was Barbara and I were dealing with. I spoke of Dr. McQuilkin's article. Then I said, "Although Barbara is displaying some of the symptoms of Alzheimer's, I'm glad the doctor is quite certain it is not that." Of course, they were very supportive and expressed great concern for us.

On October 30, 1990 we kept our appointment with Dr. Wallace. He talked with us quite positively about Barbara's condition. He had gone over the tests Dr. Wade had ordered and felt Barbara's results were normal. Dr. Wallace agreed these examinations showed Barbara's memory problems were not caused by her having had a stroke or a brain tumor. Therefore, he thought the tests confirmed that Barbara's confusion (which had cleared up considerably during the previous month) was anxiety related to stress brought on primarily by her frequent stomach upsets the previous spring and summer and too much to do. He also guessed that Barbara might have some depression (although she did not feel depressed). I did not think it was depression, but I knew depression was a possibility because it can mask itself in unusual ways. And the fact that Barbara's thinking had improved (we estimated 50%, both Barbara and I confirmed this) during the previous month "proved" it could not be Alzheimer's Disease. "If a person has that there is no improvement," Dr. Wallace assured us. So he felt quite certain Barbara's problem was not organic. I was so relieved. At that point both Drs. Wallace and Wade believed there was no need for further evaluation. Of course, both of them said that if the symptoms worsened they wanted us to come back.

But this positive change in Barbara lasted only a few weeks. Soon I could detect further deterioration. In retrospect I suppose anyone can think more clearly when he or she is not overloaded. So when some of Barbara's burden had been removed her symptoms did improve for a brief time.

In the fall of 1990 Barbara was taking an Ecology class toward keeping up her teacher certification. This involved a field trip to some farms in rural Amherst County. Barbara was very anxious about it and said she wished I would go with her. She felt she needed me. I readily agreed to accompany her. By the time the day arrived (November 17th) my father was critically ill in the hospital. Should I stay to be a support to my mother or should I go and help Barbara? I went with Barbara. (And Dad lived another seven years!) Anyway, I think it turned out to be one of the happiest days of our lives. The field trip group had a canoe race across a lake. Mrs. Johnson who taught with Barbara (and had given our Mary Beth horseback riding lessons) got in the front end of a canoe with a paddle, Barbara sat in the middle, and I paddled from the back. And we won! Barbara shouted, jumped and clapped her hands with glee. It was a joy to see her so pleased, but also sad to see her acting so much like a little girl. On the way home, Barbara expressed appreciation to me for going with her. "I feel so secure when you are with me," she said. Here again, it pleased me to know I had pleased her, but it was quite unlike her to be so dependent. She had always been such a "can do," "take charge," strong person.

Years earlier my cousin Bob Sykes had said to me, "Do you know what has been a major strength of the Sykes family?" Then he answered his own question: "The men have had the good sense to marry strong women." He started illustrating this with our Sykes grandparents, then our parents and finally ourselves. And he was absolutely right. Our grandmother, our mothers, and our wives were intelligent, wise, creative, resourceful, capable, loving and generous; they were not weak or passive. They were people to be reckoned with. They got things done. They prized being "useful." They loved to help people. There "was not a lazy bone in their bodies." And Barbara had certainly fit that pattern.

For example, about a year after our marriage Barbara drove our car with a U-Haul trailer from Wheaton, Illinois, to Decatur, Georgia (where she had never been before), found and rented an apartment for us, and got a job teaching first grade. (The reason for this was that public school started three weeks earlier than my seminary did. Because we needed the money, I remained in Wheaton for that period to continue my summer job as a laborer on construction which paid well. In due time I traveled to Georgia on a Greyhound bus.) When our children were little Barbara, by herself, had taken them from Georgia where we then lived to Kansas for visits with her family several times. After we moved to Virginia she drove back to Georgia to see friends on various occasions. In 1983 she flew alone to Germany to support some dear friends who had experienced a family tragedy.

But by 1990, a one day field trip with people she knew had become very unsettling. What was happening to her?

Chapter Two: 1991, Alzheimer's Disease Diagnosed

During 1991 Barbara would often get things mixed up and then get angry with me because I had not done what she thought she had asked. (But she had not asked.) It was frustrating for both of us. For example, I had been at an overnight church related meeting at Hat Creek near Brookneal (about 40 miles from home). When I got back to Lynchburg Barbara was at school teaching. Later in the day she telephoned from school, furious because I had not communicated with her that I had gotten back. I had never called her at school for anything other than an emergency nor would she have wanted me to. When I pointed this out she retorted that she had especially asked me to let her know this time. But she had not. I was puzzled and upset. I felt abused.

Shortly before Mary Beth went back to college near the end of August, 1991 she came into the kitchen where Barbara was trying to follow a recipe. Barbara asked Mary Beth how to measure things. Later Mary Beth said to me, "Oh, Daddy! I don't see how in the world Mama is going to teach school this year. She is so mixed up!" I suggested to Barbara that she might want to retire, but she insisted she really wanted to teach.

Barbara had felt somewhat apprehensive about school that fall because the principal under whom she had worked happily for the prior sixteen years had retired in the spring. Barbara, with "little-girl worries," expressed uncertainty about whether the new principal would like her and appreciate her work. This uncertainty in itself was a significant sign. She had never before had doubts about the acceptability of her work at school.

On Wednesday, August 28, 1991, during the teachers' orientation week before the children started coming, one of Barbara's colleagues telephoned me. She expressed great concern for Barbara. She had observed that Barbara was quite confused that morning at school about where she was supposed to be. She said it had been quite bad the previous spring, she had almost had called me then, but had thought Barbara must simply have been tired. Now, at the beginning of school, she said it seemed to her like Alzheimer's Disease. I wrote in my journal, "I feel so sad! The burden is not only what we will do in the long run, but how do I deal with it now? How do I raise it with Barbara now without hurting her? Barbara had said before she left for school that she felt very apprehensive and full of stress. We had a special time of prayer together about it. Lord, this feels lonely and scary. Give me understanding, courage and strength."

That evening when I asked Barbara about her day at first she did not mention any problem. When I pressed a little more she did say that she had worked in her room, the time had gotten away from her and she had missed the ride to the county teachers' meeting with the other teachers. The Amherst County School Board offices had moved to another building that summer and she had not been sure she could find it (she had not been there before). "I felt panic, but another teacher said she had to go over there anyway, and would take me. I got there just as the refreshments were over, but the main part of the meeting hadn't started," she said. All that made sense to me. I wondered if the teacher had based her call to me more on what had happened the year before than what had happened the day before.

On Saturday of that week Barbara and I went to buy some school supplies. She was looking forward to having the children return to her classroom after the summer vacation. They would be coming in three days, the Tuesday after Labor Day.

On that day Barbara came home from school devastated. The children had arrived. And Barbara had not known what to do. She was frightened and exhausted. "I've always been a good teacher," she sobbed. "But now I don't know what I'm supposed to do!" Her anguish reached to her depths.

Barbara did not sleep at all that night. She could not go to school the next day. She was shaking and her legs hurt. She saw Scott Wade. He called me before she saw him. I told him I really felt she needed to stop teaching. Scott did not find anything physically wrong with Barbara. But he recognized the high anxiety she was experiencing. He recommended to her that she stop teaching. At that point she was ready at least to consider that advice. Scott encouraged Barbara to have neuropsychological testing (which Dr. Wallace could arrange) to further evaluate memory loss and possible early dementia. Barbara asked me to telephone the Superintendent of Schools in Amherst County to see what the procedure would be if she did decide to quit teaching. He told me she would need to see the head of personnel whose office was in Amherst.

Barbara and I had planned to go out for a nice dinner that evening to celebrate our 36th wedding anniversary, but she did not feel like it. In long conversation she expressed her love for teaching. But she realized she could no longer do her best for the children. She asked if I would mind if she stopped teaching. I assured her that I would not, in fact reminded her that I had been encouraging her to stop for some time. She was concerned that she would get in trouble with the school board for breaking her contract. (She had always had a keen sense of duty!) I expressed a certainty that there would be no negative consequences from them when they became aware of her problem. So she decided to stop teaching. She seemed very relaxed and started talking about all the things she would then have time to do. Of course, I was very pleased that she seemed so happy about it. But I knew the next day would be hard when she had to tell the folks at school. I was so glad she was able to make her own decision. I had been afraid that one day the principal would call her in and say something like, "Mrs. Sykes, you have been an outstanding teacher in the past. But now you seem unable to do your job effectively. You need to stop immediately." Of course, I would have not blamed her principal for this; he would have had no choice. But it would have been devastating for Barbara.

I made an appointment for Barbara to see the personnel director for the Amherst County school board at her office in Amherst. Barbara asked me to go with her. "And please do the talking for me. I get so mixed up now." I reminded Barbara that the only way it would make sense to the personnel director would be if I were very frank about what the problem was. "Yes," she agreed. "You need to tell her the whole story."

So I told the personnel director about Barbara's physical problems of the past two years, starting with the shigella at Montreat in July of 1989. And I was frank about her thinking problems down through when the children came to school that week, and Dr. Wade's recommendation that she stop teaching. I knew I had to do this, but I hated it. I felt as if I were stripping my wife in front of a stranger. But the personnel director was very supportive and helpful. Although I had not so much as given a thought to disability benefits, the personnel director raised the possibility, told me how to get started and encouraged me to begin the process. I think both Barbara and I left feeling better than we had felt before we got there. We stopped by the school where Barbara had taught to see the new principal. I also told him the whole story. He too was very kind and supportive. Then Barbara talked with the other two second grade teachers with whom she had worked so closely for seventeen years. There were warm hugs shared and hot tears shed by all three of them.

All this took most of the afternoon. I was so glad I was able to "be there" for Barbara. She said when we got home, "I felt so supported by you, like you were taking care of me, but not making my decisions for me." We talked about all this most of the evening. Barbara seemed quite relieved. I was very thankful she was doing so well.

The following week I got Barbara's disability applications done, one for Social Security, the other for the Virginia Supplemental Retirement System Benefit Program. I filled them out as if she were writing, but this was way beyond her ability by then. I had her approval for what I was doing, but she took no interest in it.

"List your job duties," demanded the form. "All the job duties of second grade: planning the daily classroom work, teaching the material, being sensitive to special needs, loving the children and conveying that love, consultations with parents, playground duty, lunch room duty, bus duty, lunch money, record-keeping, planning and making attractive bulletin boards, evaluating the children's progress, grading papers, being flexible, yet keeping on track."

"Which of your duties listed above can you not perform and why?" "I can no longer perform any of them because of periods of confusion in my own mind and the resulting panic I feel. I needed and received help from others last year in doing the lunch money, attendance records, and year-end reports. On the first day the children came to school this fall (9-3-91) my mind simply would not work right. I knew I could no longer teach, although I have been an excellent teacher and have always loved it. My doctor urged me to stop trying to teach when I saw him the next day (9-4-91).

"What do you consider to be your disability?" "Periodic mental confusion, inability to concentrate and a feeling of being overwhelmed by anything new."

"Has your doctor told you to restrict your activities in any way?" "Yes. My doctor, Dr. Scott Wade, has urged me to stop teaching."

"Are your home duties, social activities or abilities to care for your personal needs limited?" "Yes. I used to be a very efficient homemaker. I loved to plan meals, cook, clean and entertain, kept a meticulous checkbook, never lost things, had everything organized. All of this has deteriorated within the past year and a half. At this point I cannot fill out this form without my husband's help."

"Occasionally I used to drive by myself on long trips. I could not think of doing that now. I still drive to the grocery store and to church (which are close to where we live). The last time I drove to the mall (which is further but very familiar to me) I got lost, so I don't do that anymore."

Barbara and I got her papers signed (she signed) and notarized and then went to Amherst to give them to the personnel director. I was glad Barbara seemed happy, but felt a deep grief at her loss of "grip" on things. I loved her so much. I was very concerned about the future, but not afraid. After all, we were in the Lord's hands, and he would supply our needs.

Later that week I was amazed to discover when I got home Barbara had told our one-day-a-week helper we would not need her any more. She had worked for us for the past sixteen years, as long as Barbara had taught at Amelon. And this sweet lady had done a great job in our home with cleaning and ironing. When I asked Barbara why she had let her go she said, "Well, we got her when I started teaching. I did need some help with the housework then. But now I'm not teaching, so I don't need her." I asked Barbara if she didn't think she could use the help. She said that she could take care of things at home herself now!

Soon after this at a meeting of the elders of our church I shared with them about Barbara's condition. I told them if they left a message for me with her, it would be unlikely I would receive it. She simply could not remember most of the time. They had special prayer for her.

A few days later when I got home Barbara was quite upset because she had read the copy Scott Wade had sent to me of his letter to the Virginia Retirement System as a part of the application for disability. There was nothing in the letter that was a surprise to me, but I don't think Barbara had "put it all together" before. The word "dementia" and the possibility of Alzheimer's seemed to bother her most. I think she felt better when I emphasized to her that in a letter supporting a disability claim a "worst-case scenario" is presented much as a doctor is required to do before you have surgery. Scott's letter was very strong.

The third week Barbara cried quite a bit. I think she was almost numb the first two weeks after she stopped teaching. Now she was really feeling it. I felt so sorry for her. I wished I could "fix" it for her, but I couldn't. We talked and talked. Although I believe I masked this from her, I felt so sad! I think I was grieving as I would have if she had died. My mind was on Barbara and her illness all the time unless I was actively engaged in something else. And then my thoughts would come right back to Barbara. I went to sleep thinking about her and her situation. I dreamed about her. I woke up thinking of her. Something awful was happening to my wife! And there seemed to be nothing I could do to change that. Would I be up to what might lie ahead? I prayed so. But I thought it might be more than I could handle spiritually, physically, emotionally, financially. What then? I felt a literal weight in my chest.

In early October I took Barbara to the Social Security interview for disability. The lady who did the interview spent almost an hour and a half with us and did a very good job. Barbara afterward remarked about how nice she was and how efficiently she did her work.

In mid-October I took Barbara to be tested by Dr. Jeffrey T. Barth at the Neuropsychology Laboratory, University of Virginia Health Sciences Center in Charlottesville. It was an all day event and was very strenuous for Barbara. She was exhausted by the end of the procedure.   In conversation with Barbara, Dr. Barth had found that she could not name either of our boys nor did she know their birthdays, how old they were, or how old she was. (I thought the stress of the test had, at least in some measure, "shut her down." For example, she usually did know our boys' names and continued to for quite a while after this.) As Dr. Barth talked with Barbara, she did know her birthday and the year she was born.   Before we left, even before the results of the tests were compiled,   Dr. Barth told me, among other things, "I don't know if you have applied for disability or not. If not, I hope you will. And if you need any more supporting evidence for disability, I will be glad to supply it. Your wife, obviously, cannot work."

I had not realized Barbara had become this disabled. Poor thing! It broke my heart! What anguishing stress she must have been under. How in the world had she functioned at all that last school year? Sheer, dogged determination, and a lot of help from one of her fellow second grade teachers, Pat Brockman. I did not know it then, but found out later that the previous year Barbara had been unable to do her paperwork for lunch money, attendance records, report cards and year end reports. Pat essentially had done it and had covered for her, thinking Barbara's confusion had been caused from exhaustion from her illnesses and that Barbara would recover her old abilities as soon as she got over her stomach upsets.

The following day Barbara and I talked most of the morning. She was very threatened by the testing in Charlottesville. Barbara said, "I feel like such a burden on you. You are so busy and you have to spend all this time filling out forms for me and taking me for tests." I assured her that I did not feel that way at all and, of course, I didn't. I just wanted to help her in any way I could.

On November 1st Dr. Wallace (our neurologist) gave Barbara and me the report from the Charlottesville tests Barbara had taken three weeks earlier. Those tests showed conclusively that her symptoms were grounded in her physiology, not her psychology. (Dr. Wallace said to me, "So Lowell, you were right and I was wrong about this." I had thought all along this was not being caused by psychological disturbance; he had been inclined to think it was.) Dr. Wallace wanted to do more physical tests. These were all scheduled for the following week.

The next week Barbara had a spinal tap, more blood work and an EEG. We would not get the results until November 20^{th,} and the report on Lyme Disease (from the spinal tap) would take a week longer than that.

At Evening Worship November 10th we had a hymn festival. I had an especially blessed experience as the choir sang the anthem version of the hymn "Beautiful Savior" as a response to the Benediction. That had been a favorite hymn for me since my youth, so I was looking forward to hearing it once again. But I was not prepared for what happened to me. (I must say I am not one given to unusual, emotional spiritual experiences.) As the choir sang I thought my heart would break with the joy of adoration as in my mind's eye I caught a glimpse of the Lord Jesus Christ in glory and this was mixed with my sadness about Barbara. Tears were pouring down my face. But it seemed the Lord was understanding and ministering to me, coming to me across the bridge of my pain, so that the sorrow itself was caught up and purified as I offered it to him who is:

"Beautiful Savior! Lord of the nations,

Son of God and Son of man.

Glory and honor, praise, adoration

Now and for evermore be thine!

I wished it would never end. But, of course, it did. I went to the door of the church and greeted the congregation as they left the service (which was my custom). After I got home I suddenly realized that the weight in my chest was gone. And, although naturally I have been very concerned about Barbara all these years, that awful weight of grief has never returned. What a gracious gift from the Lord!

On November 19th I took Barbara to the Parent-Teacher Association meeting at Amelon School where she was honored for her years of teaching there. They presented her with a silver tray and several people said some very nice things about her and her work. She looked so beautiful! Just seeing her, one would have had no idea her brain was failing. She was as attractive as ever. Everyone was very kind. Barbara cried some. I wished I could shield her from the pain of all this, but that was impossible. I could let her know that I was alongside her, but I could not remove the hurt of this diminishment for her. She was a born teacher. She had loved it and had excelled at it. To give this up, even though absolutely necessary, was giving up an important part of herself.

On November 20th Barbara and I had an interview with Miles Wallace, our neurologist. All her tests turned out negative, and the

EEG showed some area of below-average electrical activity which was incontrovertible evidence that the problem was physical. So Dr. Wallace told us Barbara had "premature aging of the brain or Alzheimer's Disease." He said we could expect it to get worse. Barbara and I ate lunch at Shoney's. She said, "You don't think he thinks I have Alzheimer's do you?" (She had been present and heard every word he had said.) I said, "He didn't say that. And you remember the doctor in Charlottesville said that although he couldn't rule out Alzheimer's, for two or three reasons he did not really think it was that." She replied, "Oh, that's good," and seemed to dismiss it. She also asked, "What do you think he meant by saying I would get worse?" I replied, "He also pointed out that everyone has some brain slowdown as he or she gets older." That seemed to put the matter to rest for her. I felt so sad. In the words of Job, "What I feared has come upon me; what I dreaded has happened…" (Job 3:25).

The next day I asked Dr. Wade if he could suggest to me about how long we might have before Barbara sank into oblivion. He said that varied greatly (from one to twenty years) and they would not hazard a guess for a particular patient. But he did advise doing things sooner rather than planning on having much of a "later." I felt sort of numb. I had both profound sadness and a deep sense of God's love, care and concern.

Barbara told me that she had seen Alyce Harrison, a dear friend. "I told her all it about it," Barbara said. "Alyce said she was so glad to know it is not Alzheimer's which she had been concerned about." Barbara must have told Alyce that. I knew I needed to try to straighten out Barbara's thinking on this issue, but not necessarily right away.

The following Sunday Barbara told me when I got home after the evening service that the person sitting next to her had laughed because Barbara had asked for help in finding the hymn. "I know she doesn't know anything is wrong with me, but she laughed at me!" I wanted to cry. It was as if a little girl had come home and cried, "Daddy, she laughed at me!" Only this was even more sad than it would have been if Barbara had been a little girl. I tried to help

Barbara by saying, "You know, if a healthy adult said to you, 'I can't find the hymn,' you would think she was joking if you didn't know anything was wrong. I'm sure she thought you were joking. She certainly didn't mean to hurt you." I'm not sure my rational explanation helped at all.

The day before Thanksgiving I received a letter from Dr. Wallace addressed to me at the church. He enclosed a couple of brochures about Alzheimer's Disease and said he deliberately had spoken in a veiled way when he had talked with Barbara and me Wednesday. He had picked up that she was very frightened of the word, "Alzheimer's," so he had not seen any point in burdening her with that term. But he thought her diagnosis was "probable Alzheimer's Disease." The reason for the word "probable" was that there was no way to positively identify that disease in a living person. (An autopsy would prove it for sure. Of course, that could not be done while a person was alive.) But when they had eliminated everything else that could cause dementia "probable Alzheimer's Disease" was what was left. Until I received this communication I had thought Dr. Wallace had meant that Barbara had either premature aging of the brain or Alzheimer's Disease. But this letter made plain he was using the terms, not as alternatives, but as synonyms. Alzheimer's Disease seems to run in some families. But, so far as anyone knew, no one else in Barbara's family had showed symptoms of having it.

Pam Ruble, a dear friend of Barbara, roasted a Thanksgiving turkey for us. Barbara planned that as a surprise for me. Laddie (home from his job with a bank in Roanoke) and Mary Beth (home from college in Bristol, Tennessee) did the rest of the cooking. I made cranberry sauce from fresh cranberries.

On Thanksgiving morning I preached at Rivermont Presbyterian from Habakkuk: "Though the fig tree does not bud and there are no grapes on the vines, though the olive crop fails and the fields produce no food, though there are no sheep in the pen and no cattle in the stalls, yet I will rejoice in the Lord, I will be joyful in God my Savior… The Sovereign Lord is my strength, he makes my feet like the feet of a deer, he enables me to go on the heights (3:17-19). I felt especially anointed and involved. I ended the sermon by quoting the hymn, "Beautiful Savior." After the service one of the ladies hugged me tight. I did not remember her doing that before. I knew she was reading between the lines of my sermon into my life situation. Many expressed appreciation. My co-pastor Wayne Meredith said, "I have some idea of how much that cost you."

Of course, I told our children about their mother's diagnosis. All of them offered to either move nearer or come back home in order to help with Barbara. We were and are blessed with great children!

Throughout the day I kept thinking that might be the last Thanksgiving when Barbara was at all aware. And that the Christmas coming up might be the last when she was "with" us in any meaningful sense.

The day after Thanksgiving while Barbara was getting her hair done I sat down with our three children. I expressed great appreciation to them all for offering to change their lives drastically in order to help me with their mother. "But," I said, "I don't want you to do that. This is primarily my responsibility. And I will do it the best I can. Of course, if something were to happen to me, then you would have to take charge of your mother's life. She could not possibly manage by herself. I hope that doesn't happen, but we never know."

Barbara and I started grocery shopping together. Buying groceries was new to me. It seemed to take me forever to find anything! I hoped the more I did it, the easier it would get.

Since the words, "Alzheimer's Disease," were so intimidating to Barbara, when referring to her disability we said, "premature aging of the brain," which seemed much less threatening to her. According to Dr. Wallace, they meant exactly the same thing. Sometimes we called it merely *the problem*.

On Christmas Eve our church was full for both the 5:00 PM and 11:00 PM services. I preached at 5:00 PM and my colleague Wayne Meredith at 11:00 PM.

Barbara had always fixed Christmas stockings for the family. But Mary Beth did it that year. Mother, Dad (who lived in Lynchburg) and my sister Sarah (from South Carolina) came. We opened our gifts together.

When Barbara opened her cranberry goblets and dishes she exclaimed with glee, "My cranberry! My cranberry! My cranberry!" She started laughing and clapping her hands. My mother said she had never seen Barbara so excited about anything. Tears came to my eyes as I saw her "little-girl-like" pleasure. That was exactly what I had hoped to accomplish with this gift. That night Barbara called her sister Charlotte to tell her about her Christmas. Barbara later informed me when she told Charlotte about the cranberry and the number of pieces Charlotte said, "Wow! That was a really nice gift." Barbara said Charlotte's mouth dropped open, although I did not know how she could have observed that over the phone!

Barbara had gotten quite interested in cranberry and ruby glass through her sister Charlotte. This became a new hobby that continued to give her pleasure. Before the previous July I do not think we had been inside an antique shop. But we were stopping at them frequently by this time. And she was able to find things she liked. She enjoyed the search. At that point she had no idea of the value of money. So if she saw something she was drawn to she would say to me, "And it's not very expensive, is it?" I told the children I could not afford to keep this up indefinitely, but I figured her ability to enjoy it would not last long, so I wanted to indulge her passion as long as she could sustain it. There were some nice antique shops on the way to and in Bristol, Virginia/Tennessee where Mary Beth was at King College, and also on the way to Beulaville, North Carolina where Powell was a pastor.

We had a delicious roast beef Christmas dinner. Barbara and Laddie (mainly Laddie) did the roast beef and I had made the pickled peach-orange gelatin salad. Barbara served the beef and carrots, potatoes and onions in a large Christmas serving/baking dish I had given her for Christmas. She used the cranberry goblets and dessert dishes and the English Wedgwood china. She was very pleased with the way the table looked and the food tasted.

The day before New Year's Eve Barbara and I left for Kathy and Powell's. We stopped in Hillsboro, NC and found an antique mall we had not known about and spent about three hours there. Barbara found some very good cups and saucers to her Autumn Leaves set. I found another cranberry dessert plate and a cranberry decanter. We arrived at Powell and Kathy's about 3:30 PM. Kathy had a great dinner. Our three-year-old grandson Chad showed us his toys. He and Barbara had a great time coloring together.

We left about 11:00 AM on New Year's Eve day and had lunch in Hillsboro at the Colonial Hotel Restaurant. It was very good. Then we looked around a little more. We stopped at an antique store on Route 29 near Altavista and bought a cranberry decanter set. We arrived back home about 5:00 PM.

Chapter Three: 1992

Early in January in my regular course of Bible reading I came to the passage in Mark 5:25-34 about the woman who was healed by touching the hem of Jesus' garment. I prayed that the Lord would heal Barbara.

In mid-January I told Barbara that I thought I ought to drop out of my Doctor of Ministry program so I would have more time to be with her. She would not hear of it. She wanted very badly for me to finish. So I guessed I would even though, with all we had gone through, I had lost my zest for it. But since my congregation had been so supportive of this program, I felt I really owed it to them to get the degree, especially since I was so near the finish line. I was due to complete the work in the spring.

I called to let Powell and Kathy know Barbara would not be going to stay with them the week I was at Hat Creek (taking a D. Min. course). She was terribly nervous about being away from home unless I was with her.

When I came in from grocery shopping Barbara was sitting on the couch in the den with her Bible in her lap. And she was crying. I asked her what was wrong. "I can't find anything," she sobbed. "What do you mean?" She had a little devotional booklet which recommended that she look up and read a particular Bible passage. But she could not do it. "I can say the books of the Bible, but I can't find anything in the Bible," she said. I asked, "Can you say the books of the Bible for me?" And she said them in perfect order, from Genesis to Revelation. But she would turn the pages back and forth, making no progress. She did not know which way to turn pages in a book, so turned this way and then that way. Sequencing had become impossible for her. (Later I told Dr. Wallace about this. He shook his head and said, "Isn't it amazing, that she can remember the books of the Bible in order that she learned so well as a child?")

She had a similar problem with the thermostat for the furnace. The numbers no longer made sense to her. She did not know whether to turn the temperature wheel to the right or to the left to make it more warm or cold. So I bought gas logs. And she could operate them for about three years because she could see whether the flame went up or down.

In early March Barbara received her first disability check from the State Retirement System, the retroactive pay for November through February. She was very glad to have it. She had been approved for disability for both the Virginia Retirement System and Social Security.

Barbara wanted to get a new vacuum cleaner (including all the attachments) with some of this disability money. So at our invitation a salesman came by the house to show us a new vacuum cleaner and carpet shampoo equipment. We bought it all. Barbara thought the upright vacuum cleaner would make house cleaning much easier for her.

Sinclair Ferguson, from Scotland, was teaching at Westminster Seminary in Philadelphia. He had preached for us at Rivermont Presbyterian Church several times. In response to my inquiry, he said he had found someone who would like to do a pulpit exchange with me: The Reverend Peter Brumby, pastor of the Evangelical Church in Whitby, North Yorkshire, England. He told me how to get in touch with Peter. (A pulpit exchange between pastors who live a sea apart usually involves exchanging pulpits, that is, each preaching in the other's church, and using each other's houses and cars for typically a month. So the major expenses of such a trip are getting to and from the other country, then buying food, and finally purchasing fuel for the car. By having a free place to stay and the free use of a car, it becomes a much less expensive journey.)

In mid-March Barbara and I spent most of an afternoon getting ready for our Hospitality Dinner. (This was a program our church had initiated in order for people to get to know one another better. Groups of four couples were assigned to each other for a dinner each quarter for a year. The dinner was held in turn by one of the couples at their house. The host-hostess were responsible for the main dish and drinks, the other couples brought the salad, vegetable and dessert.) Barbara and I had lasagna and set the table with the English china and cranberry things. I sat where Barbara had usually sat (at the end of the table nearest the kitchen) and she sat nearest the front window. I did this so I could serve the table and get things from the kitchen when needed. The lady of one of the couples (who knew nothing about Barbara's illness) teased her husband in front of the rest of us about taking a lesson from me on how to help with a dinner. Afterwards I took her aside and explained why I was doing it all. She was most sympathetic. Her mother-in-law had Alzheimer's Disease. Barbara and I finished cleaning up about 11:00 PM.

Peter Brumby could not work out a trip to America the following summer. But he wanted very much to do it the year after that (1993). So we made plans to do it then. I hoped Barbara would still be able to. I explained our situation to him. His wife Jean and their three children who were almost grown would plan to come. They wanted to do it before their children started leaving home so the whole family could come together.

At the end of March Barbara and I went to King College where Mary Beth was a student. The chapel service, held in the gymnasium, was very moving. A group acted out Jesus on the Via Dolorosa stumbling under the cross and then being placed on the cross. Mary Beth and two other girls sang a trio. It was beautiful. They passed out nails to give to people in pain or people who had helped you with your pain. One of the girls who had sung with Mary Beth and Mary Beth came to us. There were lots of tears and hugs, and a powerful sense of love. The presence of the Lord was in that place!

While in Bristol, we were riding along in the car, and neither Mary Beth nor I could remember the name of the hotel where we had stayed in Jerusalem in 1987. Barbara said, "It was the King Solomon Hotel." And it was!

In mid-April Barbara said to me, "What in the world would happen to me if something should happen to you?" I replied that we would go and talk with Carroll Freeman who was a close friend, an outstanding lawyer, and an elder in our church. We talked with Carroll. Displaying his usual compassion and expertise, he laid out for us what authority Barbara needed to sign over to me in order for me to take care of her properly and also what we needed to do to provide for Barbara if I should become incapacitated or die. We agreed and he said he would draw up the necessary papers.

By the end of April my wife had dementia and my mother was dealing with my father's latest heart attack which left him only about one half normal blood-pumping capacity, so he was not getting enough blood to his brain and was, therefore, confused much of the time. I tried to support them, care for them and pray for them.

Powell and Kathy were visiting us. When I went to tell them and their family 'goodbye' before they left to go home, I was surprised to find Powell had cut the grass for me. I knew he hated to cut grass. In fact, I was so stirred that tears came to my eyes. I wondered why. As I thought about it I realized how moved I was to have him pitch in to help me. I had been giving a lot to help others, and was glad to. But no one had seemed to be aware of my need for help. Not that I had been feeling sorry for myself. I had not been thinking along these lines at all. But Powell's kindness reminded me of my own needs of which I had not been aware before.

On Sunday morning, May 3rd I preached the Baccalaureate Sermon at King College in the chapel. It was good to see Barbara with Laddie, Powell, Kathy and Christie, one of Kathy and Powell's daughters, (Jodie, their other daughter, had kept Chad, their four-year-old son, back at the little house where Barbara and I were staying), and Mary Beth, of course, was sitting with her graduating class.

In early June Barbara, Mary Beth and I left in our car for Chicago where I was to receive my Doctor of Ministry degree from

McCormick Theological Seminary.   The ceremony was in the University of Chicago Rockefeller Chapel. What an impressive place! I remembered going to an organ recital there when I had been a student at Wheaton.

On our way to Kansas to visit Barbara's family we stopped for the night in Columbia, Missouri. As I came out of the motel office after checkout the following morning I was smiling. As I got into our car Barbara said, "You're smiling. Did you hear what I said to Mary Beth when you came out the door?" I replied, "I couldn't have heard it because the car windows were closed." She said, "Well, when I saw you come out the door I said to Mary Beth, 'There is the best man in the whole wide world!'" I took her hand and squeezed it and said, "You're the best woman for me in the whole world too!" We were so blessed to feel that way after almost 37 years of marriage!

In Kansas Charlotte, Barbara's sister, took us to several antique shops and auctions. Barbara had a ball! We bought a number of cranberry pieces, and we purchased some other things from Aunt Abbie (who dealt in antiques) in Newton. Michael Blanke, Charlotte and Everett's son-in-law, brought his paddle boat over and put it on Everett's pond. Barbara squealed with delight as she rode in the boat.

We stopped at quite a few more antique shops. We also went to a discount coat store. Barbara urged me to get a London Fog all-weather coat, so I did. She was so excited about it!

Back in Lynchburg, we went to the wedding of Amy Ruble and David Sanderlin. During the reception at the Oakwood Club as we were circulating Barbara got ahead of me. She was fine. I could see her talking with David Simms, a good friend and elder in our church. By the time I had gotten up to David, Barbara had moved on to talk with someone else. David shook his head. "I just had the nicest conversation with Barbara," he said. "If I didn't know differently, I would think nothing is wrong with her."

In mid-July Julie and Don Gamewell and their six foot, six inch 16-year-old son Zane came for a visit. Don and I had been young people in the same church back home on Long Island. He was a year older than I and had gone to Wheaton College. It was largely because of his strong recommendation I had gone to Wheaton the following year. I had not seen Don since 1960 and had never met his wife and son (they lived in Washington State). By the time of this visit, because it made Barbara so nervous to have overnight company (except our own children) I had arranged for the Gamewells to stay in a motel. Barbara had always been a most gracious hostess. But by then she felt such distress because she was not able to do what she still knew a hostess needed to do for company, I no longer had people spend the night in our home. (Barbara was not aware of this.)

In early August I was in conversation with Neil Dunnavant, pastor of the Fincastle Presbyterian Church. He told me a lady in their town who had had symptoms like Barbara's only much worse had been greatly helped with a new medicine, Cognex, which she got through a program at the University of Virginia. He thought I might like to look into it. Of course, he was right! I did want to see if there might be help for Barbara there.

Barbara and I stopped in Wytheville at Snoopers Antique Mall. Barbara was delighted when she found on her own (I was looking at something else in another aisle) some Virginia Rose, the dishes that Mother had had all through my time at home and that now my sister Sarah was collecting. We bought some for Sarah.

Right after Labor Day Barbara noticed the squeak of the school bus brakes stopping at the corner where we lived. And then the sound of the motor let her know the bus was underway again. Of course, it reminded her of school and of her sadness at not teaching anymore. She offered to tutor a boy in our neighborhood who needed extra help with his schoolwork, but nothing came of it. There had been a time when she had tutored very effectively, but those times were to be no more.

In early September Pat Brockman called and invited Barbara to their faculty luncheon at the school where Barbara had taught. The morning of the day of the lunch Barbara told me she had not slept at all the night before because she had not been able to figure out in her mind how to get to the school. So I led in my car and she followed in hers.

Some time before this I had asked my neurologist friend if he thought it was dangerous for Barbara to continue to drive. He said he didn't think so. "Usually when a person in her condition starts getting lost they no longer want to drive." His considered opinion was that she would want to stop before she had an accident and caused harm to herself or anybody else. I certainly hoped so!

Friday, September 4, 1992 was our 37th wedding anniversary. Exactly one year earlier Barbara had decided to stop teaching, and a year ago the following day I had taken her to the personnel director's office to help her resign. It had been a much better year than I had expected.

In mid-September I had an hour's visit with Miles Wallace (the neurologist). He asked me how Barbara was doing. I told him that although she was no better than the previous year, I could not observe she was any worse. He said, "Frankly, that surprises me. I'm very glad, but very surprised. I have known some who displayed symptoms like she had a year ago who, especially when they are as young as she is, within a year are not able to recognize the members of their own families. Perhaps we misdiagnosed it, but I really don't think so." I had much for which to be thankful! I asked him about Cognex for Barbara. He suggested that he refer us to a special Alzheimer's Disease clinic at the University of Virginia under the direction of his medical school professor Dr. George Hanna. I readily agreed.

On October 20th I took Barbara to Charlottesville to be examined by Dr. Hanna. We had been praying the Lord would help Barbara relax enough for them to get a realistic evaluation. She did fine and qualified for the program (to be in the program one had to be aware enough to be able to cooperate with their testing). Barbara was so proud of herself! She was delighted that she was in the program. Dr. Hanna and the others were very nice to her. She liked them a lot and did not find the interviews threatening. Because Cognex had some negative side effects they were trying other drugs that would perhaps accomplish the same positive things. So they wanted to put her in an experimental program with Ondansetron, to which we agreed. We were to go back again the following week, and from then on every four weeks during the use of this drug.

On November 3rd I took Barbara to Charlottesville for an EKG, CAT scan, interviews and the new drug. The interviews were very hard for her; she ended up in tears. We also had to wait a long time for the CAT scan. After lunch we walked around "The Lawn" of the University of Virginia, the original part of the grounds designed by Thomas Jefferson. The fall leaves were very full of color just then. We got home around 4:30. We were both very tired.

As Barbara and I were driving to visit our dear friends Sandra and David Norman in Williamsburg she said, "I have no idea which direction we're going. If something should happen to you, I would not know how to get there, or get back home." I said, "Well, Darlin', let's just pray that doesn't happen." She replied, "Well, it feels very scary." She had said the same thing on other trips we had taken around that time. It must have been awful for her.

November 10, 1992 was Barbara's 59th birthday. Although she knew it was her birthday, she could not remember how old she was even though I had told her several times. She asked me if I could cook supper and invite Mother and Dad. Mother and Dad were delighted to come. We ate in our dining room with cranberry dishes and goblets. Barbara was very pleased with how the table looked and how the food tasted. I prayed Barbara would have more happy birthdays!

On November 14th Barbara fixed corn bread and soup. It tasted so good! This was the first time in a long time she had even attempted to get a meal together. Perhaps the medicine was helping.

On Thanksgiving Day we joined my parents for dinner at Westminster Canterbury, the retirement home where they lived. It was a very good dinner and avoided the stress on Barbara (and me too) of trying to pull it off at our house. The crowd did come to our house at 6:30 PM for desserts which we served in the dining room with the cranberry dishes.

I took Barbara to Charlottesville to the Alzheimer's clinic December 1st. It went much better for her than it had the previous time.

Barbara and I decorated our Christmas tree. It was such fun doing it together like old times. She seemed to me to be more and more alert. She fixed chili for supper

On December 22nd I took Barbara to Charlottesville. She had a good experience in the evaluation. I think everyone thought she was doing better. She had a good time too. We ate lunch at Michie Tavern, just down the hill from Monticello. We looked around the Gift Shop and General Store and bought a few things.

When we got home Barbara finished wrapping the gifts. She had always wrapped such attractive gift packages. When I wrapped gift packages, they looked as if a young child had done them! That year Barbara was thrilled with the cranberry cruets I gave her.

On Christmas Day we had a great dinner supplied mainly by some wonderful church friends, Liz Broyles and Shirl Thomas.

Chapter Four: 1993

In early February I took Barbara to Charlottesville to the Alzheimer's clinic. It went well. For the next 52 weeks she would be on the experimental drug, without the possibility of a placebo as there had been during the first twelve weeks.

In March Barbara went to a church women's retreat. Of course, Barbara could not have gone if other kind women had not been willing to "look after" her which they did superbly. They got snowed in! Barbara felt it was a great adventure.

I took Barbara to Radio Shack to get another Walkman because the one our son Powell had given her had broken. She especially enjoyed listening to music on it while she walked our Sheltie Ollie around the block.

Right after Easter Powell and Chad came up to see us. We had planned to climb Sharp Top (at the Peaks of Otter, about 30 miles away), but Powell was not feeling well. Therefore, he stayed at the house while Barbara and I took Chad – almost 5-years-old then – to get the car washed, to a playground, and by our church to show him off to the staff. The forsythia bushes were in bloom. Chad learned to say "forsythia" which we had to practice a little.

Later that month Barbara and I went to the Ministry of the Laity Conference at Montreat, North Carolina in which I had a leadership role. The group at the conference responded well to my presentation on glorifying God in one's daily work. Barbara told me she thought I would be a kind old man! I think she enjoyed seeing my interacting with the others at the conference, and especially working with one fellow who was doing a D. Min. Thesis at Pittsburgh Seminary on much the same subject about which I had been lecturing.

When I took Barbara to Charlottesville near the end of May, Carol Manning, one of her examiners, felt Barbara was some better although Barbara could not answer many of the questions.

In June Barbara and I took Steve Cropper and his girlfriend Mindy Currie out to Emil's for lunch. Steve, about our own boys' age, was from Atlanta, the son of a Baptist pastor. He was the weatherman for our local television station and attended our church. Perhaps because his own mother was quite ill with Lou Gehrig's Disease (amyotrophic lateral sclerosis or ALS for short), he took a special interest in Barbara. He always sought her out after church and talked with her. She was crazy about him. When he gave the weather report on the evening news, Barbara would talk to him as if he could hear her through the television screen. Barbara urged Steve and Mindy to come with us to England. Steve said they couldn't afford it. "Well, you'll just have to start saving your coins," was her good-humored reply.

Early in July I received a very nice note from our older son Laddie in which he commended me for my patience with Barbara. He especially mentioned my obvious care for her during a supper at the Country Kitchen restaurant when she was quite confused. He wrote with deep understanding of how difficult life sometimes was for us.

Before our trip to England Pam took Barbara and helped her buy a red all-weather coat. That bright color would make it easy for me to spot her if she should get away from me in a crowd.

Shortly before we were to leave for England we got quite a scare. We were going to take both cars to the car wash in preparation for our exchange with the Brumby family. Barbara was going to follow me. She was with me when we turned onto Old Forest Road from Link Road, but another car had gotten between us. I did not worry because she knew where the car wash was – she had been there many times. It was just one block further on the right. I turned in and did not realize Barbara had not followed me. I told the man what to do for my car and then, "My wife is right behind me." "You mean she's coming right away?" "No, she's right there isn't she?" "No." I went to try to find her, but couldn't. I went back to the car wash and stood by the side of the road. I saw her coming back, called and waved and she looked at me. But she went on. I went home and, thank the Lord, she was there, but crying uncontrollably. "You lost me! I didn't know where it was," she said. I just held her and sobbed too. She had been frightened to death. I wondered how much longer she would be able to drive at all. I took care of both cars, one at a time.

We left for England July 21ˢᵗ. Barbara found some cranberry wine glasses she liked in an antique shop on the ancient Wall of Chester. I suggested to her that we might want to wait because she might find something she liked better during our time over there.

The good people of the Whitby Evangelical Church were so hospitable, bringing us flowers and food and inviting us for meals in their homes. Sybil Brown, the wife of John Brown, one of the elders, was especially kind to Barbara in that she washed, set and combed Barbara's hair each week. Barbara loved her. I found I needed to allow lots of time to get ready to go anywhere because Barbara required it by then. Before getting sick she had been so quick about everything. But by the time of our trip she was very slow. And if she felt pushed she simply shut down.

We drove down to Henley-in-Arden to visit our dear friends Mary and Bill Bell. It was a seven-hour trip. One thing I decided that day: With change and long car rides so difficult for Barbara (she got fussy and said she wished she had stayed at home), it would be wise if we pretty much stayed in the Northeast of England; there was plenty to see there and I thought Barbara would enjoy it much more than if we tried to run all over the place. She reminded me so much of a little child who is tired on a long trip and keeps asking, "When are we going to get there?"

We visited Stratford-upon-Avon with the Bells. Barbara (with Mary's help) did a transfer onto paper from a gravestone of a medieval lady of which she was very proud. I had it framed when we got back home and hung it in our front hall.

Back in Whitby we washed several loads of clothes and dried them on the outside line. The clothes smelled so fresh. Barbara said it reminded her of hanging up and taking down clothes from the line in Kansas when she was a girl.

One day Barbara said to me, "You know, when I get confused I feel panicky. And I know I get sort of mean to you. Please forgive me." It made me want to cry. I just put my arms around her and kissed her and told her how much I loved her. I think she was doing much better than I had any reason to expect. It was a wonder she was able to do as well as she did! By that time I was having to remind her to "step up" or "step down" when we were on a sidewalk and reached a curb. Otherwise, she would trip and fall.

Another day Barbara said, "It is so nice outside I wish we could sit out there." I replied, "Well, Peter told me in his note there were a couple of 'outside chairs' in the garden shed. So I got them out, made tea, and we enjoyed sitting in the warm sun.

What an enjoyable month we had in Whitby! Our daughter Mary Beth and granddaughter Christie joined us for the middle two weeks. In addition to being wonderful company, they were a great help to me with Barbara.

After Barbara and I left Whitby for the last time that year, and were approaching Chester, Barbara remembered she had forgotten to bring the dress she had left out of her suitcase to wear on the flight home. I could have kicked myself for not checking all that carefully, but it had not occurred to me. We had packed and locked the suitcases the night before and that one dress had stayed hanging in the closet to put in the "carry-on bag" so we would not have to lug the big suitcases in and out for the next few days.

By the time we got to Chester Barbara was really fussy. "Why do we have to go there again? We've already been there. I don't want to walk on the wall." Well, I insisted she come with me and walk on the wall. I knew we were headed for that little antique shop where she had seen the wine glasses she wanted (she had not found anything else that had struck her fancy). They were still in the shop and I bought them and a cranberry dish for Barbara. Her whole attitude changed! Then everything was fine.

Before we ate supper Barbara wanted her suitcase inside so she could get some more clothes out. I reluctantly went to get it. I had thought we had planned not to have to do that, at least that had been *my* plan.

That night I realized I needed to check and recheck everything for both of us whenever we left anywhere. I had thought I was doing that pretty well. But, obviously, I had not been doing it well enough that day. I also needed to be more patient when I thought Barbara had agreed with me about a plan, and then discovered she had forgotten about the plan and wanted what she wanted regardless of the plan.

The next day we drove to Evesham. Barbara *had* to go the restroom *now* and that complicated things at first. But we worked that out. At the Tourist Information Center we got a fine introduction to the Cotswolds. We visited several beautiful villages. Barbara especially enjoyed seeing some thatched roofs.

Barbara slept a good bit on the flight home. The following afternoon she said to me, "You know what I liked best about our trip? Being with you." And what I liked best about it was being with her.

I took Barbara to Charlottesville for her appointment. It went well. I was amazed that before we left home Barbara said, "Dr. Manning isn't going to be there today. I'm going to see Dr. Brashear." That was what they had told us when we were there five weeks before! With all she was forgetting, it was sometimes amazing that a spark would shine through.

In early September Pam Ruble took Barbara shopping. They found a lady's digital watch for Barbara. I had been unsuccessfully looking for one for some time because Barbara could no longer tell time with a traditional watch. I thought of all the children Barbara had taught to tell time! I had not realized it before, but it takes some quick calculating to figure the time from a traditional watch or clock which was far beyond Barbara's ability by then.

It was not long after this that Barbara was not able to get the concept of time at all. I would say something like this, "We need to leave at nine o'clock. That is thirty minutes from now." I got so used to doing that I said it to our son Powell one day. "I know that, Dad," he replied. I apologized to him for talking to him as if he were his mother.

My mother had not been at all well, so Barbara wanted to do Mother and Dad's laundry. She had always wanted to be helpful.

In early November Barbara and I voted, then I took her to get her driver's license renewed. She had trouble understanding how to describe her peripheral vision, but I got her through it. She got her license. I felt sad knowing it would probably be her last driver's license (in Virginia they were good for five years).

November 10, 1993 was Barbara's 60th birthday. Although she could not remember how old she was, she did know it was her birthday, and she liked her gifts.

Some time earlier Elaine North had come to see me in my study at the church. She said the women's circles wanted to bring in supper for us twice a week. They would bring enough for us to eat for two nights, so that would relieve me of quite a bit of cooking. I demurred. Elaine replied, "Please don't take away from us this opportunity for showing our love for you and Barbara." So I compromised. I said I would really appreciate them doing this *once* a week. But, with all the needs other people had too, I did not want to presume on their generosity. Elaine agreed. So since then they have brought in once a week enough for us to eat for two nights. That has continued through the present (2007). How thoughtful of them!

On Christmas Day Barbara, Mary Beth and I opened our gifts. It started snowing about midmorning so I went and got Mother, Dad and my sister Sarah and brought them here for dinner. What a fine dinner Liz Broyles and Shirl Thomas had fixed for us and brought over the day before!

Chapter Five: 1994

In mid January Barbara told me the women had prayed for her to be healed at their meeting. And Barbara said she felt "at peace" about it. For a while I had prayed for Barbara's healing, and some continued to urge me to do so. But by that time I had come to believe it was unlikely God would choose to heal her in this life. Of course, I believed God *could* heal Barbara and would heal her if it were his will. But I thought God was saying to me what he had said to the Apostle Paul: "To keep me from becoming conceited because of these surpassing great revelations, there was given me a thorn in my flesh, a messenger of Satan, to torment me. Three times I pleaded with the Lord to take it away from me. But he said to me, 'My grace is sufficient for you, for my power is made perfect in weakness.' Therefore, I will boast all the more gladly about my weaknesses, so that Christ's power may rest on me. That is why, for Christ's sake, I delight in weaknesses, in insults, in hardships, in persecutions, in difficulties. For when I am weak, then I am strong" (2 Corinthians 12:7-10).

In late January I had a three-day meeting in Richmond and spent quite a bit of time cooking so Barbara would have plenty to eat while I was gone. She did fine while I was away.

On February 8th I took Barbara to Charlottesville. This was the end of our three-month and twelve-month studies on Ondonsatron, the experimental drug. Barbara had deteriorated some during this time, so we were going to start the following month on a new study with a new formulation of Tacrin.

Barbara and I enjoyed watching the news and then the Winter Olympics. She really had a good time watching the ice skating.

In early March I was strangely moved when I came home to find Barbara had picked some snow crocuses and put them in a small vase. I did not remember her ever picking them before, but was very pleased and touched that she had that day. Somehow, it seemed "little girl" like.

Barbara broke up some pecans for "us" to make banana bread. It was fun to do it "together." And it turned out very well. Then we took Barbara's car to the car wash.

In early April our son Powell and his son Chad went to Charlottesville with Barbara and me. Barbara started on E-2020. I would be so grateful if it helped her.

Our twice monthly prayer group met at our house.

Barbara went to the women's circle at church.

On June 1st someone told me he had just happened to be driving behind Barbara as they were going home (he lived in our neighborhood) from church the past Sunday and twice she got in left-turn lanes and then went straight and almost got hit. I talked with her that evening about it. She had not been aware of any problem, but said, "I sure wouldn't want to hurt anybody." So I suggested we make some other arrangements for Sunday Morning (to church) and Friday mornings (to the hairdresser), the only two routes she was driving by then. That seemed quite agreeable to her for which I was thankful. I did not think she could objectify it enough to realize this meant the last of her driving. I was sad about it, but glad it had ended this way rather than with an accident or a big scare for her. Barbara said, "You won't have to sell my little car will you? I love my little car." I assured her that I would not. I felt like crying. I would not sell her car for a million dollars!

The following morning I called from my study at the church to see how Barbara was doing. She said she had talked with Pam on the phone about her "giving up driving" (these were her words). So she had realized the implications of her not driving to church and to the hairdresser. She said Pam told her she thought that was a very wise and mature decision. That pleased Barbara and she did not seem down about it. Pam called me and said she would be glad to help further. She did not want me to feel alone in it. What a dear she was!

I took Barbara to get her hair fixed. Then I had to rush back to the church to conduct First Friday Prayers. Pam picked up Barbara at the hairdresser and they got home about supper time. I was so glad Barbara did not seem upset about not driving. Pam said she would pick Barbara up for church and Sunday School from then on.

Somehow, two pictures of my Aunt Ethel had gotten misplaced. Of course, by then, lots of things got "misplaced." These pictures had been taken on Aunt Ethel's 80th birthday the previous February 4th, wearing the white orchid we had sent her. I had hoped we could find them because Aunt Ethel, to whom we had all felt very close, had died from injuries received in a fall shortly after those pictures had been taken. Towards the end of June Barbara was very happy she had found one of these two pictures. She did not know where she had found it.

On June 25th I spent most of the morning going through the closets, deciding what to send to summer storage, what to get rid of, what to put in the cedar chests. All this was very hard on Barbara because she could not get the seasons straight in her mind – so to know what to put away for the summer was very confusing to her. She felt quite anxious that afternoon.

Barbara and I worked in the basement throwing out some things, putting away empty boxes, and generally straightening up before the Synaks would come from Austria. We were planning to do an exchange with them for a month during the summer.

On Sunday, June 26th I was still in bed when Barbara awakened. She did not know where she was. "I'm lost," she said. I put my arms around her and replied, "Honey, you are with me, in our own bed in our own house." We got up and she was still disoriented, but finally seemed to get back to normal. This was a first for her – at least when I was there. I was glad I was with her that day when she felt lost. I wondered if she sometimes felt that way when I was away.

We left for Austria on July 5th. Every seat was taken on our KLM 747 plane. We flew to Amsterdam and caught another plane for Vienna. Juraj and Daniela Synak met us. They took us to their house at Bad Voslau, about 20 miles from Vienna. It was much hotter there than I had expected – they said the hottest in years. It was up in the 90s and nothing was air conditioned.

After lunch the following day, while we were still sitting at the table talking, Barbara suggested we pray right then for the Synaks on their journey to America, and especially that Daniela would be feeling better. Barbara had been very concerned about Daniela who had left with a migraine headache. So we stopped and prayed for them.

After supper we went for a walk. We circled around to the town of Bad Voslau and then circled back to the house, thereby coming from the opposite direction. In the middle of that circular route, Barbara had to "go" now! There was no place to go. I urged her to try to wait. We came to a stone wall on the other side of which was a deserted public park. We dashed behind the wall, Barbara got her panties down and squatted. While she was in the middle of doing her thing, a boy (I guess about 12 years old) came walking down the path leading his dog. As soon as he saw us, he abruptly turned around and started walking back the way he had come. And he did not look back. Barbara could not figure out how we had gotten back to the house that way. It had felt to her as if we were getting farther and farther away.

We went on the train to Vienna one day. Barbara really enjoyed it. The secret was pacing, not hurrying, not trying to do too much, not pushing. And I had a good time too.

The following day we had a quiet time doing some ironing and other housekeeping chores. Everything took us a very long time. Before this illness Barbara had done everything quickly, but that had changed radically.

Friday, July 15th was a very mixed day. We had sweet rolls for breakfast. It took us until 11:30 AM to get ready to go for a trial run to the Vienna airport (where we needed to go in a few days to pick up our daughter Mary Beth and Barbara's sister Charlotte). We had no trouble getting to the airport. It took about 45 minutes.

But then Barbara got fussy. "I'd have never come if I had known it would be this long. This is why I wish I'd just stayed home. The seat belt is cutting me. You've got to do something. It makes me so nervous. I've got to go to the bathroom. I'll never do this again." She was being so unreasonable! I was feeling frustrated! (But, of course, *she could not be reasonable.* The Alzheimer's saw to that.) I was trying to read all the signs while getting away from the airport (by this time we had already circled through the parking area and were headed back home). I had made sure (for once) Barbara had gone to the bathroom just before we had left the house. She started yelling that she was going to go "right now in the car." There was no place to stop. I kept telling her to wait just a little longer, be patient. Finally I saw a rest stop. I pulled in, but the restroom door was locked! We ran behind the little building, she stood up and "went" and I gave her my handkerchief to wipe with. She felt so relieved and started laughing about the circumstances under which she had "gone." And everything was fine from then on.

At dusk we were sitting on the terrace at the house and Barbara asked me when we were going to get Charlotte and Mary Beth. I told her she had told me earlier in the day she wasn't going. She seemed genuinely puzzled. So I merely told her again when we would be going. I think she had totally forgotten our "airport disaster" of that day.

Barbara had the hardest time with the stairs there, knowing whether to go up (to the upstairs where our bedroom was) or down (to the basement). Sometimes I could even tell her "up" and she would start down, but it did not seem to bother her.

One morning we went to the beautiful park in Baden. We walked to the top and there we could see a magnificent view of Baden, and the flowers set in formal gardens. Barbara started feeling sick while we were at the top. She began shaking and panting for breath. I thought she might be in heart failure. But we did get down the hill to the restroom, and after that she felt fine. So we went to the little park café and had a sweet. I had written some postcards. I spied a post box across the street. I asked Barbara to stay where she was while I went to mail the cards. I had just gotten them in the box when Barbara, without looking, started out into the street to come to me. I yelled, "Stop! Stop!" But she kept coming. Thank the Lord, she was not struck by a car. I would not be able to leave her even for a moment by herself on a sidewalk again.

On Wednesday, July 20th Barbara went with me to get Mary Beth and Charlotte at the airport. They arrived safely and on time

A couple of days later the four of us went to Vienna on the train. Barbara seemed to enjoy it although she complained of the midday heat. In the evening we went to a Strauss concert in a hall where Strauss had conducted. Barbara smiled often as she enjoyed hearing familiar tunes and watching the dancers.

Another day we went back to Vienna. Barbara got sort of fussy, so she and I sat on a bench while Mary Beth and Charlotte went to the American Express Office. We took the subway to the Schonbrunn Palace and did the tour of the interior. A young Englishman was our guide and Barbara especially liked him because at the beginning he said, "If anyone should feel sick or faint, please let me know. I would rather show you out than carry you out." That seemed to lower Barbara's anxiety level tremendously. We could have visited the zoo there, but Barbara did not want to because it was so hot. By the time we got back to the subway it was one of those "frantic times" for Barbara. She thought she was going to faint. It was hot, but not that hot.

Another time we tried to buy some clothes for Barbara. But she was very hard to fit, by now her stomach was much larger in proportion to her shoulders and chest. (The reason for this was that when she was home she forgot she had eaten so she ate much more than she had before.) Nothing we could find that day fit her. So she was feeling quite discouraged about the possibility of purchasing a pretty Austrian dress. We had to go home for Barbara to go to the bathroom and it was so hot she did not want to go back out.

That evening, after it got cooler, we drove to the Rose Garden in Baden and walked around. Barbara had always loved roses. She really enjoyed the formal rose gardens, especially seeing pictures being taken of a wedding party in front of the flowers.

Another day we went to Puchberg and rode the cog-rail train up the Schneeburg (Mountain). Right across from us were two men (69 and 76 years old) who had been in World War II together, prisoners of the Americans in Italy. Although they could not speak English, through gestures, a word here and there and an Austrian girl who could speak some English, I figured they were having a personal reunion after thirty years. And they both had a great sense of humor. Their eyes twinkled with it. Barbara loved them!

On Friday we drove to Salzburg and took a "Sound of Music" tour. We saw many of the places where the film was made. Barbara enjoyed it very much. Charlotte and Mary Beth wanted to visit Mozart's birthplace, but Barbara did not, so she and I sat on a bench and rested while the others did go through the house where Mozart was born.

When we got back to Mittersill (where we were staying) it was very late. For some reason the parking lot lights were out, so it was pitch black. Mary Beth dashed on ahead of us because she had to visit the ladies' room. I had my "carry all" bag on one shoulder and the picnic bag on the other, had Barbara with one hand and Charlotte with the other and led them up BEHIND me (Barbara was afraid she was going to fall off the side of the mountain), and we made it fine.

The next day we shopped in Mittersill and finally found a dress Barbara liked and it fit her, so we bought it. We were all very pleased.

On Sunday, July 31st we left right after church and drove through the tiny snip of Germany that juts into Austria near Salzburg and contains Berchesgarten. It was a beautiful drive, but it got to be one of those "frantic times" for Barbara. Her back hurt, she had to go to the bathroom and she started sobbing. She did not think we were really on the way back to where we were staying at Bad Voslau near Vienna. I stopped as soon as I could, walked with her for a few minutes, talked with her, and gave her a couple of pills for her back. Charlotte and Mary Beth took her to a restroom, only to find they needed German coins to use it and we did not have any German money! I noticed a young woman going in, and suggested to my "girls" that that woman might hold the door open for them. They asked and she did, and Barbara felt much better. Then we all felt much better!

When we got back to Bad Voslau a neighbor said he had heard on the news that that had been the hottest summer there in 150 years. Barbara would have agreed!

On August 2nd we went back to Vienna on the train. It was pleasantly cool in the morning with a strong breeze. Mary Beth and Charlotte toured the Opera building while Barbara and I sat on a bench and watched the people go by. I bought Barbara an Austrian purse and a couple pieces of Austrian china, and she was very pleased.

On August 4th a friend of the Synaks arrived at 7:20 AM to take us to the airport. I had everything ready. Just as we were getting into the van Barbara had to go to the bathroom again, and this time we had to get one of the suitcases out to get her another pair of panties. But we got away by 7:40. We got to the airport at 8:30 and Charlotte, Barbara's sister, rushed Barbara to a restroom.

We had a few hours' layover in Amsterdam and had planned to see some of the city. But Barbara's stomach hurt and she had a headache, so we simply stayed in the airport from noon until our plane left at 7:00 PM. Most of that time Barbara did not feel well, but she was willing to look around the Duty-Free shops a little. She reminded me that one of the Delft candlesticks I had brought her from Amsterdam ten years before had been broken. (Again, it was rather amazing that Barbara remembered this, since she forgot so much by that time.) I got her some new Delft candlesticks which pleased her.

Just as we were in line boarding the plane Barbara "had to go" again. I asked her if she could wait until we got on the plane, and she started crying. Mary Beth took her to the restroom. Then we got on the plane. Barbara did all right on the flight except she had to go to the restroom again and again. I wondered if panic and anxiety caused this.

On September 20th we went to Charlottesville for Barbara's examination. Serita Jane, whom Barbara liked very much, was no longer working in the program (she had left to begin her Ph. D. studies). Barbara said of her, "She'll help you out with the hard questions." Often when Barbara had been in with Serita, Carol Manning had interviewed me. She always asked me if I felt isolated, lonely. She said very often when a loved one has Alzheimer's Disease, people don't know what to say, so they say nothing, avoiding the family. And the caregiver feels isolated and abandoned. I assured her I did not feel cut off at all. With three loving children, concerned friends, our twice-monthly prayer group, my Thursday morning prayer group, a very supportive congregation, and my first Monday conversation group, I always felt cared for. For this reason I had not felt the need to join an "Alzheimer's Disease Support Group," but I realized this was a lifeline for many.

On October 18th I took Barbara to the hospital for a sonogram to see if we could discover what was the cause of Barbara chronic abdominal discomfort. Then we went grocery shopping. I spent most of the rest of the day cooking up food for the rest of the week. Scott called and said Barbara did have some gallstones, but he did not think she needed surgery at that time. He hoped we could control it with medicine.

I found Barbara's lasagna recipe. I needed to get the recipe box straightened out. In the last days of Barbara's cooking she had gotten the recipe cards all out of place and mixed up. Anyway, she was able to show me how to brown the meat and I made her lasagna recipe and put it in the freezer to have the following weekend.

Pam called and said Barbara really wanted to lose weight. I was not sure how I could help her do that with her other problems. She snacked a lot during the day, forgetting she had already eaten.

On Election Day Barbara and I voted. I had to help her.

I took Barbara to John Petrey's 3rd birthday party. He had especially wanted Barbara to come.

Barbara and I had a great weekend with Sandra and David Norman in Williamsburg where they lived at that time. David and I did a lot of walking, and Barbara and Sandra did some shopping. Sandra fixed a birthday dinner for Barbara; in fact, Sandra cooked all the meals.

I discovered Barbara had accidentally sent a couple of plastic sacks to Goodwill that contained all my pullover sweaters. I had put them in sacks in the attic the previous summer to make room in our bedroom dressers for the Synak family's things. I had gotten the sacks of sweaters down when I was up in the attic for something else, and had put them in the basement temporarily. Barbara saw them there, knew they did not belong there and gave them away. Barbara felt awful about it. I told her not to worry. (I thought she had given it to Pam with some other stuff to take to the Goodwill.) I hoped we could rescue some of it. We went over to the thrift store. One of my sweaters was still there, and they gave it back. The rest had already been bought, and were, therefore, gone for good.

Bill Gayle said Barbara needed gallbladder surgery. I called Bill's office and told them to go ahead and schedule it.

On November 30th Barbara had her gallbladder surgery. Bill came back and said everything had gone well (she had over 100 stones). He had been able to do a laparoscopic cholecystectomy, that is, the operation through three tiny punctures rather than the old procedure of a large incision, so he expected the recovery to be quick. I had a lounge chair to spend the night on. Bill said that ordinarily he would have sent her home that day, but with her other problem (meaning the Alzheimer's) he thought he had better keep her in the hospital overnight as an extra precaution.

Bill dismissed Barbara first thing the next morning. I brought her home right after she had eaten breakfast. She was doing remarkably well. She had just one shot for pain after surgery and had nothing after that for pain, nor did she ask for anything. Barbara loved Bill. She really appreciated the fact that she was recovering so nicely.

In early December I scrubbed the bathrooms. Barbara was no longer able to keep things clean but she did not realize it, so did not want me to hire someone to do the cleaning. But it was all right with her if I helped her.

On December 14th Ollie, our fourteen-year-old Sheltie, could not get up. I called Chip Godine, our good friend who was also our veterinarian, and he said he would see Ollie the next morning. Barbara was weeping, saying how she could not stand to see Ollie suffer and that we ought to have him put to sleep. He had not eaten anything for three days.

Chip came to our house. He thought Ollie might have to be put to sleep, but wanted to try increasing his prednisone to see what would happen in the next day or so. Barbara was so distressed about Ollie. She loved that dog! The next morning Ollie seemed some better. He could get up and ate a little cereal Barbara gave him. He continued to improve.

On December 20th Chip helped me put up our Christmas tree. Barbara was not able to help with that any more. She previously had eyed it and had told me if it were straight, but that was beyond her by the end of 1994. Barbara and I decorated the tree that afternoon and evening. At Barbara's request I fixed chili for supper.

Nancy Tenniswood, an old college friend who was in our wedding and lived in Michigan, called and told me Patty Karnes Brett (who also lived in Michigan) had died of breast cancer the day before. When I told Barbara she jerked as if I had slapped her. We had not known Patty was sick, but she had had this three years and had thought the Lord would heal her. Barbara sobbed and sobbed. She kept saying, "I just can't believe it!" Patty had been Barbara's maid of honor at our wedding.

Chapter Six: 1995

In the middle of the morning of January 4th Barbara called and was very upset because she could not find her purse. I went home and couldn't find it either. We went to Health Care to see Dad and got the key to their apartment from Mother.   We went there and found Barbara's purse where she had left it beside the chair she had been sitting in the day before.

We received a letter from Barry Davies in Whitby, England. They wanted to do an exchange with us during the coming summer and Barbara was eager to do it. So I started making plans.

In mid-January Wanda Eubank Murphy began working one half day every other week at our house. I thought this would help us a lot. Barbara had known Wanda through Wanda's work at Rivermont Presbyterian Church.   Barbara had always liked Wanda, and by that time was happy to have Wanda "help" her (Barbara) keep the house clean. Barbara had been noticing that things were not looking like she wanted them to. She had always been a meticulous housekeeper.

Near the end of January Barbara and I went to Bristol, Tennessee. We stayed in the King College Guest House. On Saturday we ate breakfast at the Bagel Place, then looked at antiques. I bought Barbara an old cranberry sugar shaker at the antique mall near Johnson City, then we came back and had lunch at the K. P. Duty Restaurant. Then we visited an antique mall on State Street where I bought a couple of cranberry tumblers for Barbara. I planned to give them to her for Valentine's Day since she had not realized I had purchased them.

Barbara discovered she had lost her purse. Sunday morning I called the restaurant where we had eaten the night before, and they had the purse. We went to church at Edgemont Presbyterian. Mary Beth, Barbara and I had lunch at Wendy's. On the way back to Lynchburg Barbara and I stopped at the restaurant and got her purse.

For quite a while I had thought I would try to have a study built at home to move my books to when I retired. But then I thought, "Why wait? Why not do it when Barbara is able to help plan for it and enjoy watching it go up?" So Frank Gough who would build it and Scott Glass who was an architect came over to see what I wanted and they made recommendations.

At the end of February Barbara and I shopped at Sam's Club. When we got home she did not have her umbrella, so I thought she must have left it in the ladies' room at Sam's. I called and they had found it and were saving it for us, so back we went.

We also bought a telephone with "memory" for frequently called numbers. I thought it might make it easier for Barbara because dialing a number had gotten beyond her. But by that point she could not understand the new system at all.

We had Pam and Richard Ruble over for supper. I fixed steaks on the grill, baked potatoes and tossed salad. And I baked an apple pie from Sam's Club. We ate in the dining room and used the cranberry dishes. The dinner tasted good and we enjoyed being together. This was the first time in a long time we had attempted something like this. Since it went so well, I thought we would do it again before long.

Near the end of March while I was cutting grass, Barbara came outside all upset because Mother had called and told Barbara (she thought) that Dad was being kicked out of Westminster Canterbury. I went in and called Mother. Barbara had misunderstood. Mother had simply received an official letter that Dad had been transferred to Assisted Living indefinitely. We went over to see both Mother and Dad.

On March 29th when I came home Barbara told me she had gotten lost while walking Ollie around the block. She had gone to someone's house told him her address and "some nice man" (she had no idea who) had walked her home. (I did not find out until 2007 that Ted Engelder had been a "good Samaritan" to Barbara that day. He lived on Taylor Farm Road, about three blocks from our house.) So I suggested that from then on when she took the dog she should always be able to see our house. "Don't go any farther away than that." She seemed to think that was a good idea. I hoped it would work! (It did. She never got lost again.)

I took Barbara to Charlottesville in mid-April for her regular appointment. On the way back home we stopped for an early lunch at Crossroads Store. When Barbara and I arrived in Lynchburg we realized we did not have her purse. I knew she had had it when we left the doctor's office, so it had to be at the place where we had stopped for lunch. I tried to telephone, but could not get the number. So we drove back, and, thank the Lord, it had been found in the ladies' restroom and nothing was missing. Barbara felt awful about our double drive, but it is a beautiful drive anytime, and that day, with the dogwood and redbud and all shades of new green leaves on the trees, it was magnificent! I assured her I really did not mind doing the drive again.

At the end of April Barbara and I went out to supper with Pam and Richard Ruble and Shirl and Cliff Thomas at the New London Steak House. We did this quite regularly with this group which normally included Ruth and Doug Stinespring as well.

Barbara and I attended the children's musical at the church. It was an excellent program. Barbara always enjoyed hearing children sing.

In early May the Margaret Chase Smith rose was in bloom. I cut some and brought them in the house for Barbara. She loved roses.

The following week Barbara and I went with Dianne and Jim Wright to Andre Viette's nursery in Waynesboro. We heard Viette lecture on gardening and he was very good.

In mid-May we took off for Georgia and in the evening of that same day arrived at Willia and Al Wilkes' house. The following Sunday we worshiped with them at Covenant Presbyterian and then drove back home. As I was unloading the car Chip Godine (who had kept our dog while we were gone) came over to tell me Ollie had died while we were away. He had turned 15 the previous month – old for a Sheltie. When I told Barbara tears came into her eyes. She really loved that dog, but she said she thought it was best since he had been so sick. She knew she would really miss him. We would all miss him. He had been a great dog.

The next evening we did not go to our prayer group. Barbara was very tired and also feeling sad about Ollie.

On May 26th Barbara and I went to Duplin County, North Carolina for Kathy's graduation from nursing school. We were proud that our daughter-in-law had become a Registered Nurse.

Over the years Barbara and I always had enjoyed being with my cousins Iris and Neel Rich and Betsy and Bob Sykes. In early June we met them for an "overnight" at the Peaks of Otter Restaurant and Motel near Bedford, Virginia. All of us had a good time together.

Barbara and I went to Bristol to visit Mary Beth in mid-June. Mary Beth was working at King College by then. We had a great time helping Mary Beth in her new apartment. We bought curtain rods and picture frames. I put up the rods, Barbara pressed the curtains, and Mary Beth said where she wanted things to be placed. What a nice time the three of us had working together! The apartment looked very nice and Mary Beth seemed pleased. Barbara was proud of what we had accomplished. Barbara requested we eat supper at Pizza Hut. So Mary Beth took us there for a Fathers' Day meal.

On July 4th Mother, Dad, my sister Virginia from California, my sister Sarah from South Carolina, Barbara and I ate at our house.

Dad did not know where he was. He kept asking, "Whose house is this?" Sarah gave Barbara and me a couple of very attractive King's Crown (the name of the design) tumblers with the top all ruby-flashed. We did not have any like that. She said these were an early 40th anniversary gift.

Near the end of July Barbara, her sister Charlotte, my sister Sarah and I flew to Heathrow Airport near London. We rented a car and drove to Dover. All of us, and especially Barbara, enjoyed singing the World War II popular song, "There'll Be Bluebirds Over the White Cliffs of Dover."

The next day we drove to the railway station at Salfords to catch a commuter train to Victoria Station in London. Barbara "had to go!" There was no place to "go" in the tiny Salfords station, so I took her out behind and she squatted. When we got to London we boarded a tour bus for a ride around the city. Near Westminster Abbey Barbara "had to go" again *now*. So she and I jumped off the bus to get her to a toilet. (Charlotte and Sarah did not get off the bus with us and I wondered how we would get together again.) When Barbara came out of the toilet she was crying. She thought she had been left there, could not remember how she had gotten there, and could not get out without help from a stranger. I bought her a cup of tea and a muffin, and she calmed down some. She was still so shaken she did not want to go anywhere else. I did talk her into taking a bus back to Victoria Station, and Charlotte and Sarah were waiting for us there. Barbara still did not want to go anymore, and by that time Charlotte didn't either, but Sarah went on to Westminster Abbey by herself. Pretty soon Barbara decided she was ready to go too, so she and I and Charlotte went to Westminster Abbey and found Sarah there.

I was so thankful we got through the day without a major mishap, and the memory of that day for Barbara seemed good – that is, I did not think she remembered the terror of the restroom episode, but had a pleasant memory of the trip to London. But really, London was simply too much for Barbara by that time.

We drove to Edinburgh. Barbara had always loved dogs, and had liked the story of "Greyfriars Bobby," the faithful terrier who, after his master had died, always slept on the old man's grave in the Greyfriars Church yard. So she enjoyed seeing the graves of both the master and the dog in the cemetery.

We drove from Whitby to Robin Hood's Bay where we spent a couple of hours. At an antique shop window Barbara pointed and said, "Look! That's just like what Aunt Ethel brought me from England." And it was. It was a teacup and saucer, and the saleslady said it was "Sunderland Lustre." We had not known the name of it before. We bought it. Barbara was obviously very pleased that she had found it. Then we drove to Hutten-le-Hole. Barbara remembered we had bought Mother some lily-of-the-valley perfume when we had been there two years before. So we bought some more. As confused as Barbara often was, it was amazing when she did come up with things like the cup and saucer and the perfume!

Back in Whitby we walked up the 199 steps to St. Mary's Church and from there watched the RAF's Red Arrows air show in connection with the Regatta. Magnificent! Barbara enjoyed it very much.

We visited Eden Camp (a World War II museum on the site of an old prisoner-of-war camp, near Malton) about 30 miles from Whitby. Barbara got in a fussy mood while we were waiting for it to open, but enjoyed it after we got in. That afternoon we visited Sledmere House, home of Sir Tatton Sykes, a little below Malton. It was a magnificent house with beautiful grounds.

We went to Chester and visited the antique shop where we had bought the wine glasses two years before. I bought a cranberry powder jar and a couple of tumblers for Barbara – especially appropriate that year because we were about to celebrate our "ruby" anniversary, the 40th. The same lady waited on us. She told us her name, Rhonwen Metcalf. When she discovered our "ruby" anniversary was the next month, she hugged and kissed us all! She was a Christian and an active member of a chapel in Wales.

We drove to Stratford-upon-Avon. Barbara very much wanted Charlotte to do a gravestone transfer at the same place Barbara had done one (with Mary Bell's help) two years before, so Charlotte did.

We arrived back home in Lynchburg near the end of August. Overall it was a good trip.

Soon after our return they dug the hole for the foundation of our new room. Barbara was very excited about it.

On September 2nd, a couple of days before our 40th wedding anniversary, I took Barbara out to an anniversary lunch at the Back Yard Grill, one of her favorite restaurants. Then I took her to the church "to see the flowers Rod Meek had fixed for the wedding this morning." She had always liked Rod, so was eager to see the flowers. She thought they were very nice. Then I took her down through the sanctuary toward the Cheatham Reception Center. She heard people talking in there and said, "We can't go here. Something is going on." I said, "That's all right." I took her in. She was totally surprised to find we had arrived at our Fortieth Anniversary Party which was given by our children and their spouses. What a lovely thing for them to do! They figured that even if we both were still living ten years from then, it would be unlikely that Barbara would be well enough for us to have a party. There were hosts of friends there. Nancy Tenniswood, her husband Bob and their son Steve had come all the way from Michigan for the occasion. (Nancy had been a bridesmaid in our wedding.) At this party, although Barbara had had Alzheimer's Disease for several years, she had a wonderful time! In fact, I think because of her illness, she was totally surprised. Before she got sick it was hard to surprise her because she would put things together and figure them out. This had been a very happy day!

A Tuesday in mid-September I worked some in the yard, fixed ham and beans for lunch, to which we had invited Mother and Dad. Barbara seemed more confused than usual and Dad was very sleepy – almost "out of it." Dad ate some lunch, but could not seem to come out of his stupor. I wondered how much longer he could last like this. Barbara was mad at me because I would not agree with her that there were *three* pieces to a *two*-piece outfit she had. I told her it did not matter, but it mattered to her. With both Dad and Barbara talking crazy I felt squeezed. But, to look on the positive side, it was Barbara who had wanted me to invite Mother and Dad for lunch.

Because I was planning to use some of our old living room furniture in the new study, Barbara and I went to Lancaster Galleries where she picked out a new couch and chair for our living room. I was very pleased with what she chose. Although she got quite confused about many things, she still had good taste. I was so glad we were doing all this earlier than I had originally planned because Barbara was having such a good time with it.

The next day I wrote in my journal: "It seems to me in a way 'everything that was nailed down is coming loose.' That is an overstatement, but with Barbara, Dad, etc., etc….. Lord, save me! Help me focus on you instead of the waves."

On Sunday, October 8th Dave Lane brought Barbara to Sunday School (Pam was out of town). After they got to the church, somehow Barbara thought our cat was in danger back at our house, so Lerlyne Garcia took her home to check after Sunday School. I took Barbara home with me after the 11:00 AM service. She had also left her purse at Dad's Health Care room the day before, but we did not know it until Mother called Saturday evening. Mother brought Barbara's purse to church Sunday morning.

The following day, since Barbara was not feeling well in the morning, I went home and fixed her lunch. I noticed after lunch how difficult it was getting for her to put anything away. She took such a long time, and made many false moves to get the cutting board put back. I wanted to do for her what she could not do, but not take over things she could still do. It was not always easy to get that just right!

In mid-October I did the closing on our loan for the new room. I used my Power of Attorney for Barbara's signatures because it had gotten so hard for her to do it, especially several signatures in a hurry in front of a stranger.

In mid-November we visited Powell and Kathy. It was wonderful to watch Barbara help Chad with his homework. He was now in second grade, the grade Barbara had taught for so long. Her face glowed and he was having a wonderful time. He had been reading for her.

Back in Lynchburg, they were about to finish up the new study. The furniture arrived. After all was arranged Barbara and I sat down in the new room. Barbara said, "This is beautiful! I didn't think it was going to look like this. Did you think it would?" I replied, "Yes, this is about how I had imagined it." She said, "I think it looks like a room in a wealthy person's house." I laughed and responded, "Then we'll sure have a lot of people fooled!" I was so glad Barbara liked it so well. And I was very pleased with it.

On Thanksgiving Day I preached at our 10:00 AM Service. Barbara, Mary Beth and I ate with Mother, Dad and Sarah at Westminster Canterbury. It went very well. I got Dad and Barbara's plates and went through the line for them.

The following Monday our prayer group met at our house. Everyone thought the new room was beautiful. Everyone was there (13 of us), and we fit in the new room well.

Bill Gayle gave me a very thoughtful letter in connection with our wedding anniversary. It came later than the others, so was not with them. After I had read it, I placed it on the mantel so I could easily retrieve and re-read it more slowly later. The letter went missing.   Barbara somehow knew it did not belong where I had put it, so she either moved it or threw it away. I never saw it again. Barbara had always hated clutter! At least that had not changed.

Back in 1983 I had brought Barbara a cuckoo clock from the Black Forest in Germany. She had loved it. We had had to have it repaired a couple of times. In the fall of 1995 it had stopped working again. Barbara had asked me to get it fixed, but I procrastinated too long. One day I came home and found that she had tried to fix it herself by pulling the hands off!

Barbara and I trimmed the Christmas tree. Because of the cathedral ceiling in the new study the tree was very tall, and it was really beautiful.

Barbara and I went to a Christmas Open House at Kathy and Tom Wrenn's. Being in circulating crowds like that was increasingly difficult for Barbara, but I thought she had a good time.

I took Barbara to Charlottesville. Dr. Hanna told me the E-2020 she had been taking was being found to help like Cognex without the negative side effects. They were applying to the FDA for its commercial use.

On December 30th Barbara and I and our children and their spouses went to Olan Mills for a family portrait. This had been Barbara's idea. She fell as she was being seated for the picture, but said she was not hurt. She was delighted to have had this portrait taken.

Chapter Seven: 1996

Barbara missed having a dog and said several times she wished we would get another one. I figured with her disabilities we could hardly manage a puppy. So I called Sue Woodle (from whom we had bought Ollie back in 1980) to see if she had for sale a Sheltie that was already housebroken, or if she knew of one. She said she was involved in Sheltie rescue and there was one in the animal shelter in Chesterfield County (near Richmond). So I took Barbara over there. She did not know where we were going until we got there. The dog was a collie, not a Sheltie, but Barbara immediately fell in love with him and wanted him anyway. So we brought him home. He had a damaged eye, but otherwise seemed fine. Barbara was excited about the dog. She named him "Prince." He had obviously been accustomed to staying inside. He did not jump up on the furniture. Prince seemed to be a great dog! Barbara adored him, and he was very gentle with her.

In late January I took Barbara to Scott Wade's office for a urine test, to see if her urinary tract infection had cleared up. When we got home Scott called and said she hadn't left any urine in the cup. So we went back and a nurse helped her.

In mid-February I preached on "The Transfiguration of Our Lord." I didn't decide until early that morning to include my experience during the choir's singing of "Beautiful Savior" a month or so after Barbara had to stop teaching in 1991. It was the first time I had shared it in public. I knew Barbara was going to be there, but told it in such a way I did not think she would connect it with herself. As it turned out, she slept through most of the sermon anyway. Well, it became one of those "rare moments." Tears were flowing down many faces. The choir did "Beautiful Savior" for the offertory anthem. What a wonderful response by many. I had felt led to share this and I thought, from the fruit, it really was "of the Lord."

One afternoon in early March someone called the church and said they had called Barbara and she said a toilet was running all over the floor. I called her and she told me the same thing. I went home and found the basement toilet running, but not all over the floor. Barbara in her panic had simply imagined it would.

Gary Brizendine was the Building Superintendent of our church. He had always been more than willing to do some extra work for me at our house. I asked Gary if he would like to mow my lawn regularly. He said, "Yes." He had done it for me before when we were away. Some time before I had thought I would try to get someone to do it all the time because of all the rest I had to do then. I simply felt overwhelmed when it came to finding the time. I knew I would miss it; I had always enjoyed mowing the grass. But by that time it had become burdensome because of Barbara's increasing need of me.

Barbara and I went over to see Dad. He was so weak. Mother had been feeding him – he would open his mouth, chew and swallow, but very slowly. He did not seem to have the energy to pick up the food himself. I wondered how much longer he could last.

On March 21st when I got home at supper time Barbara was sobbing. She said she felt like dying – she was so lonely, had no one to help her, had no friends. I listened and held her in my arms. Pam called in the midst of all this, but Barbara told me she would have to talk with Pam later. After Barbara had calmed down I asked if something had gone wrong that day (I knew she had been around people quite a bit that week, but I did not point that out to her). She said, "I tried to iron, but I got all confused. I couldn't get it plugged in right, and couldn't get the water in the iron. I tried and tried, but finally gave up and put it all away. And she sobbed some more. "I've always been able to iron! I feel like running away – all the way to New York. I really don't want to live, I'm so confused!" I felt awful about her feeling so badly. I got supper. She did not eat much, but did calm down a good bit.

Perhaps the time had come for me to get most of my books at home and start studying there. At least I could set it up so I could start studying at home as soon as my new co-pastor arrived which I hoped would not be too long – the church had not called anyone to that position yet.

Olympic ice skating came on TV. Barbara loved to watch that.

Sometimes I felt like I was being squeezed to death, but I was enjoying life at the same time. That did not seem to make sense. But it was true. I knew the Lord was strengthening me. My co-pastor, Wayne Meredith who had worked with me for years, had accepted a call to another church, and shortly before that our associate pastor had left to become an overseas missionary. The church needed more from me than it had in years. We had two morning services with the same sermon at both, an evening service with a different sermon, and a mid-week service with a Bible Study or devotional; I often taught Sunday School; and as I was the only pastor at that time, I had all the weddings and funerals, pastoral counseling and most of the hospital visitation. Dad and Mother were needing more from me. Barbara was needing more from me.

When I got home the last day of April Barbara was frantic because a lens had come out of her glasses, and we could not find the lens. Finally Barbara found it (I was not sure where, but someplace in our bedroom). She could not tell me where. So we went to Jay Blackburn to have it fixed. On the way home we stopped at Brown's and bought some goldfish. As we left the store Barbara ran into the propped open door and hurt her foot and leg. "The door kicked me," was the way she described it. Just as we walked into our house the phone rang and Jay Blackburn said Barbara had left her purse there, but he would bring it by on his way home from work.

On Friday, May 17th Barbara called the church about 9:00 AM sobbing, "I don't know where I am." I went right home. I think she meant, "I don't know where I am supposed to be." Because there were two things happening: the plumber was coming by and Christy Murphy was coming to take Barbara to get her hair fixed. Barbara was fine after I calmed her down and she realized she had not done anything wrong. She often was distressed because she thought she had done some unspecified wrong. That evening she told me she felt afraid much of the time. I told her I thought I ought to get someone to stay with her when I had to be away from the house. But she said she did not want that. I thought I would need to start studying at home very soon.

At the end of May I took Barbara to Westminster Canterbury to hear Elizabeth Petrey (six years old) read an essay she had written about Barbara, "My Best Older Friend." She had won first prize.

On the evening of the Fourth of July Barbara and I watched "The Sound of Music" on TV. Barbara really enjoyed it. She said she would like to go back to Austria. We also looked at our English Trip (1995) books. Barbara wanted to go back there too.

At the deacons' meeting they gave me an iron that automatically shut off if it was left face down (Barbara had been burning things). They were so thoughtful of us.

I told Vic Uotinen I did not think I could come to the Pastor Nominating Committee meetings regularly anymore. He was chairman of the committee. I simply could not leave Barbara that long.

In mid-July we went to Kitty Hawk, North Carolina to be with Kathy, Fred, Geoffrey, Katie and Jay Whitten. Barbara had such a good time. Barbara felt very close to the Whittens and they bent over backwards to make her feel comfortable.

Back home, I visited an older man in the hospital. He said that the years since his wife's stroke (he had lovingly taken care of her) had been the best of his life because he enjoyed being able to "do" for her. I felt much the same way. I would not have chosen this for Barbara for anything. But since it had been a "given" for us, my life had been very fulfilled in serving her needs. Wasn't that odd?

Perhaps it was an illustration of Jesus' words, "He who loses his life for my sake will find it." We are apt to think, "If I can only get my world to revolve around me and my needs I will be happy." But the truth is, "if we can only get our lives to revolve around God's will for us in meeting the needs of others, we will find real happiness there." Some time after Paul Tournier's wife died he wrote in his Creative Suffering, "I can truly say that I have a great grief and that I am a happy man." I knew of what he spoke.

On July 22nd Barbara and I left for Kansas at 7:30 AM. We drove all the way to Wentzville, Missouri, 786 miles! I had not planned to drive so far the first day, but Barbara traveled unusually well and was eager to keep going. She did not have to stop much (remarkable for her). Toward the end of the day she said, "This has been a wonderful day." She remarked about the beauty of the scenery. I could not remember a journey Barbara had enjoyed more.

We arrived safely at Charlotte and Everett Shaffer's in Bunker Hill, Kansas, near Russell. Charlotte is Barbara's sister. One morning I mentioned to Charlotte that several times in the past weeks Barbara had said she would love to have some good homemade cinnamon rolls "like Mama used to make." (Of course, Barbara had made them too, but I did not know where her recipe was.) Charlotte said she would be glad to give me the recipe, and that she would also show me how to do it. So Charlotte made cinnamon rolls (with me watching). They were mighty good. Barbara loved them.

As we were traveling back to Virginia, Barbara exclaimed several times, "We are having a wonderful time!" And she spoke often of the beautiful weather (it had not been awfully hot, most unusual for that time of year). And it seemed to rain only at night – like Camelot! I was so glad she had had such a good time.

On Sunday afternoon, August 11th Barbara and I drove from our home in Lynchburg to Burlington, North Carolina (120 miles) for our son Powell's installation as pastor of Westminster Presbyterian Church. We enjoyed seeing their church building and manse. (In the

Presbyterian church *the manse* is the church-owned house in which the pastor and his family live. In some denominations this residence is called *the parsonage*, in others, *the rectory*. It used to be these church-owned houses were in almost universal use. In more recent years many churches have sold their manses and the ministers have bought their own homes.)

On August 12th I started moving out of my big study at the church into both our new room at home and a smaller study at the church. That way my new colleague, John Mabray, would be able to re-do my old study at the church to suit himself. (While I was moving books a couple of older ladies walked down the hall and observed what I was doing. "Why are you moving out of your study?," they asked. I caught from their body language they thought that perhaps I was being "pushed" out. "This was my own idea," I said. "I'll be studying at home in the mornings now. Barbara needs me there. So it only makes sense that our new co-pastor have the large study here." They looked relieved, and accepted the truth of what I had said.)

On August 15th I began studying at home. Barbara was very pleased. At that point it seemed to be enough for her merely to know I was there. She understood what I was doing was important, so did not interrupt me. Actually, I thought I should be able to get more done that way than I had been able to do at the church, because at the church there were pretty constant interruptions. I fixed Barbara's lunch before I left to do pastoral work in the afternoons.

Barbara knew that on a particular day Catherine and John Mabray would be telling their children in Louisiana about their move to Lynchburg. Always very sensitive to children and their needs, Barbara was concerned about how they would react to the news and wanted us to pray for them, which we did.

In late September I took over the washing and drying of our clothes. Barbara seemed very glad to have me do it. I had been afraid she had been getting things quite mixed up along these lines for a while anyway. I had been finding lint she had rightly taken out of the dryer dropped in potted plants instead of the trash for some time. It was when I found soap powder in the dryer I knew I had to intervene. This was about the last thing she had held on to, except rinsing the dishes. (She had stopped using soap on the dishes, so I tried to wash them and then let her rinse them.) She continued to dress herself, but that was getting harder for her.

The last Saturday night in September I had laid out Barbara's clothes for the next day, had run her bath water (which she could no longer do), saw that she got her nightgown on after her bath, and I was working in my home study. When I came out Barbara had taken off her night gown and put on her clothes for Sunday! A first.

On October 21st, Barbara showed me that she had removed the toilet paper roll and the wooden stick it stayed on and wanted me to find them. I searched and searched and could not locate them. She started jumping and screaming, "I hate you! I hate you! I hate everybody – except Prince! I'm going to run away." I asked her why and she said, "Because nobody will help me." It was as if I had hidden the thing from her, which she might have thought. I assured her it was not important, that I would get a new one the next day. But she wanted the old one! It had been broken for a long time anyway, and we had needed to replace it. Anyway, this was the first time she had done this to me. And she cried and cried and cried. It must have been horrible for her. I had been very blessed up to that point that Barbara had not been hostile to me. I hoped this did not mark the beginning of a general hostility towards me. It did not. Although we did have other episodes like this, they were few and far between.

On November 2nd Mary Beth helped Barbara go through her clothes – getting rid of a lot of things that no longer fit her.

On November 4th Barbara could not get her bra on for the first time. Since I had not done it before, it took me a while to figure it out, but we finally managed to get it on. I wondered if this were just a fluke or if she would not be able to do this from then on.

On Election Day we voted. I helped Barbara vote. Anyway, we voted for her fellow Kansan Bob Dole. The next day we found out he had lost to Bill Clinton.

Tuesday of Thanksgiving week I took Barbara to Charlottesville. Paula Damgaard (the nurse who essentially ran the program) told me that the drug Barbara had been taking experimentally was about to go on the market by prescription. It would be called "Aricept," and we could get it filled in Lynchburg. We had only one more appointment in Charlottesville. We would miss the Charlottesville visits after having gone regularly for four years. They had been pleasant trips for Barbara and me, and Barbara had looked forward to seeing her "friends," those doing the tests and evaluations, there. They were all outstanding people.

We had our larger family at our house for Thanksgiving dinner. As I had expected, Barbara thoroughly enjoyed having everyone over, because by then she did not think it was her job to "get the dinner on" or to clean it up. So she was relaxed and perfectly content to let us do it while she visited with those who were sitting around.

At that stage in Barbara's illness she would ask me to help her get dressed. She could still put on the garments, but I handed them to her in the order she needed to put them on.

On Thanksgiving Day I found Barbara had poured the cat food in the litter box. First time for this. So I scooped it out. This was another job we might need to begin doing "together."

One night at the end of November I was feeling dog-tired; I just couldn't hold my eyes open. So Barbara and I went to bed at 9:00 PM, something I never did except on Saturday nights because I always got up at 4:00 AM on Sundays.

On December 7th when we got up Barbara asked what day it was. I told her, "Saturday." She said, "Oh, that's good. I love having him (meaning "you, Lowell") with me to do things together." Barbara often spoke to me in the third person by then.

I took Barbara to an open house at Amelon School to celebrate the opening of the new library and wing. All her old school friends were delighted to see her. She had a very nice time.

On Sunday, December 15th after church Barbara and I had dinner at Judy and Lee Aylor's. They had several people, but thoughtfully sat us with just a few (large tables with several people talking at once confused Barbara even more than usual). Barbara had a very nice time.

Barbara wanted very badly to find some ribbon candy for Dad for Christmas. She remembered it was one of his favorites. We looked several places, but she felt certain we could find some at the mall. They did not have any at the candy store, but we did find some at Leggett's. Barbara was delighted!

On Christmas Eve Mary Beth went and picked up Mother and Elaine North from Westminster Canterbury and brought them and Barbara to the 7:00 PM Service. Laddie was there too. I spent from 8:45 to about 9:45 with them at home. I got home from the 11:00 PM service about 1:00 AM, and sat up 'til about 2:00 AM.

On Christmas Day I got up about 6, Barbara at 7, and Mary Beth at 8. Then we opened our gifts. Barbara was thrilled with the portrait of herself painted by Barbara Mayer. It was a complete surprise to my Barbara because it was painted from a photograph. She could not figure out why there was not one of me, too!

The last Sunday in December although both morning and evening I had helped Barbara get dressed and she had everything on when I had left for church, but by the time Pam picked her up she had gotten her panties off and her panty hose were back on! She had on a three-piece outfit – skirt, blouse and sweater. Evidently this was too much for her to keep straight.

Powell asked me if we had any duct tape. I did not know. Barbara said, "Yes, we do, and I know where it is!" She went to the basement and brought it up to Powell. This was amazing! One of those "shafts of light." By that time she hardly knew where anything was. I would not have believed this if I had not seen it.

In our 1996 Christmas Letter we said, among other things:

With Barbara's increasing disability it seemed wise for Lowell to begin doing his studying at home this year. So the books he uses most were moved from the church study to the new home study we had built onto our house last year for this purpose.

Nineteen ninety-six has been, perhaps, the busiest year of our lives. Lowell's co-pastor for the past twelve years accepted a call to another church in January. Shortly before that our associate pastor had left to be an overseas missionary. So Lowell was the only pastor at Rivermont Presbyterian Church for nine months – a heavy responsibility in a church of almost 1,000 active members.

We are delighted to report that John Mabray from Monroe, Louisiana has recently become our new co-pastor. He is God's answer to our prayers: doctrinally sound, full of passion for Jesus Christ clothed in his glorious gospel, an outstanding preacher, a "people person," and committed to his wife Catherine and their three children. He is thirty-nine years old – a year younger than Lowell was when we came here over twenty-two years ago.

Chapter Eight: 1997

In mid-January Barbara and I went to pick up her framed portrait. It was lovely. I hung it over the fire place in our den. Barbara loved it too, but she could not figure out why there was not one of me to hang beside it. "We are supposed to go together," she said. I tried to explain, but she just did not get it.

In mid-February I drove to a church conference in Florida. On the way I left Barbara with her dear friend Willia Wilkes in Augusta, Georgia. Willia really wanted Barbara to come and Barbara was anxious to spend some time with Willia. The visit went very well.

For several months I had been having a severe pain in my knee. At the end of February I had an MRI. It turned out I did have a torn meniscus. Surgery would correct it, but with so much going on, I hardly felt I had time for surgery.

In mid-March Barbara and I took Janice, Rodney, Sarah, Abbie, Amanda and Richard Suddith and Janice Hatton to supper at the Lodge of the Fisherman. Barbara had especially wanted to do this because of Richard Hatton's death while we were in Georgia and Florida (Richard was Janice Hatton's husband and Janice Suddith's father).

Frances and Andy Sale had us over to their house for supper one night. On the way home Barbara said, "They are really nice people. He is such a funny man!" (Andy had told some hilarious stories from the early days of his pastoral work. He was a great storyteller.)

I arranged to have my knee surgery. Powell thought he could come in for a couple of days.

In mid-April I stopped by the house about 2:00 PM to see how Barbara was doing. She was hungry; although I had shown her where I had left food in the refrigerator, she had not gotten it. I asked her why not. She said, "I didn't know what to do." So I put it in the microwave and set it on the table and she ate. This made me wonder if I could keep working much longer. From then on when Wanda was at our house Wednesday mornings (and I was at the church), I asked her to put Barbara's lunch on the table before she left, which she was glad to do.

When I went to the basement one morning to do the washing I discovered Barbara had put dog food in the container with the basement towels. Although Barbara knew she was out of dog food upstairs, she did not know what to do about it even though I had told her she could bring some up from the basement. She said, "I just don't understand."

On April 28th I had my knee surgery. I got up early to take Barbara to Pam Ruble's for the day. Powell arrived in time to take me to the hospital. All went well. Powell brought me home about 9:00 PM.

The next day Powell and Barbara and I had lunch at Milano's. Then Powell went back home to North Carolina. He was such a wonderful help. After Powell left Barbara tried to "help me." She wanted to, but she couldn't. This was so obvious now, because I was quite limited in what I could do. And when I tried to go through it "step-by-step" with her she thought I was fussing (which I was not) and she got upset. So I simply needed to do what I could myself – and let the rest go. People had been great to bring in meals, but I still had to carry them to the table which was a whole new ball game because I was on crutches. I finally figured out I could bring dishes from the stove to the table by moving them around the counter, a step at a time, while I moved another step on the crutches.

Wanda took Barbara shopping. They got some sheets, towels and wash cloths. And they bought me a pillow that said, "This can't be happening." Wanda was really wonderful with Barbara.

My own temporary disability freshly reminded me of all Barbara could not do. I had gradually taken over everything, and now since I could not both carry things and walk with crutches, I saw she could not follow the simplest directions. I had gotten supper on the table with the round about process I described, and we sat down to eat. I had neglected to put the napkins on the table. I felt exhausted so I asked Barbara if she could get them (they were on a shelf in the cupboard right behind her). She tried, but could not. I said, "They are lower down." But she interpreted that as "deeper in." She kept reaching further and further back on the top shelf. She started crying, "I want to help you, but I can't. I don't know what to do." I said, "Don't worry. We'll do it together. We always help each other." So I got up and got the napkins and she was fine.

Right after that Mary Beth called to see how I was doing. I told her what had just happened, and she said, "I'm coming home! I'll plan to stay two or three days." What a great help that would be, although I hated to have her take the time off work. It would be great to see her.

May 1st my Thursday morning (6:30 AM) prayer group met in my new home study for the first time. Mary Beth arrived about 1:00 PM. She took Barbara and picked up some things we needed. I was not able to drive yet.

A couple of days later Mary Beth left to go back to work. She had certainly accomplished a lot at our house. My knee was so swollen it throbbed with every heartbeat, although I was taking pretty strong pain medicine.

I had been having a terrible time. The pain in my knee had spread to my whole leg which had become an aching mass. Rodney

Laughon took me to see the doctor who drained the accumulated fluid which was causing so much pain. I did not know exactly how much he got out of it, but it looked to be about a pint of purple-bloody sludge. I could feel the throbbing lessening as the liquid was drained off.

The following day I could hardly believe the difference. My leg did not ache! I still did not have all the normal use of it, but I could bend it a little. I drove to the grocery store and did fine.

On May 13th Alyce and Lionel Harrison took Barbara and me to Charlottesville. This would be Barbara's last trip to the clinic where we had been going for the past five years. Paula Damgaard hugged Barbara as we left and there were tears in Paula's eyes. They had been good *to* Barbara and so good *for* Barbara. Now the medicine was available by prescription so Barbara would continue on it under Scott Wade's supervision.

In mid-May the *Easy Voice Service* started on our phone. I hoped I could get Barbara able to use it, but that was impossible. One was supposed to be able to simply speak a person's name into the phone to have it ring that number, but she could never seem to get the hang of it.

On Sunday, June 8th Barbara and I were eating an early supper about 4:00 PM because I had a committee meeting at the church at 5:00 PM. Barbara started complaining of a heaviness in her chest, and pain in her shoulder and neck. She was not nauseated, sweaty or short of breath. Diane and Jim Morgan were picking cherries in our yard, so I asked Diane (who is a Registered Nurse) if she would come in and check Barbara. She said Barbara's pulse was steady. I called Scott Wade and he said to take her to the Emergency Room right away. Scott and Dr. Joe Pond examined her. They could not find out what was happening, but said she neither had had a heart attack nor was she in the process of having one. They wanted to keep her overnight, do another test the next day and observe her. Needless to say, I missed my committee meeting. I was not scheduled to preach that evening anyway. I spent the night with Barbara in the hospital on a cot Scott asked them to bring in for me.

The next day Pam Ruble stayed with Barbara in the hospital while I kept some appointments. Powell came in the middle of the day. Barbara had an echocardiogram, which made her nauseated, but nothing was wrong with her heart. We got home from the hospital about 8:00 PM.

On June 15th John Winter called from Whitby in England. His wife Elizabeth had cancer and they were planning to do a bone marrow transplant that fall. The Whitby Evangelical Church had granted him a two month leave so he could tend to his wife and their two young children. He wondered if I could substitute for him for the months of October and November. I told him I could not possibly be gone two months, but I thought I could come for the month of October. Barbara wanted to go. I called Charlotte to see if she could go with us. She could. Since it worked with our schedule at Rivermont Church, we started making plans.

One afternoon in late June we had quite a thunderstorm and our power was off until about 9:15 PM. So, although I had planned to attend a Long-Range Planning Committee meeting, I stayed home with Barbara. We ate in the bay of my home study, because there was plenty of natural light. Barbara still loved to watch the birds.

We went to Myrtle Beach, South Carolina July 19th–26th. Our children joined us there. What a great time we all had together. Barbara kept thinking the condo in which we were staying was Powell and Kathy's new house. She told them she liked it very much. Barbara had the most fun I have ever seen her have in the water (the pool outside our door). She was so advanced in her illness she did not worry about getting her hair wet!

After the evening service August 3rd Wilma and Joe Ernsberger and Barbara and I went out for ice cream. Barbara enjoyed it so much.

Tuesday, August 12th was my birthday. It never registered with Barbara that it was my birthday, although I received birthday cards and calls and Mother took Barbara and me out to lunch. And that made me sad about Barbara's deteriorating condition. She had not been able to personally get me a gift for years. But up until then she had urged me to get something for myself from her. There was no longer thought of anything like that.

And Barbara was asking the same questions over and over. I'll have to admit, it sometimes got on my nerves, but I tried to remember that she was speaking from her then-diminished perception of reality. *She* did not realize she was repeating herself. If I tried to "straighten her out" it only made matters worse. I needed to attempt to enter her "reality," and talk with her accordingly (by patiently answering the same questions again and again and again). What never "worked" was my trying to insist she enter my reality, because of course, she couldn't.

The following Sunday morning Barbara seemed more confused than usual. I realized I might not be able to leave her alone much longer whether she wanted a companion or not. I felt the weight of all this the whole day. By then she was sitting in a chair beside my desk while I studied at home in the mornings. She seemed content to let me study. She simply wanted to be where I was. And it was working.

In late August we had a staff picnic at the church. Barbara went with me. Although she could still take herself to the bathroom at home, she could no longer go to a restroom in a strange place by herself. So when she needed to "go" Ellen Geisert, our church business administrator, took her. In a few minutes Ellen came to get me, frightened. Barbara was bleeding badly. Ellen guarded the door while I went in. When I got the blood washed away, I could see it was coming from her rectum. I got things back together as best I could, took Barbara home and got her cleaned up. For the first time she was not totally against having surgery. So much bleeding had scared her, and it had frightened me too.

We went to the Barter Theatre in Abingdon, Virginia to see *Camelot*. That was one of Barbara's favorites and she enjoyed it very much.

The last Sunday in August we went to church with Mary Beth in Johnson City. Then we had a quick lunch at Wendy's. I had planned to go by Bluefield to visit relatives there, but long before we got to the place where we would have turned off for Bluefield, Barbara became sort of hysterical and panicked, so I decided not to try it. I felt pretty discouraged. Barbara was so confused. A couple of times on the way home I got her into a ladies' room, and she did not know where to go in there, she couldn't find the stall. It was getting harder and harder for her, and therefore for me.

On Labor Day Barbara slept until 10:00 AM, which was most unusual for her. But she seemed exhausted. As confused as she was I was sure it took more energy than I could imagine for her just to get through every day.

I called Pam to see if she could spend the next Friday night with Barbara so I could go to the church Officers' Retreat at Hat Creek. Pam could not because of a shower for their daughter in Richmond. So I called to see if Mother could do it. She seemed delighted that I asked her and planned on staying with Barbara while I was gone.

September 4th was Barbara's and my 42nd wedding anniversary, but it simply did not register with her. That night we planned to go out to dinner with the Rubles, the Thomases and the Stinesprings. Going out with them had nothing to do with our anniversary; we did this with these couples quite regularly. If Barbara had been more aware of things like our anniversary I would have had them do it on a different date. But I thought under the circumstances both Barbara and I would enjoy it. And we did. I said nothing of our anniversary to the others.

The following week I took Barbara to Dr. Wade. She did not have a urinary tract infection, but he did give me some medicine for her hemorrhoids and thought she might well need surgery for that when we got back from England. He also gave me some medicine to give her for anxiety.

I went to a one-day church meeting out of town. Mother came to our house about 11:00 AM, took Barbara out to lunch and stayed until I got back about 5:30 PM.

On September 22nd Barbara and I went to see Dad. There was no response from him at all. He was not in a coma; it was more like a stupor. I knew he could not last long like that. I hated to go to England with him in that shape. But I had promised John Winter I would cover for him while he took care of his family in this huge crisis with his wife's health. It was not as if we were simply going on a vacation. I told Mother that if Dad should die while we were gone, we could not come back early. She understood.

The next morning, the last Sunday in September, the day before we were to leave for England, our dog Prince had a huge accident in the house. That had never happened before. That morning when I had every minute tightly planned I walked into the kitchen and smelled something awful. I turned on the light in the dining room and discovered Prince had had diarrhea all over the carpet. While I was shoveling and scrubbing, Barbara came out. She wanted to help me. (She had always been the "super" helper.) But I knew she could not. I was afraid she would walk in it and get it all over herself. So I told her the best way to help me would be if she could go back to bed and rest a while. So she did that while I cleaned up the mess. Then I got myself and Barbara ready. And I did not have time to go over my sermon before leaving for church.

The next day we drove to Baltimore-Washington International Airport and we met Charlotte's plane. I had given Barbara a tranquilizer Scott had prescribed before we left home and she had done beautifully all day. She did not even need to stop on our way to Baltimore, except when we were stopping anyway.

The following day we arrived safely in London. We visited Ely and its beautiful cathedral. A great day! As we came back to the room Barbara said, "We have really been having fun today!" The tranquilizer Scott prescribed seemed to be making a positive difference.

We arrived in Whitby October 3rd. The following day our son Laddie called to say Dad was very ill with pneumonia and a high fever. They would not be surprised if he did not pull through this. I called Mother. She was doing pretty well. She said she had spent a couple of hours the previous day simply looking into his glazed eyes. He was unresponsive. Then she said, "I love you." And he asked, "What for?" and she replied, "For all your money." And he smiled. I had heard them do that exchange (a game of theirs) many, many times.

Following lunch the next day we visited an antique shop down the hill from where we were staying and found three Sunderland Lustre cups and saucers. Barbara was so happy. "Oh, please get them," she said, so we did. She was very pleased, and, of course, that pleased me.

On October 14th we visited Stratford-upon-Avon. Barbara wanted Charlotte to do a transfer (as Barbara had done with Mary Bell's help in 1993). So we went to that place and Charlotte did one of Anne Boleyn.

Alex Green, a Church of Scotland minister from Strathblane (about 15 minutes north of Glasgow) telephoned to see if I would do an exchange with him July of the following year. I told him our circumstances and that therefore it would be unlikely we could do it, but I would try to find someone else who could.

We went down to the harbor in Whitby to see a replica of Captain Cook's ship *Endeavor* come in. It was windy and cold, but Barbara did very well. She enjoyed seeing the ship.

On October 21st we had just walked in the door a few minutes after 9:00 PM when the phone rang. It was Mother telling me Dad had died a couple of hours before (1:20 PM their time). Barbara was very sad about Dad's death. She cried quite a bit and had a couple episodes of real sobbing. She loved Dad, and he had loved her. Although I was very sorry not to be there with Mother at a time like that, she was well taken care of, first by our son Laddie, then our other children, then the larger family, and, of course, the church family. I loved Dad too and would miss him a lot.

On October 28th we had a good flight back on Iceland Air. I expected this would be our last long trip.

For several weeks before we had gone to England I had been putting Barbara's lipstick and rouge on her. She wanted to have them applied, but could no longer do it herself.

By November 2nd I noticed Barbara was worse. She could not find the basement door to let the cat up. She would hear the cat crying and look for her, but did not know to open the basement door.

When Barbara had a bowel movement she did not get herself clean, so, if I was home, I washed her bottom with a soapy wash cloth.

If Barbara washed dishes, she did not get them clean and did not rinse them, so I tried to beat her to it. But she still remained cheerful most of the time. I kept wondering how long it would be before I could no longer leave her alone, although she insisted she did not want anyone to stay with her.

Barbara and I had our annual physical exams November 5th. My blood pressure was up (for the first time). Other than Barbara's *big problem* she was fine.

A few days later one of the ladies told me the Rivermont Presbyterian Women had decided to bring us meals *twice* a week. I think I would have objected if Scott had not found my blood pressure up. Maybe I had been trying to do too much.

Our prayer group met at our house on Barbara's birthday. Amber Hoke brought a birthday cake. It was a beautifully decorated, delicious coconut cake. I was not sure it had sunk into Barbara's head that it was *her* birthday. I got the impression at one point that she thought it was Amber's birthday. Anyway, she had a good time.

November 21st I took Barbara to see Bill Gayle, a friend and surgeon, to see about her rectal bleeding. He said she did not need surgery, but he could treat it right away with a cauterization and twice again at three-week intervals, and she ought to be fine. It was not painful for her either during or after the treatment.

None of those I asked were able to do an exchange with Alex Green in Strathblane, Scotland the following summer. So I called him to say we would come. I knew this was probably pushing it with Barbara as "out of it" as she was by then.

On the evening of December 5th when I drove into our driveway at home I could see Barbara sitting at the dining room front window looking out and when I got in she said she "had been crying all day, because I thought you might have left me." That killed me. I hugged her and assured her I would never leave her. I was surprised – that day especially because I had been there all morning, then Lerlyne Garcia took her to get her hair done and out to lunch, so Barbara really had not been there that long by herself. I came in at 4:30 PM. I thought Lerlyne must have mentioned missing us at the Deacons' Party the night before, because Barbara said people did not invite us anymore. ("I don't think they like me.") Well, I explained to her that a big crowd at a large party made her nervous, and, although we had been invited, I had declined for us both. But I do not think she understood what I was trying to say. Life was getting tougher, as I had known it would. But I hated to have her feel abandoned by me or anyone else.

As Mother was leaving church the first Sunday in December she told me she had fallen again that morning, but had not hurt herself—her walker had caught on a rug. I wished I could do more for her, but with all I had on my plate at home and at church, I hardly thought I could do more than I was doing.

A couple of weeks later I ran into Bill Gayle in the hospital. He asked how Barbara was doing. I told him since that treatment he had given her she had not shed a drop of blood. He said he did not need to see her the following week as he had planned. "If it's not broke, don't fix it," he said. I was so glad she was apparently over it. Bill did say if she had any more trouble to let him know.

When I got home in the afternoon Barbara had a white sock on plus one of the colored socks I had put on her that morning. She also had several panties scattered about. I did not know why, and neither did she. She was not upset, but said she had just gotten confused. Later she said she was afraid when she got her clothes all mixed up and did not know what to do. I asked her if she would like for me to get someone to come and stay with her when I had to be away. She said, "No, I can take care of myself." But I knew I might have to make such arrangements before very long whether she wanted me to or not. Perhaps the main reason she was still asserting this little bit of independence was that, by that time, her short-term memory was so poor, she did not remember the times she felt afraid.

In mid December I found a CD of the old record of the Robert Shaw Chorale's "Joy to the World," which we had and used and loved for years. Our record had become so badly scratched we had not been able to use it for a long time. Barbara was delighted to be able to listen to this beautiful, familiar music again.

On Christmas Day Barbara did not know how to open her gifts. I handed them to her, she waited for me to unwrap them for her, and then she picked up the contents of the package and showed interest.

By the last day of the year, Barbara was very tired. I thought having so many people around had worn her out, not that she had done anything, but having a crowd changed our routine. She asked me to help her get ready for bed at 8:00 PM. I did; she went to bed and fell asleep right away.

Chapter Nine: 1998

Barbara and I watched most of *The Search for Red October* on television. I was watching more television and videos than I ever had before because Barbara felt that when we both did this we were "doing something together." So, it was worth it. One evening I had suggested to Barbara that perhaps she was watching too much television. She started to cry and said, "I don't think that's very nice of you to say. That's the only thing I can do." I felt awful for making her feel so badly. Because she was right. She could no longer read, clean, cook, wash or iron. Watching television, even though she could not follow a story line, was all she could do.

In mid-January I had a Church Session Meeting after Evening Worship (the Church Session is the body of elders that governs a local Presbyterian church). During my meeting Barbara went home with Marie Seiger. Marie was always so kind to her.

Later that week Barbara and I went to the Plaza and bought a quilt for our bed, something she had wanted very much to do. Someone had told her that they were having a good sale on quilts.

On the first Monday in February my discussion group met. I asked them if they could start meeting in my home study. I simply could not leave Barbara alone any more in the evening. Of course, the group was glad to accommodate.

Mary Beth was very excited that my mother wanted to come to Bristol and Johnson City with Barbara and me at the end of that month. For the past three years while Dad had been so sick Mother had not left Lynchburg, and then her knee had become so painful she couldn't. So we were especially glad she felt up to it at this time.

In mid-February Barbara seemed quite anxious one day, so I took her with me to Amherst to pick up the Nova (her old car which had been in for servicing). Then she and I visited the sick in the hospital together.

Adriana Ribeiro took Barbara for lunch and the afternoon at her house. Barbara enjoyed being with her.

Barbara and I took Frances and Andy Sale for dinner at the Lodge of the Fisherman. We enjoyed it very much.

On Valentine's Day Barbara and I drove over to the cemetery to see Dad's gravestone in place. I sang "Happy Valentine's Day" to Barbara and gave her some gifts. I asked her to sing it to me, and she sang, "Happy Birthday to Barbara."

On Friday, February 20th we went to the Inauguration of Greg Jordan as the twenty-first president of King College, held in the First Presbyterian Church, Bristol. It lasted two hours, but Barbara did very well. Then we drove around the King campus for Mother to see it. Because it was cold and rainy we did not walk around. We had lunch at a favorite restaurant, K. P. Duty on State Street. Mary Beth fixed a delicious supper for us at her apartment. We watched the Winter Olympics on television.

Back in Lynchburg, one evening I went with Paul Mudrick to a book review by Bob Weimer. Paul's wife Gail stayed with Barbara at our house.

Another evening we had supper with Mother at Westminster Canterbury. Then Barbara stayed with Mother while I went to the Long-Range Planning Committee Meeting.

The last day of February I took Mother shopping for a dress for her birthday. (Barbara went with us.) Mother found three dresses on the second floor at Belks. She was very pleased.

By early March I knew I could not leave Barbara alone for any extended period of time. I would get Barbara ready and then take her to Mother's for the day while I went about my pastoral work.

When I came into the house one morning from taking our dog Prince out Barbara said she would like for us to sing. I asked what and she started singing, "There's a Land that Is Fairer than Day." This was the first time in a long time she had suggested singing. And then we sang a few more, including "When I Survey the Wondrous Cross" and "Heavenly Sunshine."

March 11th was Mother's 89th birthday. Barbara and I took her to lunch at Meriwether's Restaurant.

In mid-March I got my email working for the first time. Powell had gotten his the previous week, so we had a good time sending messages back and forth.

One day Barbara called Powell and Kathy's daughter Jodie in Burlington, North Carolina by automatic dialing and told her she (Barbara) was too hot and needed a drink, but did not know what to do. (Jodie could not get Barbara to hang up the phone, so she went to a neighbor's house to call for help for Barbara.) When I got home Gary Brizendine (the building superintendent at our church) was there because Powell had called Rivermont Church. Later Powell called me and suggested I change the way Barbara called the number that rang at their house so it would ring at our church in Lynchburg. But I had lost the directions on how to set the phone up. So I simply removed it and replaced it with another phone.

I knew we were very near having to have someone at home with Barbara whenever I was gone. I would come home and find wads of toilet paper all over in drawers, on the dressers. I tried to show her, but she simply did not get it. So I decided I did not need to talk about it any more. I just needed to pick it up, flush it down and keep my mouth shut!

A bowel movement had gotten impossible for Barbara to handle by herself. So I tried to get that taken care of first thing in the morning, not always successfully.

On March 23rd our prayer group met at our house. Barbara always enjoyed seeing the people who were in our group.

Near the end of March I called a lady in our church to see if she would be able to sit with Barbara as a paid companion. I had not known she was now working full-time at another job.

Four different women from our church took Barbara one Friday a month to get her hair fixed and then to lunch. How kind of them!

On Sunday, March 29th Pam had to be out of town, so instead of asking anyone else to take Barbara to church, I took her with me at 7:30 AM. She sat with Dot Spencer and Janice Hatton during the 8:30 service, then Janice took Barbara with her to Sunday School. Then at the 11:00 AM service Barbara sat with Kay Uotinen. She never realized she had been to two services. I think this way she was much less anxious than she would have been if someone other than Pam had come for her.

Pam called and suggested that I might be able to get Sherri Lindstrom to stay with Barbara. Sherri, a member of Rivermont Presbyterian, had helped with Kitty Davenport's mother and had done an outstanding job.

On April 9th (Maundy Thursday) Sherri said she would help me with Barbara.

On Monday April 20th Sherri sat with Barbara for the first time. Barbara enjoyed Sherri very much. I was so grateful to have found such a good person for Barbara.

Barbara enjoyed having Sherri with her three afternoons that week. She thought of Sherri as a friend who had come to visit her.

After evening church the last Sunday in April Barbara and I went to Billy Joe's ice cream parlor with Janice and Roger Dixon and Barbara and Fred Mayer. My Barbara enjoyed it very much.

One day while Sherri was with Barbara she made a spool doll "with" Barbara (Sherri actually did it, but said she and Barbara had done it together). Barbara was so proud of it and was eager to show me when I got home. It was sitting on the mantel. Barbara talked and talked about it. She said, "I am so happy!"

In mid-May I had a Church Session meeting after evening worship. Barbara stayed with Mary and Joe Spencer while I was at the meeting.

On May 19th when we got up Barbara said, "Is Sherri coming today?" "No," I replied. "Today is my day off and I'll be here with you." "Oh," she said in a disappointed voice. When Sherri was there she gave her undivided time to Barbara. When I was there, I took care of Barbara, but had lots of other things to do around the house.

I got the potted plants outside and planted the impatiens. Barbara sat on the porch and watched me most of the day.

Barbara and Sherri went out to a farm and picked strawberries near the end of May. Barbara had a ball! We had strawberry shortcake for supper that night.

On May 25th Mary Beth called and asked if May 22nd the following year would be clear for her and Alan Marcum's wedding at Rivermont Church. I thought so, but would have to check the master schedule at the church to make sure. I checked and May 22, 1999 was open. So they planned their wedding for that day. I prayed Barbara could hold out until then at least.

In the middle of June Charlotte called to say that because she had another tear in her retina she would not be able to go to Scotland with us. There was nothing to do at that point, but to go on and trust the Lord to work it out. But this would make the trip for us much more difficult.

I called Alex Green in Strathblane, Scotland to ask if there were a lady in his church who would be willing to sit with Barbara in church when I was leading the service and preaching. He said, "Yes."

On June 21st we had a hard time getting the cat Lucy into the carrier. (Mary Beth was going to keep the cat while we are away.) Barbara cried because Mary Beth was taking Lucy away. "Don't take my kitty, don't take my kitty," she sobbed. I tried to explain to her that this was only for while we are away in Scotland, but she did not understand.

I bought some pads that strap on the body for Barbara. But she absolutely refused to wear them. "I'm no baby! I'm not going to wear diapers!" I would have to save them for when she became a little less aware.

On June 29th we left for Scotland. I could not find a handicap restroom for Barbara in the Baltimore-Washington Airport, so ended up taking Barbara to the men's room handicapped stall, a first for us. I felt odd doing that, but I had no choice. There was no way at this point that she could go into a restroom by herself and find her way around. As we came out of the stall one fellow looked quite startled. But it was obvious Barbara was not paying any attention to anyone else there. And on the plane it was quite a trick to take her to the restroom! There was hardly room for one person in those small spaces. We were literally belly to belly. We both got tickled and laughed and laughed.

Early the next morning we changed planes in Iceland, and there was a unisex handicapped restroom there right off the public waiting room with plenty of space for luggage! It would have been so helpful in our situation if these had been located in many places. The flight from Iceland to Glasgow was not long. I was so grateful we had arrived safely and that Barbara was OK.

That first night in Scotland we both slept very well. We had breakfast, then I bathed and dressed Barbara, then did the same for myself.

Barbara and I walked to the village (a short walk of two or three blocks), but Barbara's legs almost gave out. We had to stop a couple of times for her to rest. I had not remembered her having trouble walking before.

Monica and Geoffrey Philips came by the manse. Geoffrey would open the church at 10:15 on Sunday mornings and Monica who was a retired nurse would sit with Barbara during worship.

Barbara was having trouble walking. This was not obvious, but she simply gave out after a very short walk. Therefore, we were severely limited what we could do. Even a short walk around the village was very difficult, and to ride much in the car got us away from restrooms. So I guessed we would stay at the manse most of the time which was all right with me.

Barbara gave me a scare in the night. I got up to go to the bathroom and did not even realize she was not in bed with me. I found her in the hall with a dress on she had gotten out of a closet in another bedroom. It was one of her dresses; we had hung several in that other room. In the morning I found a light on downstairs that I was sure I had turned off the night before. It must have been very frightening for her, although when I found her she did not appear to be afraid. She simply said, "I am confused." It was a real mercy she had not fallen down the stairs!

Barbara had been talking about wanting to go to see our friends in Whitby (England), but I really did not see how I could manage it with her restroom problems. I had to help her find the toilet even when we were already in the bathroom at the house. She had tried to sit on the edge of the bathtub several times.

Peter Brumby called from Whitby. He and Jean wondered if we would like for them to come up July 21, spend the night with us and then take us for two nights to Gairlock – 240 miles north on the west coast – way up through the Highlands. How kind of them to offer! We were happy to accept.

Barbara was in a good mood most of the time, but was sleeping a lot during the day – as well as sleeping well at night.

Monica and Geoff took us to Aberfoyle to a woolen mill where we saw a sheep show and wool spinning. I bought Barbara a woolen suit. We also got her a couple of very attractive blouses which she picked out herself.

On July 14th Isobelle Brown and Isabelle Kelman took Barbara to the Kelmans' house while Brian Kelman took me on a long walk up Conic Hill that overlooks Loch Lomond and John Young went with us. Stunningly beautiful views! Brian had packed a lunch for us. Shortly after they brought me back to the manse Nancy Sharp and Marie Forgey returned Barbara to me. She had had a good day too.

On July 16th Barbara asked me, "Am I married?" She had never asked that before. I assured her that she was, that we were, and that seemed to settle it with her for the time being.

The next day David Hawks took me for a nice hike while his wife Judy kept Barbara. A few days later Isobelle and Jim Brown took us to lunch at a hotel at the edge of Lake Menteith (the only *lake* in Scotland – they are normally called *lochs* in that beautiful land). Afterwards Isobelle and Barbara stayed in the sitting room of the hotel while Jim and I rode a boat to the island which contained the ruins of Inchmahome Priory.

Jean and Peter Brumby drove us through the Scottish Highlands to Gairlock. Barbara got quite fussy during the trip. We arrived at the home of Janet and Donny Macrae. What warm, hospitable people they were! Barbara especially loved their little dog. I noticed the Macraes had a canister of "Wet Ones" by the toilet. I thought it would be a good idea for me to buy some to keep handy in our bathroom at home for cleaning Barbara after she had had a bowel movement.

We drove back to Strathblane by way of Inverness. There was so much we could have seen there, but we still had a long way to go and Barbara was very tired. I would have loved to pop down to Loch Ness which was nearby, but thought it would be unwise. We arrived back in Strathblane safely. We had been so blessed by the Brumbys and the Macraes! We were sad to have Jean and Peter leave us to return home to Whitby.

As Barbara and I were leaving Scotland an Icelandic Air agent said they were upgrading us to "Business Class" because of Barbara's disability. How nice! There was great food and service in "Business Class."

Barbara and I had a planned couple of days' layover in Iceland. We went to the hotel shop and bought gifts to take home. (Actually we had them mailed home since Barbara could no longer carry anything and my shoulders and hands were already full of our carry-on luggage.) The clerk in the hotel shop, Maria Steffansdatter, was very helpful. She reminded me of our Mary Beth. Maria was sympathetic about Barbara. Her grandmother had Alzheimer's. Maria even offered to take us (the next day, her day off) to see the huge Lutheran Cathedral which was near where she lived, and she gave me her home telephone number.

We went for a van tour of the city. The driver was a committed Christian whose father was a pastor. He knew a friend of ours! Barbara had a terrible time getting in and out of the van. I noticed she was walking with her shoulders slumped, like Dad had done during his last years. So sad. We ate supper at the hotel, but Barbara ate very little. She seemed quite anxious and kept asking me the same questions over and over. I was very certain this would be our last trip. I tried to get Barbara to take a short walk that evening. But she wanted to return to the hotel immediately. When we got back to the room she wanted to do something, so we watched CNN News. But Barbara kept ringing her hands and walking around the room.

Before we had left Scotland I had bought some "Wet Ones." They were perfect for her bathroom needs. They were so much more efficient than a washcloth.

Barbara kept putting her napkin in her food on her plate, and she tried to eat her cereal at breakfast with the spoon upside down. When I tried to help her she said, "When you do that you scare me." I told her I was just trying to help, but rational explanations did not make any sense to her.

I did not called Maria. It had been so kind of her to offer, but Barbara was not up to going over and seeing the big church (I did write a note of appreciation when we got home, and received a gracious reply from Maria).

I took Barbara to the restroom just before we got on the bus for the airport. It was about a forty-minute ride. Barbara wet her pants while I was getting our bags off the bus at the airport, but it did not seem to bother her much.

When we got to the ticket counter I told the agent we needed an aisle seat and one next to it if possible, because I needed to be able to get Barbara to the restroom as easily as possible. They did not have any left, so again they put us in "Business Class" where we had very comfortable seats (only two on each side of the aisle instead of the usual three). We had outstanding food and service. The flight to Baltimore was very good.

Driving back to Lynchburg on the last day of July we hit the Washington traffic at the wrong time. So it took us two hours to go forty miles. During that time, when there was no place to "go," Barbara really had to "go," and agreed to use the female urinal I had brought. For the first attempt I got it way too far forward, and, although Barbara was standing outside the car (with thousands of cars slowly creeping by), a clear stream shot behind her to the car seat! The next time I got the urinal back further, but still not far enough. About half of the urine went into the receptacle. The other half dribbled down the back of the urinal all over her slacks. But it did not seem to bother her. I grabbed one of my tee shirts out of a suit case and tried to sop up the seat (the first time) and her slacks (the second). We did get to our house about 1:00 PM. I felt so relieved and grateful to the Lord to have had a safe trip all the way to Scotland and back!

On August 10th a member of our church telephoned. His wife had found out earlier in the day that she had a very aggressive breast cancer. I called Mother to see if Barbara could stay with her while I went over to see the distressed family. Mother was not in her apartment, so I took Barbara with me on this pastoral visit.

The next day Barbara kept asking me to take her home. I told her we were at home, but she said she did not feel like she was home. I felt so sorry for her. I surely did hope this was temporary.

In mid-August I bought a bathtub chair to use with Barbara. Getting seated in the tub had become frightening to her; she just did not know what to do, even when I was helping and telling her each step. I had been bathing her for quite a while before this. When I started giving Barbara a bath I had asked a nurse to show me how and she had said she would be glad to. But before she did I think I figured it out pretty well. So I told the nurse I did not think I needed to have her demonstrate to me how to bathe Barbara. Back when I had asked for the help, as I had thought more about it, I had been afraid it might have been embarrassing to Barbara. But by the summer of 1998 I did not think it would have bothered Barbara at all.

I got a big scare one afternoon. Barbara and I were visiting Mother. Barbara went into Mother's bathroom. We heard a crash. I ran in there. Barbara had tried to sit on the toilet, but instead sat on the edge of the bathtub and fell right in. She was stuck on her back, cross ways in the tub, and "hurt" and frightened. I got her out, brought her home and gave her some Ibuprofen. I did examine her and she did not seem to have anything really wrong. Mainly she was shaken up – and so was I!

A lady in our church sent me a list of seventeen people she had asked (and who had agreed) to sit as volunteers from time to time with Barbara. I hoped this would enable me to "keep going" at the church one more year. Since I could not leave Barbara alone I simply could not do my job adequately at the church for another year without this kind of help. Sherri came in the daytime, but sometimes I needed help in the evening.

Barbara stayed with Mother one afternoon, but kept asking where I was.

I happened to be home when one of the ladies brought Barbara back from her hair appointment and lunch. Somehow, the one who had taken Barbara had locked her keys and Barbara in the car. Barbara was fine; she did not realize her predicament. But at first neither could she pull the lock button up. She simply did not get it. But I kept calm and kept talking to her, and she finally did it. She did not mention it afterwards, so it must not have scared her.

Over my lifetime I had seen many people, including some pastors, yearning for retirement. They had counted the years, the months, the weeks, and the days between where they were and that *golden day* when they would stop working. Either they had not liked their jobs in the first place or they had become tired of what they were doing and were eager to move on to something else or to doing nothing. That had never been true of me. I had always loved being a pastor. The church which I was serving was flourishing. God was apparently continuing to make my ministry effective. If it had not been for Barbara's special needs, I might have stayed on indefinitely. I had known some pastors who had remained far too long past their prime. They had been blind to what had been plain to everyone else. That could have been my temptation. But Barbara's disabilities were increasing to such an extent, I heard the Lord calling me through her very handicaps to lay down God's pastoral call to me and take up God's call to care for my wife full-time. The church could find another pastor. But Barbara had only one husband – me.

On August 26th I had lunch with my colleague John Mabray. I talked with him about my need to retire the following year and about soon publicly announcing my retirement plans.

The next day I took Barbara to our dentist for a regular cleaning, and he found an abscess. She had complained periodically (but not regularly) about a sore in her mouth, but I had thought it was a canker sore. Anyway, she needed a root canal.

September 4th was our 43rd wedding anniversary. I felt sad because at that point Barbara simply could not take it or anything like it in. I did not mention the anniversary to her because it seemed less stressful (to me anyway) to simply let it go. We planned to have our picture taken for the church directory that afternoon, and then go to have supper with Mother. Since Barbara got her hair done that day I thought it would the best time for the picture.

I took Barbara to Adriana Ribeiro's while I went to our Officers' Retreat at Hat Creek and led the Communion Service. I could not be away from Barbara at night anymore, so I had missed the night session the day before.

By the end of September Barbara for the first time started having bowel movement accidents. She did not seem to realize she was the one who had done it. The first time she still had her nightgown on during breakfast, so it went all over the place. I hoped this was a fluke and not the beginning of a new trend.

Also, I had to change Barbara's place at the table because she had forgotten how to put both hands around the seat of her chair to pull herself up to the table. And I could not push her on the carpet. So when I changed her place I was able to push her chair on the bare floor and it worked. (I put her chair on a carpet remnant square. That way I was able to push the chair forward under the table without scratching the floor.)

On the first Sunday night in October there was a beautiful moon. I took Barbara outside to show it to her. I asked her what it was, and she did not know. I said, "Is it the sun?" She replied, "Yes! That's it!" When I told her what it was it didn't seem to register with her.

Pam called and said she had found a couple of dresses at a new shop in the Galleria downtown she thought might work for Barbara to wear to Mary Beth and Alan's wedding. We went down and bought them. Barbara did not object at all, but neither was she excited about it. She just could not grasp it.

Barbara had not had any more bowel movement accidents, so I guessed she had had a bug for a couple of days. I was very thankful we did not have to deal with that every day (at least, not yet).

On October 18th I told the elders of our church of my retirement plans at the end of August 1999. The saddest part of it for me was in telling Barbara afterwards and getting no response at all. By that time she did not understand what retirement was.

The next day I mailed the following letter to the congregation:

Dear Rivermont Presbyterian Church Family,

I believe God is calling me to retire as co-pastor of Rivermont Presbyterian Church at the end of August 1999. The enclosed article by Robertson McQuilkin says much better than I can why. I read this piece when it first came out in Christianity Today in 1990. Its substance has been a guide to me as I have sought to be faithful to the Lord, to my wife Barbara, and to you, the most supportive and loving congregation for which any pastor could hope.

Barbara and I began struggling with her memory loss over ten years ago. Three years later came the diagnosis from the physicians, 'Alzheimer's Disease.' By the time the doctors told us this Barbara could no longer cook. Countless numbers of you kindly have brought us meals! Nor could Barbara manage going through a church service by herself. Several of you have sat with her at church and Sunday School. For many years Barbara's decline was gradual. She was able to stay at home alone when I needed to be away from the house in connection with my pastoral work. But during the past few months she has deteriorated quite rapidly. I have not been able to leave her alone since April. From that time I have had to have a companion with her when I have needed to be away during the day, and many others of you on a volunteer basis have stayed with her when I have had to tend to my work away from home at other times. Four women in our church, one at a time, have faithfully taken her to get her hair done and then out to lunch each week for years. The way Barbara's disease has progressed lately, I feel certain that by next year she will need me full-time.

Some might be thinking, 'Why announce your retirement almost a year before it will take place?' I admit this goes against all general advice. But we are brothers and sisters in the Lord. I do not think we are to play games with each other. I am convinced it would not be right for me to know in my heart what I believe God is calling me to do, while letting those responsible for planning Rivermont Presbyterian's future staff needs stumble around in the dark. If you know my intentions this far ahead your own planning can be much more informed. And, because God is blessing our congregation so abundantly, wise planning is critical. Having a perceptive strategy is only good stewardship.

Believe me, I do not intend simply to drift into retirement during this last year. Although my activities away from home are already curtailed because of Barbara's needs, I pray that the Lord will enable me to have a fruitful final year at the church. If I did not suppose this were possible, I would retire immediately.

There will be more opportunities for me to thank you for all your support over the years and especially during these years that Barbara has been ill. But I want you to know now that without your help, the support of superb co-pastors and the assistance of an outstanding staff, I neither could have carried on until now, nor could I contemplate continuing another year. You are a great congregation for which I thank the Lord daily. May the Lord continue to guide and bless us all.

Yours in the love of Christ,
Lowell Beach Sykes

In late October I was cooking one morning and Barbara was standing just a step behind me. I had my hands full, and asked her to go sit in her rocking chair. She tried to, but could not. Before she got there, she put her hands out as if to feel the chair (like she was blind) – but she was not there yet. So she got on her knees on the floor and then sat on the floor and seemed surprised, not afraid. I quickly washed my hands and went over and helped her up. I wondered if her depth perception was way off. She had never done that before.

I could not get one of our disabled church members out of my mind. I had visited her in a nursing home. She was by then in a fetal position. She could not speak, but did try to hit me when I had prayer with her. And she had been such a sweet lady! She had been diagnosed with Alzheimer's Disease some time after Barbara, was a good bit older than Barbara and had gone down much faster. I prayed the Lord would either take Barbara before she got to that stage or so work in me that I could handle it as a believer in Jesus Christ should.

On the first Sunday in November we worshiped in Kingsport, Tennessee at the Marcum family's Baptist church. On the way back we called Laddie in Roanoke, went by to see his new apartment and then ate together in a Chinese Restaurant. Barbara enjoyed seeing Laddie, but the rest of the afternoon was awful for her. She was very confused, afraid, having to stop often and sobbing lots of the time. I had no idea what was at the bottom of it. Probably simply too much going on.

Barbara, Mother and I ate Barbara's birthday supper November 10th at Main Street Eatery. Barbara had increasing difficulty feeding herself, but she got through it all right.

A few days later Barbara and I went to Grave's Mountain Lodge with Sandra and David Norman. David and I went for a hike while Barbara stayed with Sandra in the Lodge. We had adjoining rooms and we visited in their room until it was time to go to bed. Sandra was so good with Barbara.

Some people in our church told me they were going to help contribute to the cost of having more help with Barbara. I was so moved that when I tried to respond with appreciation, I broke down. In that time of acute need to be surrounded by friends and caring people like that was quite overwhelming!

One evening I went outside to put the garbage can on the curb. When I got back inside Barbara had dropped an open liter of Coke on the carpet in the dining room. It took some time to clean up.

The next morning Barbara went to the bathroom and did not make it to the toilet. She wet all over herself and the floor, and it took a while to get her and the bathroom cleaned up. She did not seem to know how the mess had gotten there.

About that time another evening Barbara was trying to sit in her rocking chair and missed. She landed on the floor. I helped her up. I was so glad she was not really hurt.

We had Papa John's pizza for supper one night. By then we did not eat pizza regularly. But we both liked it and it was easy for Barbara to manage.

On Thanksgiving evening we gathered at our house for dessert. My brother Ern (from New York) and Alan played their guitars and we all sang. We had a very enjoyable evening. Barbara loved it when people sang.

The first Saturday in December I did not go to presbytery (the body of elders which governs the Presbyterian Church in a nearby region) because I did not think it was fair to ask a volunteer to keep Barbara all day on a Saturday in December. So Barbara went with me as I bought a wreath for the front door and a Christmas tree which I put in a bucket of water.

One afternoon I took Barbara to Mary and Joe Spencer's while I performed a wedding ceremony. After that Barbara and I ate at the Chinese Restaurant at Boonsboro Shopping Center. When we got home Barbara wet her pants, but had not said anything about needing to go.

Our prayer group met at the Rosenthals' for our annual Christmas party. Barbara enjoyed it.

One day in the middle of December Barbara kept asking where Mary Beth was. I told her Mary Beth was at her home in Bristol, and that she would be coming here in a couple of days for Christmas. Barbara was really missing her.

The next Sunday evening, when I came in from church Mary Beth was crying. She said, "Oh, Daddy! Mama doesn't know who I am. We knew this would happen, but I hadn't expected it yet. This is so hard! She asked me who I was. I told her, 'You are my mama and Daddy is my daddy,' but she said, 'I'm not your mama.'" I assured Mary Beth that I thought this was only temporary; Mama had had a lot of people around and many things going on the past several days. At least I hoped it was only temporary.

The next day Barbara did know Mary Beth. So Mary Beth left for Bristol feeling better.

Eating had gotten harder for Barbara. She would eat a little and then "give up" by saying she had had enough. So I started feeding her some. And I could imagine it would not be too long before I would need to feed her everything she ate. It was easier for her to pick up something in her hand to eat than to try to manipulate a fork and spoon. She had not been able to cut food with a knife for some time.

New Year's Eve we spent a quiet evening at home. As I looked back over the year I thanked the Lord for his faithfulness to us throughout this year. Even as life had gotten much harder for us, the Lord had provided.

In our Christmas Letter that year, among other things, I wrote:

As most of you know, about ten years ago Barbara and I began struggling with her memory loss. Three years later the physicians said, "Alzheimer's Disease." Unlike many people with Alzheimer's, Barbara is and has been gracious, sweet and loving throughout these years of slow decline. During the past several months her deterioration has been more rapid. Since April I have had to have a companion with her when I have had to be away from home in connection with my pastoral work. Barbara is most content when I am with her. Therefore, I feel called by God to retire at the end of next summer so that I can be with and minister to Barbara full-time. I announced this to the Rivermont Presbyterian congregation in October. I could not have worked this long if it had not been for their loving understanding, support and help.

This past summer Barbara and I did an exchange with an evangelical Church of Scotland minister, Alex Green and his family. We spent a month in the manse of the Parish Church of Strathblane (just north of Glasgow). The good people of that congregation were a great blessing to us, helping with Barbara in many kind and generous ways. This trip showed me it would be our last. We were pushing the outer edges of what is possible for Barbara now. But I do thank the Lord for several wonderful trips since Barbara became ill. Little did I dream, when the doctors advised me in 1991 that if there were things I wanted to do with Barbara I'd better do them quickly because we might not have much time, that the Lord would give us several years during which we would be able to travel with enjoyment and make new friends. Great memories!

Chapter Ten: 1999

On New Year's Day I was very aware the new year would bring vast change to Barbara and me of which I was aware – and I also knew there would be some changes of which I knew nothing at all. I prayed:

Change and decay in all around I see,
O Thou who changest not, abide with me.
(from the hymn, *Abide with Me*, by Henry F. Lyte, 1847)

By early January whenever Barbara got up in the night to urinate I had to get up with her. She could not find the toilet even though the light was on in our bedroom bathroom, and also she could not pull her gown up when she sat down on the toilet. A couple of times she had sat without pulling up the gown and, of course, had soaked the gown. But I was very thankful she still knew when she had to go for both #1 and #2. There would be a big change in her needs when that ability was lost.

By January 12th, when I took Mother and Barbara to lunch at Main Street Eatery, I had to put every bite in Barbara's mouth. This was new.

By mid-January Barbara did not notice anything on television. She only complained about it if she thought something sounded "silly" or "scary."

Barbara could no longer find her way around the bed – nor did she know where to lie down to have her head hit the pillow right. So I walked her around the bed, sat her on the right spot, pulled her legs up and drew the covers over her. She had the most beautiful smile when I was "tucking her in," whether to bed at night or for a nap on the couch. It must have made her feel secure and cared for. She could no longer find her way to the bathroom from the bed.

One night at 3:00 AM Barbara got up to go to the bathroom. Then she was up every five minutes or so (and, of course, so was I), so neither of us got any more sleep. I was glad that did not yet happen often.

Also, Barbara's "shuffling" was worse and she tended to walk bent over from the waist. She could straighten up when I ask her to, but she did not unless I asked.

Barbara was speaking much less. Earlier she had asked me the same questions over and over. Now it was rare for her to say anything, except sometimes to tell me she was hungry or thirsty, hot or cold.

On Sunday evening, January 24th there was a Missions Service so Vic Uotinen, our Director of Missions, preached. I sat with Barbara in the congregation. She kept trying to stand up at inappropriate times. So as not to interrupt the sermon, I took her to the Family Room and we listened to the sermon over the speaker. It was a fine sermon and there was a great crowd. We did not stay for the "tasting" of African food. Barbara was simply too agitated. I wondered how much longer she would be able to attend worship.

In late February I took Barbara with me while I did some premarital counseling. It worked fine. The couple was most understanding.

On February 25th Mary Beth was having her pre-wedding pictures taken at the photographer's in Forest. A few days before she had said to me, "Daddy, Mama is going down so fast now, she may not be able to have pictures taken at the wedding in May. Let's get her in some of these pre-wedding pictures." I thought it was a good idea too. So that morning I took Barbara to get her hair done, then brought her home and put on her the dress we planned for her to wear to the wedding, then took her to the photographer's where we met Mary Beth.

Tears came to my eyes when I saw the photographer taking pictures of Mary Beth in her wedding gown and veil, and again when I saw her together with Barbara having some pictures taken. Although no mention of this had been made beforehand, Mary Beth insisted that there be a picture of me with them. Later I was so glad Mary Beth did this. Although we did get some pictures of Barbara at the wedding, by that time she was not able to hold her head up, even when we asked her to. Nor was she able to smile for a picture as she had for the February photos.

On March 9th Barbara fell on the floor because she "missed" her rocking chair when she tried to sit down. She was scared but not hurt.

In mid-March Barbara wet while she was sitting on her glider rocker. She had never done that before. Of course, I changed her clothes. I was out of Spick and Span, so did not have anything with which to properly clean the chair, but I would not have known how to get down inside anyway. I hoped I could keep the house from smelling like a run-down nursing home!

On March 22nd I had a hard time getting Barbara up the steps at Marie Seiger's house. This had not been a problem before.

A few evenings later the Rubles, the Stinesprings, the Thomases and we went to supper at Boodles Restaurant. I ordered Barbara things she could pick up with her fingers – the only things she could eat now without being fed. She had no idea how to manage a knife, fork or spoon.

After the Easter services Jean and Peter Brumby who were visiting from England came over for a couple of hours. Jean was a wonderful communicator with Barbara. She put her hands on Barbara's cheeks and talked with her, and Barbara beamed with joy.

(Perhaps Jean, as an outstanding teacher of young children, had discovered this method was especially effective with them.)

Barbara and I went to the Department of Motor Vehicles to pick up a handicap sign for the car so we could park closer to entrances. Walking was increasingly difficult for her.

On April 7th we had a good trip to Bluefield – excellent with Barbara's new medicine for "overactive bladder control." After we got back I told Scott we should have gotten that years ago. He said it had been available only about six months.

The following Saturday Mary Beth was given a nice shower at the church. Barbara needed to come home about an hour into it. They called me and I went and got her.

In-mid April Barbara and I went to Richmond. We arrived at Kathy and Fred Whitten's. The red bud and dogwood trees were beautiful on the trip, but Barbara could not appreciate them at all – something she had previously loved.

Barbara stayed with Kathy while I went to Paul Porter and Alison Sinclair's wedding rehearsal. I asked the blessing for the rehearsal dinner but skipped eating so I could get back and put Barbara to bed. But when I arrived Kathy had already done it – including giving Barbara a bath! Kathy told me she had asked Barbara if she would like a bath before she went to bed and Barbara had said, "Yes." Kathy could not get Barbara to sit in the tub (of course, she did not know I use a bathtub chair for her), so she had soaped her up and rinsed her off with the hand-held shower head. Kathy told me Barbara had said several times during her bath, "I need that man!" Sometimes she said that to me, meaning, "I need you." She no longer knew my name. Barbara was sound asleep in bed when I got back to Kathy and Fred's.

April 24th Mary Beth had another shower. Barbara did not go – sad, but it was better not to attempt to drag her through it.

Catherine and John Mabray had Ralph Davis, our Bible Conference preacher, and Barbara and me over for supper. I had to feed Barbara, but that did not seem to bother anybody.

April 26th our prayer group met at Susan and Chris Burch's. I was not sure Barbara and I would be able to do this much longer. Barbara interrupted several times. If she should start "speaking out" in church we would have to stop that, too.

It had not been long since Barbara would come from the bedroom into the den when she woke up. But she was not able to do that any longer. A couple of times after my morning prayer group (which met in my home study) I had found her standing in our bedroom, not upset, but not knowing what to do. She always smiled when she saw me. So from that time on, the mornings when I had prayer group, I would go back every few minutes to check to see if she was awake yet. I could not bear the thought of her standing in the bedroom and not knowing what to do.

At breakfast one morning I had to pick up the pieces of orange and banana and grapes I had prepared for Barbara and put them in her mouth. She could not seem to do that for herself any longer. Until a few days before she could. When I picked them up for her she was very cooperative in opening her mouth and chewing and swallowing the food.

On Sunday, May 2nd Sherri came at 7:30 AM and stayed with Barbara, taking her to the 11:00 AM service. This seemed to work well. Sherri was also able to get a pair of panty hose on Barbara – the new dress Barbara had on was too short for her knee highs. I would have to find out from Sherri how she had done it because Barbara would need panty hose with the dress we had bought for her to wear to Mary Beth's wedding.

A couple of days later I picked up Mother so she could stay with Barbara while I grocery shopped and planted the summer bulbs. Then Mother stayed with Barbara while I went to a Church Session meeting. Barbara wet the couch while Mother was with her.

We went out to supper with the Thomases, the Stinesprings and the Rubles. I had to feed Barbara every bite.

On May 7th when Sherri came in she said Barbara had had two accidents (urinating) when Wanda had been here. Wanda had changed Barbara and washed her clothes. That morning Barbara had a bowel movement in bed. I was afraid I was going to have to have her wear some kind of protective stuff on her bottom. I knew she would not like it, although I thought she would be less aware of it than she had been the previous summer when I had tried to get her to wear a pad. At that time she had absolutely refused! I did try one thing that seemed to feel uncomfortable to her. So I attempted putting an absorbent pad in her regular panties. She seemed to be tolerating that. I hoped it would help!

I cut some roses for Barbara and some tree peonies, but these things she used to love did not seem to register with her by then.

On Mother's Day Barbara and I had dinner with Mother at Westminster Canterbury. Since I had to feed Barbara, we took a table at the back of the dining room with Barbara's back to the crowd, so as not to "put her on display."

May 12th Barbara wet the couch in my study at home when she woke from her nap. So I had to quickly (it was almost time for me to go) change her clothes, wash her, wash the couch with *Spic and Span* (much later my son-in-law Alan recommended *Febreze* which I found to be most effective in such situations) before the caregiver came to sit with her. That evening I ordered some pads and absorbent panties from the Vermont Country Store to try to contain Barbara's increasingly frequent accidents. I knew I must do better at managing this!

Sunday, May 16th Mary Beth had a time with Barbara in church. Barbara kept talking out loud, getting up, and did not like it when Mary Beth told her to sit down. Mary Beth was wondering if Barbara should be at the wedding at all. And she was feeling guilty about this. She talked it over with Pam Ruble. Pam very wisely said, "Mary Beth, your mother was always the 'perfect lady.' She was both dignified and gracious. She never would have wanted to make a spectacle of herself. And, of course, you would not want to parade her inappropriate interruptions before your wedding guests either. She would be mortified if she could know she had 'spoiled' your wedding. Try to think of it from your mother's point of view."

I called Scott Wade. He suggested upping Barbara's dosage of tranquilizer and see how it did the next few days. Mary Beth cried a lot about Barbara's rapid descent the past few weeks. That morning had been the first time Mary Beth had experienced Barbara being that way. She said, "I was so hoping she could play her part at the wedding. And a week before to discover this is just so sad!" And it was.

A couple of days later Mary Beth said she thought it would be nice to set up a frame of a 5" x 7" picture of her and one of Barbara at the reception. I thought it was very sweet of her and said so. Then Mary Beth left to do some errands. As I went down the basement stairs to do the laundry, thinking about the pictures, I started to sob. My reaction surprised me. I had not shed tears over this in a long time. But I had the thought, "To set up a picture of Barbara at the reception is to act as if she were dead. And in many ways she is dead. But she's not dead!" And my grief over her poured out. I prayed I could get through the wedding the following Saturday without acting like a blubbering idiot!

Our dog Prince adored Barbara. He would always lie at her feet. But by that time when Barbara would get up to walk away from

her chair, the dog would not jump up. So Barbara would fall over him.
She had not been seriously hurt, but it would be only a matter of time.
I knew we were going to have to give the dog away. I did not think
Barbara would notice if he were gone. A year before she had wept
when she thought Mary Beth had been taking the cat away, just to
keep the cat for us while we were in Scotland. But things were very
different now.

When Wanda came back I apologized for Barbara's accidents
when Wanda had last been at our house two weeks before. "Aw,
that's all right. That's how life is right now. I should have asked her
if she needed to go more often. I love Barbara." How sweet of Wanda
to have such an attitude! Wanda also suggested I ask the Pfisters if
they would take Prince which was a great idea. They lived out in the
country with plenty of room. He would have a good home with them
if they would take him.

Barbara and her sister Charlotte got their hair done two days
before the wedding. That evening we had a nice dessert in the Blue
Room at Westminster Canterbury for members of the family who were
already in town. Afterwards Charlotte got Barbara to laughing a lot.
It was fun to see Barbara that engaged.

The next day at the Bridesmaids' Luncheon Barbara did very
well – as well as she could.   The rehearsal dinner was a barbeque
under a tent that had been set up for the occasion behind the church. It
was very nice. Barbara said, "I know who Chad is," which was more
than she had said in quite a while (Chad was our almost eleven year
old grandson).

Saturday, May 22nd was Mary Beth and Alan's wedding day.
We had feared Barbara might not be able to sit through it. (We had a
plan B: if Barbara started acting up Sherri who was sitting nearby
would simply take her out.) But Barbara did sit between Laddie and
Charlotte and was perfectly quiet. There was not a hitch!

The reception was lovely. We did not think it would be right to put Barbara through that, so had arranged that Sherri would take Barbara home immediately after the wedding ceremony. Of course, Barbara did not feel she was missing anything. She had not known what was going on when she was there.

Just as Mary Beth and Alan were getting in the car to pull away Mary Beth said, "Oh, Daddy! This has been a perfect day!" I was so glad for her, because there are not many perfect days in this fallen world. As Margaret Clarkson pointed out in one of her books, "In this world there is no unmitigated joy. But, for the Christian, neither is there unmitigated sorrow. Because in Christ, even our darkest clouds are shot through with glory!"

The really heartrending part of Mary Beth and Alan's wedding day for me had been that Barbara could not enjoy it. I remembered how involved she had been in planning and organizing our boys' weddings and receptions. That she had missed in any meaningful sense her daughter's wedding was profoundly sad to me. She would have had such a wonderful time doing all the mother-of-the-bride things! But I was grateful she had been able to physically attend the wedding. We had not been sure that could happen until it happened.

A couple of days after the wedding LoisAnn Pfister and her girls came by to take Prince. He had been a great dog for us. But with Barbara falling over him several times, this had to happen. And Barbara who used to love him so, at that point did not know he was gone.

The first Friday and Saturday in June we had an overnight meeting of presbytery at Hampden-Sydney College. Sherri stayed with Barbara the whole time I was gone. And everything went well at home as I had thought it would. This was the first time since I had not been able to leave Barbara alone that I had left her overnight. A few months before I think my being away might have caused her distress. She used to ask Sherri over and over again when I was coming back. But that almost never happened any more.

June 21st we had our prayer group supper at the Laughon's. It was our last meeting until the fall. I did not think we (Barbara and I) could continue in the fall. It was getting quite hard for her to sit there during the study-discussion.

On July 2nd Barbara wet three times in the evening. I was glad I had put a pad under her. But I did need to wash her and her clothes and the pads. I finally put the "potty panties" on her, those which have an absorbent "saddle." And she did not complain for the first time. I did not think she was aware of anything different. I wondered if something else were wrong with her.

The next day I woke up and Barbara was not in bed with me. I called her and she answered from the bathroom. She was standing in front of the shower and had had diarrhea all over the place! So, I washed her and the bathroom and put a load of stuff in the washing machine, and then went back to bed.

The following night I woke up and found Barbara sitting in the bathroom floor, and she had wet. I supposed she had thought she had sat on the toilet seat, but she had missed it. She was not crying or scared, just sitting there. So I got her up, washed and changed her, and she slept well the rest of the night. It seemed to me I must have been so tired I had not awakened when she needed to get up.

The afternoon of July 6th Barbara had a bowel movement in her pants. While I was trying to get them off she fell with one hand down into the toilet and her other hand over the bathtub with bowel movement all over the place, including all over her and me! I was surprised she had not hurt herself, nor did she seem frightened. (I burst out laughing. I figured it was better to laugh than to cry.) Barbara did not say anything. Some time later, after I had gotten everything cleaned up, she said, "I'm sorry I didn't do right." I hugged her and told her she did not do anything wrong. And I reminded her that we worked together.

On July 15th we had a time! Barbara and I had gone to Westminster Canterbury to pick up Mother for supper at the Lodge of the Fisherman. When I got out of the car to get Mother and then put her in the car, I found the door was locked. I figured I must have accidentally pushed the lock when I had gotten out. I had turned the air conditioning on "high" because the car had been hot when Barbara and I had gotten in. My spare key was not in my wallet. I had no idea when it had fallen out. We had to call a locksmith, so Barbara was in the car with the air conditioning blowing hard on her for about an hour! I could read her lips saying, "I'm cold! I'm freezing!" Of course, if she had been able to think normally she could have opened the car door from the inside. But she did not even try. As soon as we got to her she was fine. She had forgotten all about it. Nothing much registered with her by that time.

Since I had a meeting at the church at 7:00 PM, we stopped by the Burger King and bought some food to take home. The car locked again, but this time I had the key in my pocket. And this time I knew I had not locked the car.

I got to my meeting just on time. Mother stayed at our house with Barbara. I stopped to get gas on the way home – and the car locked again with the key in it. Terry Schwartz was getting gas at the same time and I asked her if she could bring me home so I could get the other keys. Of course she was glad to help. I got the other set of keys and drove Barbara's car back to the station. I left the Subaru keys there to have it worked on the next day.

When I got back home Barbara was on the floor and Mother (who was 90 by then) was trying to get her up! I got Barbara off the floor and asked Mother please not to attempt such a thing again. It would have been horrible to have come home and found them both on the floor! Even though she was cheerfully willing, I did not think I should leave Mother alone with Barbara anymore. It was not fair to put her in such jeopardy.

On July 22nd Barbara and I had supper at the Landmark with the Rubles, the Thomases and the Stinesprings. I had to feed Barbara every bite.

On July 28th when I got home Sherri told me when Barbara was sitting on the toilet she said with a big smile, "My husband is a great guy!" That made me happy because by this time she rarely said much unless she said, "I am so tired!"

By the middle of August Barbara no longer told me when she needed to go to the bathroom. I simply had to watch her as you would a young child to see if I thought she needed to go. The moment she woke up from a nap I rushed with her to the bathroom. If I was not getting her up in the morning and she got up herself, she was apt to have a bowel movement standing by the side of the bed and then she tended to walk in it! I was becoming an expert at "clean up." And I did not gag anymore.

Mary Beth, remembering how I always had gagged and carried on about things like that when the children were growing up said to me, "Daddy, how do you stand it?" I replied, "Well, I have decided it is time for me to grow up and assume my responsibility. You know, when something like this happened when you were growing up I would start gagging and Mama would take care of it. Now it's my turn."

In mid-August I took Barbara to see David Wilson, our dermatologist. Barbara had a breaking out on her face. He prescribed an antibiotic in liquid form so she would not have to try to swallow capsules (the way that particular medicine usually came). For some time I had been crushing her pills and putting them in apple sauce because she could no longer swallow them whole.

A few days later Barbara had three bowel movements, only the first one in the toilet. She no longer recognized the feeling of when she needed to go. I knew I would have to put diapers on her before long, but I hated to start that, though I really did not think she would notice by then.

Sunday, August 29th was my last Sunday as pastor of Rivermont Presbyterian Church. What a blessed day! The Lord had been so good to me! We had a huge crowd. I preached from the text from which I had preached for my first sermon at Rivermont twenty-five years before: Colossians 1:18c, "That in all things Christ might have the supremacy!"

The worship was awesome! The music, both the hymn singing and the anthems, lifted me to the gate of heaven. There were about one hundred people in the choir because our organist and choirmaster, David Charles Campbell, had invited back all he was able to contact who had sung in the choir during any of the twenty-five years of my ministry there. Some of the singers traveled great distances to get there for that special occasion. Following the service there was a very nice reception. Sherri had taken Barbara home right after the service. No point in dragging her through what would have been for her a cruel ordeal.

I experienced no sadness that day, only joy in and thanksgiving to the Lord, except for the sadness that Barbara was not able to enjoy it. Although she had been there, she had had no idea of what was happening.

A couple of weeks later we went to Bluefield (about 160 miles each way) to visit my aunt. When we got home Barbara had wet herself. But she had not said anything about it. I had put absorbent panties on her so there was no run off. I had stopped and tried to get her to go in a restroom four times, but she never did.

On September 22nd I bought a Certificate of Deposit at a new bank in town because they were offering a better rate than most to get people in the door. When the lady who was waiting on me finished with our business she said, "Mr. Sykes, did your wife use to teach school?" "Yes," I replied. "At Amelon in Amherst County?" "Yes." "Both my children had her for second grade. She was the best teacher they ever had! She didn't put up with any nonsense. But they knew she loved them. And they loved her and learned a lot." How nice of her to tell me that!

At the end of September for the first time Barbara wet the bed. I had kept a pad on her side of the bed for some time (just in case) and I was so glad because it meant only washing that pad, her nightgown and herself, and not having to unmake and remake the whole bed.

I was greatly moved while I was feeding Barbara her supper. I was watching the video of the 11:00 AM Service from August 29th at Rivermont. As the congregation sang "Glorify Your Name" Barbara started singing with them in a clear, beautiful voice. I almost wept. When I tried to get her to do it again later, she couldn't.

One afternoon Barbara and I went to have her Scottish wool suit altered. Since she had not been able to feed herself, she had lost some weight.

Barbara and I went to the "visitation" for Lindsay Butler, Jr. There was a very large crowd and we had to wait quite a while in line to speak to the family. It about did Barbara in, but she did not complain. She rarely complained about anything by that time.

In early October I ordered a cell phone to keep in the car for safety. At that point, if the car should have broken down, Barbara would not have been able to walk with me to get help and I would not have been able to leave her alone while I went by myself.

At the end of October Barbara and I went to Williamsburg to visit Sandra and David Norman. On the trip I listened to The Notebook which was very moving. It was about a wife with Alzheimer's Disease. It had been recommended and loaned to me by my friend Joe Seiffert. David and I headed for Chincoteague Island while Barbara stayed with Sandra. What a nice trip. Barbara did fine with Sandra as I had known she would.

In early November Barbara had her eyes examined. Our ophthalmologist, Bill Hobbs, said everything looked healthy. Of course, he could not tell how well she could see because she could not read the chart. At home she had been pulling her glasses off and dropping them (not throwing them) on the floor. There was probably no longer any point in trying to have her wear them.

On November 9th Barbara and I went to the Alyce and Lionel Harrisons at the lake for a "birthday lunch" for Barbara of fried oysters which she loved. After lunch Barbara took a nap.

The next evening I bought "take out" suppers from Main Street Eatery. It was so much simpler to eat at home by then.

By the end of November Barbara was having bedwetting accidents (and chair wetting, too) much more frequently. I ordered super absorbent underpants for her.

Our daughter-in-law Kathy brought some "Depends" which we put on Barbara. She did not notice anything was different.

On December 13th I had just gotten out of the shower which is off our bedroom and was drying off when Barbara who had been sitting in a chair in the bedroom stood up and had a grand mal seizure. It threw her to the floor. She was thrashing and blood was running from her mouth (I think she must have bitten her tongue or cheek). I ran and joined her on the floor. I thought she was dying! I kept praying, "Lord, help her, please don't take her yet! Don't let her die!" Such a prayer may not have made rational sense, as sick as she was, but it showed me that on an emotional level I was not ready yet to part with her. When she stopped jerking she was unconscious and breathing very deeply. As she was in this deep sleep it reminded me of the epileptic fit a fellow had had the night I graduated from high school. I was holding Barbara's head up and finally got her up. She seemed quite disoriented, but not really hurt. She ate a good breakfast, but was very restless all morning. Barbara had had small involuntary jerks first thing in the morning for quite a while. When these occurred she would often look puzzled and say, "I didn't do that. It wasn't me." But this was the first major seizure she had had. I hoped we could avoid another one.

The Rubles, the Thomases and the Stinesprings came over to help me decorate our tree. There was lots of laughter, and Barbara joined right in. She really enjoyed herself.

One afternoon Barbara and I went to an open house at Sandra and Jay Spencer's. They had just a small group, most of whom knew Barbara well. It was very nice. Barbara was tired when we got back, but I think she had enjoyed it.

On December 20th I went and looked at wheelchairs. It was increasingly difficult for Barbara to walk any distance at all. I thought it would be particularly useful when I took Barbara to church or the store.

Ever since Barbara's big (grand mal) seizure there had been times when she had not been cooperative with me and when she said hateful things. That had never been true before. This hurt because I thought I was doing my best for her. Also, her balance seemed off. She was prone to falling, not just because she tripped or missed a chair, but because she lost her balance. I wondered if she had had a mini-stroke.

After the grand mal seizure Barbara started sleeping most of the day. The pattern seemed to be that she would sleep until around 9:30 AM. Then I would get her up, dress her, and feed her a little. She would not eat much. And then she would go back to sleep until I woke her at 4:00 PM.

Mother's mind seemed to be failing. I knew she had been under a lot of strain. But I was trying to help her discover whether or not she had paid her newspaper bill, and I had a hard time keeping her "on task." I thought I would have to take over paying her bills, or at least helping her with it each month.

Barbara fell out of bed one night. I had a hard time getting her up. Finally I did get her to the bathroom, but she went down on the floor again there, and vomited all over herself. Her food had not been digested at all, although she had eaten five hours earlier there was no "sour smell." I got her cleaned up and back to bed and she slept through the night. (This happened at midnight.) She was very unsteady on her feet.

I bought a rail for Barbara's side of the bed at a children's shop. I hoped this would keep her from falling out of bed!

On December 18th Sherri stayed with Barbara while I went to Burlington, North Carolina to attend Christie's (Kathy and Powell's daughter) marriage to Jim Miller at Westminster Presbyterian Church. The church was beautifully decorated for Christmas. I had to leave right after the wedding to get back home so Sherri and her husband could get to a dinner to which they had been invited. I hated to leave before the festivities were over, but it seemed that had become a way of life for me.

Powell said to me, "Dad, one of the most important things about a marriage is the husband and wife being able to talk with each other. That means so much to me – being able to communicate with Kathy. Don't you miss that with Mom?" Of course I did – every day, every moment. This was a constant sadness.

On December 22nd Barbara got progressively worse with her ability to stand and even sit without falling over. I got in touch with Scott at home at 9:00 PM. He urged me to take Barbara to the emergency room. A female doctor from Scott's office was already there. I think she thought Barbara was having a stroke (which I had wondered about). They put us in a regular room. Barbara was very restless. Scott called Dr. Octavio (Tavi) de Marchena, a neurologist. He came by to see Barbara in the hospital. He told me that not all Alzheimer's Disease patients had seizures. But when one's neurological system was under attack (as anyone's with Alzheimer's was), the chances of having seizures went way up. And if a person had one seizure the chances of having more increased. He decided Barbara was taking too high a dose of the dilantin which she had been put on following the big seizure. I was to reduce the dose.

A white Christmas! Unusual for Lynchburg. We had a nice dinner and ate in the dining room. Barbara was still very groggy. Scott said to further reduce her dose if necessary.

On December 29th I read that most of Barbara's recently acquired negative symptoms could be caused by dilantin. I thought I might simply stop it. That morning I played racquetball with Greg Alty, a surgeon friend, and talked with him about the medicine. He wanted me to call Scott (since Scott had prescribed it), but Scott was visiting his parents in Kentucky. So, on my own I stopped the dilantin.

I did talk to Harold Riley, a friend who was a retired neurologist. He thought I ought to call our regular neurologist the following day – but said I was right to stop the dilantin.

The next day Dr. de Marchena said I did the right thing to stop the medicine. We needed to wait until Barbara had recovered from this, and then start another anti-seizure medicine the following week.

On the last day of the year Barbara was back to her "pre-dilantin" self. She ate a good breakfast, lunch and supper.

In part of our Christmas letter that year I wrote:

Barbara has gone down considerably this past year in her struggle with Alzheimer's Disease. That is the main reason I retired – having served 25 years – from Rivermont Presbyterian Church at the end of August – so that I could care for Barbara full-time.

Chapter Eleven: 2000

On January 3rd I went by Lincare and got a wheelchair for Barbara. She did not need it in the house yet, but it would help greatly when we went anywhere else, especially to the store.

Barbara had not slept – she took no nap the day before, did not sleep that night and did not nap that day. I had no idea why. I surely did hope she would sleep the next night. I was about ready to pass out.

On January 4th I wrote in my journal, "Barbara did sleep well last night. Thank you, Lord. I got an email from Toby Cook saying he was praying for us last night." (By that time Toby and his wife Barbara were living in Kansas City. We had gotten to know them when they had lived in Lynchburg.)

Barbara was very "antsy" all day. She "talked" much more than usual. Most of the time I could not figure out what she meant. But once she said, clearly, "Please give me a quarter." I said, "I don't have a quarter, but I'll give you a dollar – or – better than that, I'll give you twenty dollars." I handed her a twenty dollar bill. I asked what she wanted to do with it. "Buy you something," she said. I asked what she wanted to buy and she said, "I don't know." Then I asked if she wanted me to keep the $20 safe for her. She said, "Yes." That was the most conversation we had had in a long, long time.

January 5th Scott called. He and Dr. de Marchena wanted to start Barbara on a new (for her) anticonvulsive drug right away – Tegretol. I hoped it would have the desired effect without negative side effects.

The next day Scott sent Barbara some Elevil to try to help her sleep. She had wakened at 3:30 AM, and I finally had given in at 4:30 and had gotten her dressed and fed. I brought her into the study for my prayer group because she was constantly "up and down," and when she came into the meeting she kept talking ("jabbering" would be a better description).

That night Barbara was in a stupor. I was afraid the new medicine was effecting her the same way the other had. I planned to cut back the dose from 2 to 1 the next day to see if it would help. She could not hold up her head at all, and it was very difficult to feed her at supper because her chin was practically resting on her chest.

The next day I stopped Barbara's new medicine. She was still in a stupor and yet did not sleep in the daytime at all, and not well at night.

In mid-January I started helping Mother get her bills paid. I planned to do that regularly from then on.

January 20th we had about three inches of snow. A couple of young men stopped by to see if they could shovel our driveways and walk. Since I could not go out and spend that much time away from Barbara with no one with her in the house, I was glad to hire them to do it.

That evening the television was on – I wasn't paying attention – but a congregation sang the hymn, "Love Lifted Me." "That's nice," Barbara said, I asked if she would sing it with me, and she said she would. So we sang together. She smiled and smiled. I asked her if she would like to call Charlotte and sing for her. She replied, "Let's do!" So I did and we did and then Charlotte sang it with us. And Barbara was more responsive to her than usual in the conversation. This was one of those precious times that happened only rarely by then.

On January 22nd Barbara got her hair fixed. Lorene could not get her to lie back to wash her hair, so we each stood on one side of her and helped her lean over the sink.

February 8th I took both Mother and Barbara to the dentist. Barbara did fairly well (with my help) getting her teeth cleaned. At the end the hygienist said, "Would you like a pink toothbrush or a blue one." Barbara replied, "I'll take a blue one." I was amazed! That was much more than she usually said by then.

A few days later Powell was visiting us and said, "Dad, you and Mom look like you are having a good time! She looks so good!" I was glad. We generally did have a good time, and she did look great!

In mid-February I worked on tax stuff all day, except for having lunch with Mother and then going to the business office and getting Mother's bill straight and paid. With Mother's glad agreement they were going to send the bill to me from then on. Mother was having increasing difficulty keeping track of her bills.

I played racquetball with John Mabray. He had asked me the week before if I would consider putting Barbara in respite care in a nursing home for a few days so he and I could go to the Banner of Truth Ministers' Conference in Pennsylvania that coming May. I told him I would love to go, but simply could not leave Barbara. He asked me to reconsider. "I don't think it would do her any harm at all, and I think it would do you a lot of good." So I told him I would think about it further.

That afternoon I called some nursing homes to inquire about "respite care." I still needed to visit them, but they were going to send me some material through the mail.

February 18th I called Willia Wilkes, an old and dear friend of Barbara, and told her that because of Barbara's condition I would not attempt to bring her to Augusta, Georgia the following month. Willia had long before invited us to stay with her and said she would take care of Barbara while I preached at Lakemont Presbyterian Church (where I had served from 1965-1974) for the church's 50th anniversary. She was very sad that Barbara had declined so much.

February 22nd we had lunch with Mother. Then she went with Barbara and me and we looked at the Medical Care Center as a possibility for Respite Care for Barbara if I decided to go with John in May. I did not think I would look further. This was in a good location (right across the street from our doctor's office) just in case they should need him for Barbara while I would be gone. Barbara did not react at all, she was quite unaware of her environment by then. And this was the reason I thought I could seriously consider respite care at that point. A year earlier Barbara would have been distressed without me in a strange place and I would not have thought about leaving her even for a few days, but by now, I thought she would feel fine.

I sent in my registration and check for the Banner of Truth Conference in May. If it turned out I could not go, it would be a donation to a good cause.

In early March I spent a good bit of time on the phone trying to get Medicare straightened out. It seemed there were three divisions: the doctor, the hospital and medical supplies. All of them wrongly had records that showed we had some other primary provider. All I had gotten straight earlier had been the second division. And their computers were not connected with each other. Sounded crazy to me. I felt like having a tantrum!

On March 10th Mary Beth came home to stay with Barbara while Mother and I went to Augusta. We arrived safely at my sister Sarah's in Aiken, South Carolina.

The next day we had a "birthday brunch" at Shoney's. It was Mother's 91st birthday.

I went to the anniversary supper at Lakemont Church in Augusta which was just 25 miles from Sarah's house.

Sunday, March 12th was a great day at Lakemont Church! The only sad part of it for me was that Barbara could not enjoy it too. She had loved Lakemont Church and Augusta so. I got back to Lynchburg about 7:20 PM (Mother was staying on with Sarah for a few more weeks).

March 25th Barbara had vomiting and diarrhea all day. Since she could not anticipate the eruptions, it got pretty interesting. I spent that day cleaning Barbara, her clothes and the bedding – including the ruffle around the bottom of the bed.

Sunday, March 26th we stayed home from church. I thought we might have more of what we had had the day before, but we did not. Barbara was exhausted from all the "activity" of the previous day. She slept most of the morning after breakfast and then most of the afternoon after lunch. I hoped she would sleep that night.

In early April I called the Medical Care Center and made arrangements for Barbara to stay there 24 hours the following week as a "trial." If it went well I would plan to go with John at the end of May to the conference in Pennsylvania. If it did not go well, I would not go.

About that time Barbara said, out of the blue, "I'll be dead by Monday." I tried to respond, but by that time she wasn't saying anything at all. She had not said anything like that before, nor did she say anything like that later. I wondered what was going on in her mind. There was no way for me to know.

I wrote the following to the nursing home:

Barbara Powell Sykes

Barbara Sykes was an extremely capable and loving person, pastor's wife, mother, second grade public school teacher and Sunday school teacher. Her specialty was young children. She loved nothing better than to take a child who was having trouble learning and work with him or her until he or she was able to master whatever the lesson was. Barbara was an excellent cook and housekeeper. Whatever it was, she did it quickly and thoroughly. She was the "detail" person in the family. She knew where everything was. She never lost anything. She loved to "do" for others. For example, just a few months ago a woman came up to me and said, "I'll never forget Barbara's kindness to us. When our daughter was planning to get married my husband had been laid off from work. We didn't have any money, so we were not planning to have a reception. When Barbara heard about it she said, 'Of course, we are going to have a reception! I'll take care of everything.' And she did!"

When she was only in her early fifties Barbara began forgetting things. At first the doctor thought Barbara was merely too busy. But the forgetfulness kept getting worse. After about three years of this and doing all the tests twice the doctor said, "Her diagnosis is probable Alzheimer's Disease." That was in 1991. At first her decline was very gradual. But for the past three years she has been quite disabled and has not been capable of caring for herself at all.

I have been her primary caregiver. For nine or ten hours a week I have had a companion with her so I can do errands and get some exercise.

Barbara was in an experimental program at the University of Virginia hospital where she was on Aricept for three years before it came on the market. Since that time she has been on it by means of a prescription. She also takes Detrol to help with her "overactive bladder." It has made a real difference. She used to have to get up at night about four times. Now she sometimes gets up once and often not at all. She takes one or two Mellaril tablets about an hour before going to bed at night and occasionally takes one Mellaril tablet in the daytime to relieve anxiety. Just before she goes to bed she takes some Metamucil in a glass of water. She has a terrible time now trying to swallow pills, so I crush them and give them to her in applesauce. Occasionally (not often) she does not want to take her medicine. I tell her, "The doctor wants you to have this," and she takes it immediately.

Barbara's medicine schedule: After breakfast, 1 Detrol, After supper, 1 Detrol, 1 Aricept, One hour before bed, 1 or 2 Mellaril Just before bed, 1 glass Metamucil.

Barbara usually goes to bed at 10 PM and gets up at various times between 6:30 and 8:30 AM.

Barbara likes most foods. The only exceptions I can think of are raw onions, tuna fish and raw or cooked green peppers. She likes fruit juice, sweet iced tea and Diet Coke. She no longer drinks coffee or hot tea. For breakfast I usually give her a banana, an orange, red seedless grapes, and a cinnamon roll. Many times, while I am feeding her, she looks at my face. If I am smiling at her, she seems reassured. If I am not smiling she somehow feels something is wrong.

Barbara cannot feed herself, toilet herself, wipe herself, dress herself, bathe herself. Occasionally she says she needs to go to the bathroom. More often, by carefully observing Barbara (as one would a very young child) I know when she needs to go to the bathroom, but sometimes we have accidents. Wearing an absorbent pad helps when this does happen. You might want to put diapers on her. Sometimes when I think she needs to urinate, but she can't seem to think what to do after she is seated on the toilet, it helps get her started if I run some water in the lavatory. I use "Wet Ones" to clean her after a bowel movement. Also, when she is sitting in a chair, she sometimes stands up and then tries to sit back down and misses the chair, sitting down hard on the floor. I try to keep a very close eye on her to keep this from happening. Usually when she is either in bed or sitting in a chair and she needs to urinate or have a bowel movement she gets up, but then doesn't know what to do. Walking is difficult for Barbara. She *walks best when I take both her hands in mine and I walk backwards. This is the reason I use a wheelchair for her when we have to walk any distance, like going to church or to the store. She does not mind being given a bath. But she is afraid to step into the tub with me behind her. So I get into the tub, stepping into the water in front of her, turn towards her, take both her hands and encourage her to come into the tub towards me, and that usually works fine. I use a bathtub chair for her. I no longer brush Barbara's teeth because she cannot "swish and spit." She simply gags. We do get her teeth cleaned at the dentist's every three months. For the past year she repeatedly has pulled her glasses off and dropped them on the floor. So I don't even try to have her wear them anymore. Very often from the time she gets up in the morning until after breakfast she has a number of small, involuntary jerks. She often makes an involuntary guttural sound when this happens. Nothing needs to be done about this. She often feels cold – even when it is not cold. At these times when I take her hands they are cold, even though I do not feel cold at all.*

I think Barbara would be most content where others are around – in other words, it would be better for her to sit with others in the lounge rather than alone in her room. She tends to feel afraid if she feels she is alone. I usually have music playing on the radio or the television on unless she is going to sleep at night. She can't follow anything on the radio or television, but the quiet noise seems calming to her. Loud noises or several conversations going on at once distress her. In the daytime she seems to prefer taking her naps sitting up in her chair rather than lying down.

Barbara is never hostile to me or her companion – quite unusual with this disease, I'm told. I really love taking care of her. She knows I'm familiar, but she no longer knows my name. Sometimes she will ask me, "Who are you?" Sometimes she will beg me to take her home when we are at home. I simply try to reassure her. Sometimes (not usually) Barbara will not want me to take her clothes off in connection with going to bed. I try to distract her or make a joke out of it and that usually works fine.

I hope this "trial" twenty-four hours at the Medical Care Center will go well for her. If it does, I will plan to be away three days and three nights in late May. If this doesn't go well, I will not plan to go in May. One or two of her friends may come by. Her companion, Sherri Lindstrom, will come to be with her from 11:30 AM to 3:30 PM on Friday. I think it would be best if I did not come by during this time. However, I will plan to telephone from time to time. If she seems unduly distressed I would appreciate your telephoning me and I will come immediately and take her home. If all goes well, I will plan to come by for Barbara at 4:00 PM tomorrow. If she soils any clothes, I will take them home and wash them.

Lowell B. Sykes
April 2000

I got Barbara to the Medical Care Center at 4:00 PM. She was fine, but I had a hard time leaving her there without sobbing. She was so unaware of her surroundings I thought she would be fine.

I telephoned twice that evening and Barbara was OK. She had eaten a good supper. At 10:10 PM she had gotten up out of bed and was sitting in the lounge. The nurse said Barbara was not upset at all.

The next morning I called about 6:30 AM to see what kind of a night Barbara had had. The nurse said Barbara had still been up when she came on duty at 11:00 PM. The nurse then put Barbara to bed and she had slept soundly all night and was still asleep.

I called again at 10:00 AM and the 7-3 nurse said Barbara had not seemed to be upset at all and had eaten a good breakfast.

I picked Barbara up about 3:30 PM. She was fine and made no reference to it afterwards. So I thought I could safely plan to go to the conference the following month.

On Palm Sunday we worshiped at Rivermont Church. What a magnificent morning service! Since Barbara had done so well in the morning we went back for Evening Worship. But Barbara was very restless by then. For the first time we sat in the middle of the right side of the congregation where they had cut a pew so a wheelchair could be accommodated.

On April 19th Sherri took Barbara to have her teeth cleaned at the dentist's office. But they were not able to do it because Barbara would not lie back and open her mouth.

On April 22nd Barbara, Mother and I left for Myrtle Beach at 8:00 AM. It took us seven hours and fifteen minutes (362 miles). Alan, Mary Beth and (Alan's son) Josh arrived shortly after we got there.

We decided that Mother and I, Lord willing, would attend the 8:30 service at a nearby Lutheran church – Easter Day – and Mary Beth and Alan and Josh would go to the 11:00 AM service. That way we would not have to attempt to drag Barbara through what we imagined would be large Easter crowds.

On Easter Day we did as we had planned the day before. It worked very well.

On Thursday I took the whole crowd to supper at Bennett's Calabash Seafood Buffet. (By that time Powell and his family and Barbara's sister Charlotte had joined us.) At the end of the meal Barbara got upset (we did not know why) and started pinching Charlotte who was sitting next to her. She would not stop. So Powell changed places with Charlotte and that seemed to end the episode. I was glad this kind of thing was very unusual with Barbara. But it had gotten so that if she got upset with someone, including me, she would start to pinch – hard! I hoped this would not last! She also tried to bite a couple of times (although she did not attempt that on this occasion). As Barbara descended further into Alzheimer's Disease she typically became more childlike, rather than mean or hostile.

On May 4th Mother telephoned. She did not think she could get to the dentist because she said the van did not run that day. I could not take her because of a prior appointment. I told her I thought the van did run on Tuesday and Thursday. She checked and found I was right. Her mind was slipping more.

On Sunday evening, May 7th I drove to Diamond Hill Presbyterian Church, out in the country from Rustburg. I would be preaching there Sunday through Wednesday nights. Lorene Payne, who had been Barbara's hairdresser ever since we had moved to Lynchburg (1974), was spending these evenings with Barbara. Sherri was away that week. But Sherri was the one who had found out Lorene was a certified Home Health Caregiver as well as a beautician.

On May 10th Glen Murphy (who worked at Rivermont Church and often fixed things at my house) installed a handheld showerhead in the hall bathroom, which would make it easier to rinse Barbara off when I bathed her.

Marie Seiger stayed with Barbara in the middle of the day. Barbara had a big bowel movement accident Marie had to deal with. I realized this job was getting too difficult for volunteers.

On May 14th Barbara and I went to both Morning and Evening Worship at Rivermont. Barbara tried to sing the hymns and say the Apostles' Creed and the Lord's Prayer.

May 22nd I took Barbara to the Medical Care Center at 4:00 PM. Both Sherri and Lorene planned to go by there to see about her, and Pam was going to check on Barbara too.

John and I were refreshed at the conference. When I got back I picked Barbara up from the nursing home. She was fine, but very tired. I took her to get her hair done.

Sunday May 28th Barbara had to go to the bathroom just as the service started at Rivermont, so we stayed in the Family Room for the rest of the service.

On June 1st our friend and dentist Raine Sydnor tried to clean Barbara's teeth himself, but did not have much success, even with both his assistant and me trying to help. Barbara would not open her mouth. We planned to try again in a couple of weeks.

On June 6th Barbara had not urinated since just before we went to bed the night before at 10:00 PM. And it was time for us to go over and meet Mother for lunch at 12:30 PM. We did have lunch with Mother and then took her to the airport. We got Mother checked in at the airport at 2:00 PM for a 3:07 PM flight to Charlotte and then to California to visit my sister Virginia and her family. We left before Mother's plane did because I felt I needed to get Barbara to the doctor because she still had not urinated! While we were in the doctor's waiting room I took Barbara to the rest room again (at 3:15 PM). And she did urinate. We got to see a doctor not long after that. He did not know why she went so long. He did take some blood to test and said he would call me if he found anything wrong. Since he did not call I figured he found things normal. A doctor has to treat someone in Barbara's condition much like a very young child who cannot tell where it hurts. The doctor has to figure it out on his own – if he can!

On Mother's way back from California her plane was cancelled from San Francisco. She was able to book another flight via Washington, so she got to Lynchburg at 10:45 PM instead of 6:17 PM – but she had a good trip. Barbara did very well even though she was up much later than usual.

On June 22nd I took Barbara to Raine Sydnor again. He had a bit better success cleaning her teeth by having her sit in his chair and himself sitting "below" her on the patient's chair. He said her teeth looked healthy.

Sunday, July 2nd we worshiped at Rivermont. Barbara sang all the hymns with me.

On July 6th Lorene stayed with Barbara from 11:00 AM to 4:00 PM. Lorene also did Barbara's hair at the house. That worked out very well.

At that point noise in a restaurant made Barbara very nervous. I thought that perhaps she had lost the ability to "filter" sound. (By this I mean, thata normal person can concentrate on what a dinner partner is saying and ignore the din coming from other tables. But I thought Barbara could no longer do that.)

On July 18th we visited Mother. She wasn't feeling well, so I brought her washing home to do.

On July 24th Barbara and I went to the Laughon's for a farewell supper for the Ribeiros who were moving to Grand Rapids, Michigan where Paulo would be teaching at Calvin College. We would miss them. Adriana (who was a physician but had stayed at home with their children since becoming a mother) had been wonderful to help with Barbara. It had gotten so that Adriana was coming to our house rather than have Barbara over at hers because they had a long flight of steps up to their door that had become almost impossible for Barbara to manage.

July 25th the Rubles, the Thomases and we ate together at the Red Lobster. This had become very difficult, but our friends wanted us to continue doing this with them as long as we could.

The next day I helped Mother with sorting through lots of "stacks" of things. I worked from 10:30 AM to 1:00 PM. Then we ate lunch. We picked up Barbara from our house (Sherri had to leave at 2:00 PM that day) and took Mother to the dermatologist. Then we dropped some stuff off at the Goodwill (some of Dad's old clothes I had cleaned out). I had lots more to do at Mother's, but was glad for the good start I had gotten. She seemed very pleased.

Shirley Hobbs stayed with Barbara while I went over some things with our friend and lawyer Dan Sweeney – especially what would be done if I should die before Barbara. There would be enough monthly income to keep her in a nursing home plus my life insurance. The financial squeeze would come if we both had to be in a nursing home at the same time for very long. If that should happen the money would run out quickly.

When I got home Barbara had had a bowel movement in her pants and would not let Shirley change her. What a mess! But I got her and her clothes cleaned up. While I was washing her – she was standing up in the bathroom – she urinated! More fun!

Around that time Barbara had been getting very restless in the late afternoons until bedtime. She would walk around the den, and even would open the door to the back porch and would walk out there and sit down in the rocker. She did not seem to be upset, just much more active than she had been for a long time. She also would sit on the edge of the table we ate from. I had to keep a keen eye on her to make sure she did not fall.

On August 7th my First Monday Discussion Group met at my home study. Barbara was so restless I could not stay with the group, even with her in the room with us.

On August 12th Sherri stayed with Barbara so I could fly to Chattanooga to preach for Tom Goodrich's ordination at the Signal Mountain Presbyterian Church. I got back the following evening.

Barbara was fine. Sherri said Barbara had eaten well, but since I had had no supper I pulled some pizza out of the freezer. After I took it out of the microwave and started to eat, Barbara stood up and started coming toward me saying, "Good. Good." I asked her if she wanted some pizza and she said, "Yes!" So, of course, I fed her some. She loved pizza!

August 20th I tried giving Barbara two Mellarils before we went to church. It seemed to work because she was quiet during the service.

Lorene Payne came to stay with Barbara the next day and would the day following that.

I took Barbara to Raine for a cleaning of her teeth. She let him do more than she had the last time.

On August 29th our dear friends from college days Ellie and Jim Gustafson were finishing a visit with us. As they were leaving Ellie hugged me and cried hard – she had not cried before when they had left. I was sure she was upset about Barbara. She said, "There is such a sense of peace in your home – even under these trying circumstances." And I think there was.

The Rubles, the Stinesprings and we ate at Red Lobster. Barbara was very restless, so she and I left as soon as we had eaten. The others understood.

On Sunday, September 3rd Barbara was very restless at church. We had to leave between the bread and the wine of the Lord's Supper. She continued to be restless all afternoon and into the evening.

Sunday, September 10th I started preaching twice a month at the Pisgah Presbyterian Church (in the country about twenty miles from our house).

Sunday, September 24th Barbara Bennett came into Rivermont church and sat on a back pew with me (I had my Barbara in her wheel chair beside me.) Barbara Bennett was surprised and said, "Barbara has gone down so fast." But I told her, "It hasn't been fast – just a long time now." My Barbara was very quiet during the service.

The next day while I was "walking" Barbara to her chair in the den I tripped over the chair and almost fell down. I did fall over the chair. But, thank the Lord, Barbara did not fall. The following day I could feel it in my back. I hoped it would not amount to much.

On October 5th Barbara got a permanent. She had needed one for quite a while, but by then, with Barbara's disability, Lorene could not handle it alone. That day Sherri was able to help Lorene with Barbara.

On October 10th I could have been hurt badly. By then when I stood Barbara up at the toilet after she had had a bowel movement, I would step into the bathtub so as to be able to hold her up with one of my arms hooked under her armpit and clean her with my other hand. The bathroom was very narrow, hardly wide enough for me to do the necessary work with Barbara. Just as I was stepping into the tub, Barbara tried to cross her legs. My foot caught her leg and I was airborne – heading face down into the tub! I knew I was going to be hurt seriously. But, thank the Lord, I was not – just some bangs and bruises. My heart was pounding hard, but I was fine.

On October 12th Barbara and I went to the Lodge of the Fisherman with and Frances and Andy Sale. They took us and asked if we could do it once a month. That was extremely thoughtful of them, because they had not known Barbara before she had gotten sick. And by that time she was not easy – she kept getting up and wanting to go home.

The next day I sat with Barbara during her hair appointment. She did not want to stay under the dryer, kept trying to pull her curlers out, and was generally unhappy.

Barbara had been very restless all day. Whew! I was glad this happened only occasionally so far.

On the evening of October 17th I took Mother, my sister Virginia, her husband Keith and Barbara to Main Street Eatery. The food was, as usual, excellent, but it was very noisy because a German Club from one of the Lynchburg schools was there – about 20 or 25 high school students. They did not misbehave at all, but with all those hard surfaces the din of noise was pretty bad, and it about drove Barbara wild. So we ate and left as quickly as we could.

Then we went to Billy Joe's Restaurant for ice cream. It was quiet there. I asked Barbara what kind of ice cream she would like. At that point she usually said, "I don't know," or did not answer at all. But she replied with animation, "Chakit!" And smiled broadly. So I got her chocolate with hot fudge topping. I fed her all of hers and half of mine! She was animated and tried to talk (gibberish) several times. It made me so happy when she was that way – quite rare at that point.

On October 19th we got Barbara's teeth cleaned. Raine did it with his assistant's and my help. He was able to do more than the last time.

A few days later Barbara fell out of bed – pushed through the child's rail I had gotten for her – onto her stomach and face. I could not get her up for quite a while, but finally did. Nothing was broken, but she did have a "skinned" knee and a red place on her face where she had rubbed hard on the carpet.

The next night Barbara slept very little, so we got up about 3:00 AM. I had her dressed and fed before the prayer group got to the house at 6:30 AM. Scott said he would send some new medicine to try to help Barbara sleep.

We had lunch with Mother at Westminster Canterbury and then took her for a ride out Trents Ferry Road to Eagle Eyrie. It seemed we could have a better visit that way. Otherwise Barbara kept wanting "to go."

Another day we had lunch with Mother and another lady at Westminster Canterbury. Barbara embarrassed me when said, "Grandmother, you're ugly!" And a few minutes later Barbara said to the other lady, "You're fat!" Of course, I apologized for her. With a little child you can teach them better. With Barbara things only got worse. She almost never spoke, even a very short sentence by then, so it was especially a shame when her few words were hurtful. I did not think she was trying to be mean. She was simply saying what was on her mind. Her civilizing self-control was pretty much gone.

On November 16th Mother had a serious heart attack. In the hospital she said to me, "Whether I live or die, I belong to the Lord." She was resting in him.

On November 27th Barbara fell out of bed again, even with the rail up. I was not sure how she did it. I wondered if I needed to get a hospital bed sooner rather than later.

I found out I could buy an adult bed rail (which I had not known existed) that Barbara would not be able to push out. So I went to Lincare and ordered one.

That night I placed two pillows between Barbara and the rail, so she could not roll over into the rail.

On December 1st I picked up and installed the new bed rail. I did not think Barbara would be able to roll out with this up.

The following Sunday Barbara and I worshiped at Rivermont Church. After church I took Barbara to the hospital to see Mother. Mother looked good. Barbara was freezing!

A couple of days later Mother came out of the hospital to Health Care at Westminster Canterbury. I visited her in the hospital before she was dismissed. She seemed very weak.

I ran into a friend in the grocery store. The week before he had spent a few hours at our house. In the store he said, "I haven't been able to get you out of my mind the last few days! I keep thinking, 'Lowell is really trapped at home.'" I replied, "I can see why it might look that way. But I don't feel trapped at all. I know God has as surely called me to this ministry of helping Barbara as he did to the pastoral ministry. So I am happy and content to be where the Lord has called me to be. And I love taking care of Barbara." And I meant every word.

Sherri stayed with Barbara later than usual so I could visit Mother. She was still very weak. I was glad I had been able to visit her almost every day since her heart attack. It was often hard for her to reach the phone in her Health Care room, so I hesitated to call her. I did not know why the aides did not leave the phone where she could reach it easily. It ought to have been obvious, but it did not seem to occur to them. I complained regularly, was promised it would not happen again, but it usually did.

The Christmas CDs were playing. One time Barbara said, "That's pretty." That was quite a lot for her to say by then. She had had loose bowels that day, so I had been quite busy.

On December 17th we worshiped at Rivermont Church in the morning. I tried to take Barbara back to the evening service but we had to leave after about 30 minutes. She started talking loudly during worship.

The following Friday while Barbara got her hair done I visited Mother and Sarah. When I got back to the hair shop Barbara had had a bowel movement in her pants. Lorene had cleaned it up.

On Christmas Eve Barbara did very well during the church service. She sang most of the carols.

Barbara and I had a quiet Christmas Day. I opened Barbara's gifts for her and told her about them. But she was not able to show any interest. We visited Mother and Sarah in the afternoon.

On December 28th Barbara did not sleep at all in the night, so, of course, neither did I. But it was more than worth it because once she said, "I love you," which she had not said without being prompted for a long time. We came out to our family room and I put on some new CDs of children singing children's songs. At one point Barbara said, "Sweet children!" She seemed much more alert than usual all night long.

Chapter Twelve: 2001

On January 9th I took Barbara to see Raine Sydnor. She was so sleepy he was able to do more cleaning of her teeth than usual.

One night about that time Barbara did not sleep at all well. While we were sitting in the den in the middle of the night she said, out of the blue, "I have a good husband. I love you..." Amazing! This showed something did go on in her mind at least occasionally, probably more often than that, but it was rarely expressed at that point.

I had lunch with Harold Riley. I told him Barbara has not had that early morning jerking since she had been on the Ativan (which Scott had prescribed for sleep), and he said he had often used that medicine for seizure control. I had not realized that.

Pam stayed with Barbara while I was with Harold. I showed her how I put Barbara on the toilet (pulled down her panties and pad from behind while she was facing the toilet, and then turned her around and sat her down). When I got home Pam told me she did it "my way" and had no trouble at all. The last time, which had been quite a while before, she had tried doing it from the front and Barbara had not let her. Our Mary Beth pointed out that one instinctively resists having someone pull down her panties. Barbara certainly did unless it was done from behind, and sometimes even then.

We went to see Mother at Westminster Canterbury. They were talking about her going to Assisted Living before long. This would be a "step up" from the skilled care unit where she had been since her heart attack. Great! They said she needed to walk more. I had a talk with Don Lowery, a nurse there. He said Mother could walk as much as she felt like it. But no one had told her that! I could not understand why.

Barbara was pulling on and twisting her hair. Paula Petrey noticed and mentioned it when she brought in supper for us.

February 2nd – 5th so I could visit Mary Beth and Alan in Tennessee, Sherri stayed with Barbara twenty-four hours a day until Monday morning when Lorene Payne came and stayed until after my First Monday Discussion Group met at our house. All went well.

On February 7th Lauren Blake Sykes was born at 5:00 PM. Both she and her mother were doing fine. Our son Laddie was the proud and happy father. How thrilled Barbara would have been to have known she had a new granddaughter! Of course, I told her, but it did not appear to register.

On February 10th Glen fixed a showerhead that could be handheld in the bathroom off our bedroom. I bathed Barbara that way and it worked very well. I put her bathtub chair in the shower and it was much easier for her to step into the shower than to lift her leg high enough for me to get her into the bathtub.

I had a nice visit with Mother. She was working hard in physical therapy, and had not used oxygen since seeing the doctor.

Barbara did not sleep much one night about that time, so we sat in the family room. She was very talkative (mostly jabber) but many times she said, "I love you." A blessed time!

On February 21st Mother told me she liked her new room in Assisted Living, and that if she could not go back to her apartment it was, in her words, "another bridge to cross. I've been thinking a lot about the bridges in my life. When the Lord has called me to walk over a new bridge, he has always given me the strength to do it." She still hoped she could get back to her apartment, but was not as concerned about the possibility of leaving it permanently as she had been at first. I met Debrah Raessler (who was head of Assisted Living for Westminster Canterbury) in Mother's apartment to see what furniture we might move (at that point temporarily) to Mother's Assisted Living room.

On the following Monday Mother moved to Assisted Living. The room looked very nice with her things in it. I thought she was very pleased.

On the last day of February our son Powell came up from North Carolina in order to stay with Barbara the following day, so that I could go to presbytery and vote on a very important issue in our denomination. Powell had never taken care of his mother before, but he said it was time he learned how. Powell is a pastor who is also an excellent musician and songwriter. While with his mother that day, the seeds were planted for the following song which he actually completed later:

WANDERING PILGRIM

Wandering pilgrim, rest with me
Gentle the night and melody
Near journey's end, dawn coming when
Jesus appears and life begins
Do you hear my song? Can you see His light?
Mystery unfolds but only for you
Triumphant at last, you've fought the good fight
Well done!

Seems like forever you've been here
Trick of perspective and never clear
Eternal now finally in doubt
Temp'ral illusion shaken out
I will miss you so, I already do
Are you rememb'ring sweet days in the past

Or worshiping now, aware in the new
Kingdom?

Flesh cannot win eternal gain
What's sown and what's raised is not the same
Tent falling down, you won't be found
Unclothed, but housed on promised ground
Absent from me, if not quite from your body
Present with Him who died for your sin
Stranger no more, home permanently
Welcome!

Powell attached the following notes about his song:

I wrote the words to this song in 2005, though the chord progression I developed a few years earlier while "baby-sitting" my mother, who has advanced Alzheimer's Disease. My father had to be away at a meeting that day. I knew then it would become a song about my mother. Where is she now? Her body is here. But where is she, all the things that made her wonderful? In 2006 a thorough examination led the doctors to declare that her brain is the most deteriorated by Alzheimer's that they have ever seen, but they have never seen an Alzheimer's patient live this long either, and attribute that to the "exquisite" care she receives from my father. In the meantime, is she remembering the past? Is she dreaming? Or is she already conscious in heaven, worshiping Jesus? I don't know. But she is not abandoned. The line "stranger no more" is a play on the meaning of Mom's name: "Barbara" means "stranger." Here we're all pilgrims and strangers; the name "Barbara" acknowledges this.

I can never hear this song, or even read the words without shedding some tears. There is so much we do not know! The Apostle Paul's words in the 8th chapter of his letter to the Romans speak directly to our uncertainty:

If God is for us, who can be against us? He who did not spare his own Son but gave him up for us all, how will he not also with him graciously give us all things? Who shall bring any charge against God's elect? It is God who justifies. Who is to condemn? Christ Jesus is the one who died – more than that, who was raised – who is at the right hand of God, who indeed is interceding for us. Who shall separate us from the love of Christ? Shall tribulation, or distress, or persecution, or famine, or nakedness, or danger, or sword?... No, in all these things we are more than conquerors through him who loved us. For I am sure (absolutely persuaded) *that neither death nor life, nor angels nor rulers, nor things present nor things to come, nor powers, nor height nor depth, nor anything else in all creation will be able to separate us from the love of God in Christ Jesus our Lord* (Romans 8:31b-39). And, really, this is all we need to know for sure! This is more than enough.

Every time my mother, Ruth Beach Sykes, talked to me she told me how much she liked her new room. I got the impression she was thinking she might choose to stay there permanently.

On March 5th I had supper with Mother during which she decided to stay in Assisted Living (Hearthside). I thought she felt more secure there, and she also knew that was what I had hoped she would do. (I knew, but she did not, that Westminster Canterbury was going to make this decision for her if she did not. They knew even before she had had her heart attack the previous November that the apartment was getting away from her. So I was very glad she made that decision for herself.) She had always accepted her diminishments gracefully, and this was no exception.

On March 9th Barbara got her hair done. Lorene had ordered a dryer attachment that fit like a shower cap, so the drying would be easier. By then Barbara could not keep her head up enough to have the regular dryer work properly. Her chin was practically on her chest most of the time.

Sunday, March 11th was Mother's 92nd birthday.   I preached at Pisgah.   I had thought I might be able to take Mother and her niece to church (my cousin, Peg Beach Ungerleider was visiting from New Jersey), but realized Mother was not strong enough to sit through a service.   But I did take Mother and Peg out to a birthday brunch at a restaurant.   While Mother sat at our table, I fixed her plate from the buffet and she ate well.

On March 16th Sherri was able to stay with Barbara while I took Mother to see the cardiologist. He was pleased with her progress, and said he would not need to see her again for six months unless she felt the need to see him sooner.

On March 19th I worked some at Mother's old apartment – took more china and things to her new place for her to decide what to keep and what to distribute to the family at that time. As I walked into her new room (she had not known I would be coming) she said, "I was just thinking how lonely I would be if you weren't here to come to see me." That made me wish I could go see her more. But she was very aware of my responsibilities with Barbara.   Mother was never demanding.   In fact, she always urged me not to do so much for her with all she knew I had to do at home.

March 31st I took Barbara to the dentist for a cleaning. I held her head back with my two hands, the dental assistant held Barbara's hands and the tray under Barbara's mouth and Raine did the cleaning. He got more done this time than we had been able to do in a long time. I almost fell over when Barbara said, "Oh, shit!" (She had never in her life used that kind of language! Nor, so far as I know, did she ever do it again.) I was so embarrassed.   But Raine said not to worry, it was the second time that day one of his patients had said that – the other was a child.

One night about that time Barbara did not sleep at all. She was very talkative (mostly jabber).   Once I made out, "I asked Lowell about that yesterday." She had not said "Lowell" in a very long time. She also said, "This is a pretty house," and "I love you." Since she went for days and days without saying anything at all, it was worth a night awake to hear her sweet voice.

On March 22nd about 9:30 AM (while I was feeding Barbara her breakfast) I called Mother to see how she was doing. She said she was not feeling well. She had gone to breakfast but had eaten little because she felt she was having trouble getting her breath. I asked her to open her door and tell the nurse (whose station was just across the hall from Mother's room) she was not feeling well so the nurse would check on her. And then I said I thought it would be wise for Mother to lie down. She said she would.

Marlene, our caregiver that day, was due to come and sit with Barbara at 10:00 AM. She got here at 9:50 AM. A couple of minutes later Westminster Canterbury called and said Mother was very sick, perhaps dying. I was able to go over there right away. Mother was unconscious and had vomited. The nurse told me she had heard Mother fall and went in to see about her. (She must have fallen on her way to the door to tell the nurse she was not feeling well.) Mother was having a seizure when the nurse got there, and then had another one. The nurse could not get a pulse. By the time I arrived the pulse was 35. They thought Mother was in the process of leaving this world. She was perspiring a lot. The ambulance took her to the emergency room. Years earlier Mother had signed a "Do Not Resuscitate" order. So they did not do anything on the way or at the hospital to jump-start her heart. But she came around on her own. When she regained consciousness she knew the month and the year in response to the doctor's questions. And when he asked her where she was, she looked around and said, "Well, I guess I'm in the hospital." (Of course, she had been unconscious during her trip there, so had to figure that out by her new surroundings.) Mott Robertson (the doctor) said to me, "Your mother is one tough lady!" He admitted her to ICU and ordered several tests, hoping to see what had caused this episode. I stayed with Mother in the room until she went to sleep. Later in the day I went back to the hospital and Mother was still asleep. I stayed until I had to go back home to let Marlene leave at 3:00 PM.

I had clothes Barbara had had a bowel movement accident in (with Marlene) and clothes Mother had vomited on to wash. I was getting lots of laundry experience!

Late in the afternoon I called ICU and Mother was still asleep. Later the nurse made the call to me for Mother, and then Mother and I had a nice telephone visit. She thought it was early morning. She had no memory of our phone conversation that morning, or of her getting sick. Her voice sounded good.

That evening Powell and Kathy and Chad arrived a little before bedtime. They had come to Lynchburg especially to celebrate Kathy's mother's birthday the following day. We went to bed about 10:00 PM

At 11:30 PM the phone rang. I awakened out of a deep sleep. The nurse said Mother's pulse had dropped back into the 30's and she had told Mother (who was fully alert) that she was calling me. Mother asked her not to because she knew I could not leave Barbara. But the nurse told Mother she felt she had to call me because of Mother's dangerously low pulse. So Mother asked her to be sure to tell me not to come. Well, I knew I could not go because I could not leave Barbara alone in the house. I said, "Tell her I love her," and hung up. I had forgotten Powell and his family were here! Powell tapped on our bedroom door and said Kathy had heard the phone ring and wondered if anything was wrong. I told him and then it dawned on me, "I can go to the hospital!" I immediately got dressed and went.

Mother was surprised but pleased to see me. I told her how I had been able to come because Powell and his family were at our house. She had forgotten they were with me although we had been scheduled to eat lunch with her at Westminster Canterbury the next day.

We had a wonderful one-and-a-half hour conversation. Mother said, "I may be dying, but I don't feel like I'm dying. I don't even feel sick!" She said she had no pain, no feeling of weakness, no shortness of breath, no discomfort at all. It was as if she were on her bed at home and we were having a good talk. She said, "If this is the Lord's time to call me home, I've looked forward for years to being in his presence; if he has work yet for me to do in this world, that is all right too. I rest in his gracious hands."

About 1:00 AM Mother insisted I go on back home. I told her I did not want to leave her, but she said she was feeling fine and did not want me to lose any more sleep. I suggested that perhaps she would rest (which I knew she needed) better if I were not there to talk to (she had talked almost non-stop). She sort of chuckled and said, "Perhaps that's right. It's hard not to talk to you while you are here." I had prayer with her, we told each other, "I love you," I kissed her on the forehead and I left.

At 2:30 AM the nurse called again. She said Mother had slipped into unconsciousness. I went back to the hospital, and stood by Mother's bed, rubbing her hands and commending her to the Lord's gracious keeping. There was a "death dew" on her brow. I sang softly, "My Jesus, I love thee, I know thou art mine… I'll sing when the death dew lies cold on my brow, 'If ever I loved thee, my Jesus, 'tis now.'" She fell asleep in Jesus at 4:17 AM on March 23rd. How I would miss her!

On March 26th my sister Sarah arrived from South Carolina. Christy and Bert Murphy stayed with Barbara at our house while I took Sarah to the funeral home. When we got back Christy asked if Barbara had called my mother "Grandmother." From the time we had had our children, that was the name Barbara had used for Mother. Christy said she had wondered because twice, very clearly, Barbara had said, "Grandmother" while Sarah and I were gone. Of course Barbara had heard all the talk of Mother's death including the phone calls I had made to inform the family. But Barbara had shown no sign that she had taken in any of this. More must have been going on inside her head than was apparent. Barbara had always loved Mother. And Mother had loved Barbara.

On April 7th Sherri stayed with Barbara so I could help my sisters Sarah and Virginia go through and clean out Mother's apartment. There was a lot to do!

The evening of April 12th Frances and Andy Sale and Judy and Bill Gayle brought supper and ate at our house with us. Mary Beth had helped me prepare the dining room for company. Everything looked very nice.

In late April I was enjoying emails from our son Powell in Russia! He was very tired, but felt his teaching was going well. He had been invited to preach Sunday. He said he wished I could be with him because he knew I would enjoy it so much. I would have, but was perfectly content to be at home which was my calling by then and it was good.

It became increasingly difficult to feed Barbara because she sat with her face almost on the table. One positive thing: Lorene discovered Barbara would drink more from a straw. So I began giving her liquids that way, too.

On May 3rd I took Barbara to have her eyes examined. Faye Hughey (one of our part-time companions) went with us to help. So Faye was holding Barbara's hands, I was holding her head back, and our ophthalmologist Bill Hobbs was trying to examine her eyes. She tried to fight him off and said, "I'll kill you!" There was not much Bill could do. He said he thought there was not any point in bringing her back unless she had an eye infection or something like that. Of course it had been some time since he had been able to tell what she could see anyway because she had not been able to read the chart. She kept her eyes closed through the days nearly all the time by then.

Barbara had been having less and less control of bathroom needs. One evening she soaked two pads and pants through the pad she wore. So the next day I tried diapers. I did not know how to get them on tight, so she wet through that too! Great fun!

On May 10th I wrote in my journal: "What a morning! Our caregiver was supposed to be here at 10:00 AM. I had an appointment with Raine Sydnor to get two crowns put on at 10:45 AM. When our helper wasn't here at 10:10 I called the agency to see if they had heard from her. They had not. I told them I would have to take Barbara with me to the dentist. If our missing helper called, I asked them to have her meet us there. Barbara and I left at 10:25 AM We got there in time. We sat Barbara in another chair – just outside the dentist's cubicle where I was. After a while a woman (who schedules for the agency) came and sat with Barbara. Then our own helper came. Her son had had an emergency at the hospital."

It was getting harder to bathe Barbara. Quite a while earlier I had had to give up trying to get her into the bathtub. So I had been washing her in the stall shower in the bathroom off our bedroom. But there was hardly room enough for both of us to get in there. One night Barbara almost fell over as I was getting her out of the shower stall. Maybe I could figure out a better way – that is, a way that worked better with the updated disabilities. I thought of the handicap shower Mother had had in her Assisted Living place with just one tiny step to get into it. I wondered if I could do something like that at our house.

In mid-May as I was bringing Barbara's breakfast to the table she had a grand mal seizure. She was already at the table. She smashed her face into the table. I was able to grab her from behind and keep her from falling on the floor. At first I thought she had bitten her lip, but then I was not sure if it was that or if she had cut it on the table edge. As she started coming out of the deep sleep which followed the seizure she kept saying, "Dear Lord... O God! ...Dear Lord." This kept up for almost an hour. Wanda came in and said, "The Lord is helping you, Barbara." (Wanda came after the seizure, but during the time Barbara was praying.) Then, when Barbara stopped that, she was very restless, and continued so all day. I had planned to play racquetball while Wanda was there, but canceled it because of what had happened. Barbara ate well. It had been about one-and-a-half years since the first major seizure; I hoped it would be at least that long before the next one. (Because of the negative side effects of the anticonvulsive medicines on Barbara, we had discontinued them all.)

On May 17th I wrote in my journal: "Barbara didn't sleep a wink all day yesterday and, although we went to bed at 10:00 PM we had to get back up because she was so restless. We went back to bed about 1:00 AM. Today she has been (in her chair) in such a deep sleep I've been able to feed her only one orange, and that with difficulty. Scott wanted me to put her in the hospital this evening, but I want to wait until tomorrow to see if she improves, because it is so much easier for me to care for her at home. Scott said, "OK," but he is afraid she might drag me down to the floor because she is so 'rag dollish' today – she can't carry her own weight at all."

The next day Barbara seemed much more normal (for her). She was drooling lots more than usual, probably because her mouth hurt where she had bit or cut it. The day after that Barbara seemed more like her old self, that is, up to where she had been before she had had the seizure.

On May 22nd I went by Lincare and bought a couple more pads for Barbara. Also, I tried a new way of giving her a bath that seemed to work pretty well. I put the bathtub chair right against the edge of the tub. Then I soaped the top of the chair and had her sit on it from the outside of the tub. With her on the soapy top I could rotate her around and put her feet into the water. Then I got her out the opposite way so she never had to step into or step out of the tub. The hardest part was getting her to stand up so I could wash and rinse her bottom. Maybe a bed bath would be needed before long.

Sherri would be able to help us only occasionally after that month (May) for the summer. She was in nursing school and had to keep up with that schedule. I would have to make other arrangements for Sundays when I preached.

A new woman from the agency came (temporarily). She was very sweet, but really not strong enough to handle Barbara with confidence. The woman was 75 years old. I felt sorry for her, that she needed to work that hard at her age.

On Sunday, July 1st Barbara and I tried to worship at Rivermont Presbyterian. But just before the service started Barbara stood, so I took her to the restroom. We didn't make it in time! The pad was soiled with a bowel movement! So I had to take it off. Then, in the middle of the sermon Barbara had diarrhea! I did have a pad on the wheel chair seat which kept it from running on the floor. We simply had to go home. I will not describe what it was like to clean Barbara up, and then the clothes. But I got it done. It was pretty bad, but could have been worse!

I had been thinking more about building a "handicap" bathroom for Barbara off our bedroom. I talked about it with our friend Frank Gough who was a builder. It might cost more than I could afford, but it would be worth quite a bit if it meant I could care for Barbara at home longer.

On July 2nd I wrote in my journal: "Last night I had a horrible dream: I was assisting Barbara down the front steps of the church, but in my dream there were many, many more steps than there actually are. Carroll Freeman, our friend and lawyer, was quite a way down the steps in front of us. He fell down hard. I told Barbara to hang onto the rail and not move, and I dashed to Carroll. He was dead. As I looked up to go back to Barbara she jumped forward, and hit her head as she fell down the steps, and I "knew" she had broken her neck. I woke up with my heart pounding, and couldn't go back to sleep." (As a matter of fact, Carroll Freeman, who in 1992 had drawn up the documents we needed in light of Barbara's Alzheimer's Disease, about five years later had been diagnosed himself with a terminal illness. He was ten years younger than we were. I grieved over Carroll's decline. He would die the day before Christmas, 2003.)

On July 5th while I was dressing Barbara she had another major seizure. I had hold of both her wrists. We were standing in front of the dresser and her legs buckled, but I let her down to the floor gently and kept her from banging her head. A little blood did dribble down the corner of her mouth. I thought she had bitten her tongue. It had been seven weeks since the last one. In spite of all this I was able to get behind her and lift her up to the bed. It did not take her as long to wake up as it had the last time. And she ate a good breakfast and was quite normal (for her) the rest of the day.

The next day Barbara was in pretty much of a stupor, similar to the day after the other seizures. It was hard to get any food or liquid into her.

On Sunday, July 8th I preached at Pisgah Church. Barbara was still very tired. She also had a large black and blue place on the top of one of her feet. She must have hit it on the bottom of the dresser while she was thrashing around on the floor during the seizure.

By the next day Barbara seemed to be back to her "normal." She ate a good breakfast and lunch.

Barbara started a new anti-seizure medicine. I hoped it would be effective.

That night Barbara didn't go to sleep night until 3:00 AM! I wondered if it were the new medicine.

On Sunday, July 15th Barbara woke up at 3:00 AM, and was "wired up," constant movement. It must have been the new medicine. Lorene stayed with Barbara while I went to preach. Lorene said she bet Barbara got up and down from her chair a thousand times while I was at church! Barbara continued to be very active all afternoon. I called Scott. He said to stop the medicine.

Barbara slept very well that night. She was so sleepy I was not able to feed her breakfast the next day.

On July 22nd Neel Rich showed me the Hoyer Lift he used with his wife Iris who is my first cousin. I did not need that yet, but it would help with Barbara as she got to where she carried less of her own weight on her legs.

On July 24th they got the hole dug for the foundation of the new bathroom. Frank said they would pour the footings the next day. It was exciting actually to be started! However, unlike the pleasure Barbara experienced when we built the new study back in 1995, by 2001 she knew nothing about the handicap bathroom although she was at the house the whole time.

Sunday, July 29th it was pouring rain when Barbara and I went to Rivermont Church. We both got wet as I tried to hold the umbrella and push the wheel chair at the same time. In the middle of David Etheridge's sermon Barbara had to go to the bathroom. I took her. And she had a good bowel movement. Then we stayed in the Family Room and listened to the service over the speaker. A young man was in the Family Room too. After the service I introduced myself and he said he was Jef Flippin. I guessed he had grown two feet since I had seen him last! He said his spurt of growth had happened in the past year. He kindly suggested he help us to the car and hold the umbrella. Although it was not raining as hard as it had been when we arrived, I was grateful for his help.

On August 10th I ordered two cherry twin beds and orthopedic mattresses and springs for our bedroom when we got back into it – we had had to move across the hall while the new bathroom was being built. I hated to get twin beds, but thought it would be easier to care for Barbara in her own bed. The new beds would be simple, but attractive and adequate in our bedroom. I did not think we needed a hospital bed yet and Lorene agreed.

On August 15th the agency called me and said their Home Health Care workers would no longer be able transport people (their insurance company's policy). They would make some special arrangements for the next couple of weeks, then I would need to do something else about getting Barbara to the hairdresser once a week. I thought I would ask Lorene to do Barbara's hair at our house on Tuesdays when she was there anyway, starting in September.

The last day of August Barbara and I went to Kathy and Powell's (a two and one half hour drive). I had put diapers on Barbara and we made the trip fine. She was wet when we arrived, but it hadn't leaked.

Kathy was able to get some rails for our bed. I would sleep better, knowing Barbara would not be able to fall out.

While Lorene was fixing Barbara's hair at our house September 4th (which she planned to do from then on), Barbara tipped over backwards in the chair. She was not hurt, but it frightened us.

The next night Barbara fell out of bed about midnight. She was not hurt. I did not sleep anymore. I could not figure out how she had done it unless I had forgotten to pull up the rail on her side of the bed when we had retired for the night.

I picked up a "Gait Belt" for Barbara. It gave something by which a caregiver could hold her up. Lorene seemed to think it might help.

Barbara did not sleep at all well the night of September 10th. She jabbered a lot. But once I did hear her say clearly, "I love you!" How sweet! But I was tired! I fed Barbara her breakfast at 6:00 AM.

About 10:00 AM September 11th I was reading and Frank Gough came to the door. That was not unusual because he and his people were in the midst of building our new bathroom. But the first thing he asked was if I had heard the terrible news. "What news?" I asked. "That the World Trade Center in New York and the Pentagon in Washington, D. C., have been attacked!" We turned on the television and watched the horror unfold before us. I did not think either of us would forget that day the rest of our lives!

They delivered our twin beds. Justin Petrey brought supper his mother had fixed for us. While he was here he helped me put the twin beds in place in our redone bedroom and they looked nice.

On October 17th I started using a loose-fitting seat belt on Barbara when she was in her rocking chair. Barbara did not even realize she was wearing it, but it kept her from standing with the possibility of falling. I thought I would use it for her regularly when I had to be out of the room where she was. She would be much safer, and I would feel less anxious about her.

I gave Barbara her first bath in the shower of the new bathroom. I sat her on her shower seat and used the handheld shower head. It worked very well. The heat lights were great! Barbara did not complain once about being cold, which she had been doing a lot previously when she had gotten a bath.

We slept in our new twin beds in our old bedroom for the first time. We both slept well, maybe because we were so tired from not sleeping the night before!

Then we went through a period of Barbara not sleeping well three nights in a row. I became exhausted.

On Reformation Sunday I preached at Pisgah on "Needed: A New Reformation." Then I came home and took a nap before Lorene left because Barbara had not gone to sleep until 6:00 AM that morning! So, although we gained an hour that night, I did not feel as if I had!

On November 6th I ordered a Hoyer Lift after getting a prescription for it from Scott. I had thought they said they would bring it that day, but they didn't (not that I was in that much of a rush for it). But my back had started hurting, and I figured I needed some help in lifting Barbara, especially when I bathed her.

They brought the Hoyer Lift the next day. The net sling which I needed to bathe Barbara would be delivered in a couple of days.

On November 10th, Barbara's birthday, I spread one of the vinyl tablecloths to keep the water off the floor, and bathed Barbara with the shower curtain open. It seemed to work very well. We got our flu shots the next day at the doctor's office.

I had started using a full diaper on Barbara at night. But I could not seem to get them tight enough, so they leaked.

Barbara and I drove to Kathy and Powell's for Thanksgiving. Kathy had a great dinner, and it was wonderful to be together.

The next month Sarah and I went to the Christmas Eve Service at Rivermont Church at 7:00 PM while Mary Beth and Alan stayed with Barbara. And they went and we stayed home at 11:00 PM.

In that year's Christmas letter I shared the following:

Although Barbara is very severely handicapped now, it is a joy for me to take care of her. She is a dear! We have just built a handicap bathroom at the house. This way I can bathe Barbara much more easily and safely. In addition to preaching regularly the 2nd and 4th Sundays of each month at the little Pisgah Presbyterian Church (twenty miles from here), I have filled in at several other churches as well. I am blessed to have outstanding part-time help at home with Barbara so I can do this.

Chapter Thirteen: 2002

On January 17th Ellie and Jim Gustafson came and we ate at the Lodge of the Fisherman. Bev Cosby followed us out to the car and talked a few minutes. (Bev died suddenly a few days later.) Barbara had four bowel movements that day! I was glad all was functioning!

Mary Anne and Jack Voelkel, old friends from our college days, visited us. Mary Anne said she deeply appreciated my keeping Barbara looking so pretty with earrings, necklace and lipstick. (Later I had to stop the lipstick because Barbara would try to eat it while I was applying it to her lips.) Mary Anne and Jack both commented on the sense of "peace" there was in our home. Ellie and Jim had said the same thing when they had visited a couple of weeks before, for which I thanked the Lord. It was his gift.

Lorene's Westminster Canterbury patient died (she was 100). So Lorene could stay here later in the afternoons. I thought I would ask her to do that some, though of course, she might get another patient.

On February 7th Faye could not come so they sent someone else. She did fine, but when I got home she was in the middle of cleaning up a huge bowel movement mess.

A couple of weeks later Gail Mudrick stayed with Barbara so I could go to the Rivermont Readers' meeting. Paul Mudrick led an outstanding study.

Barbara had been humming with the music playing on the CD quite a bit. It sounded so sweet.

On Easter Day I took Barbara to Rivermont Church. John Mabray preached a powerful sermon. Barbara had a bowel movement in her pants at church. I had put a big absorbent pad on her over her small pad, so nothing leaked out. When we got home I got her clothes off, put her in the shower, and "hosed her down." We had a huge mess, but nothing I could not handle.

Nancy Tenniswood came from Michigan for a visit. She had been a bridesmaid in our wedding, we had visited them at their home in 1992, they had come to our 40th Wedding Anniversary party in 1995, and Nancy's husband Bob had since died. When Nancy was making plans for her trip she asked, "Do you think Barbara still will know me?" I replied that Barbara had not known me for several years. It was great to see Nancy. She was very distressed about Barbara's much more deteriorated condition. One day Barbara sang with me, the first time in quite a while. Nancy was so pleased. The next day Barbara was unable to sing.

One evening an advertisement came on television where they sang, "Your Cheatin' Heart." Barbara got tickled. I picked it up and sang that phrase over and over again with an exaggerated country twang accent, and she laughed and laughed.

On April 13th Barbara had not slept well the night before. About an hour after her breakfast she threw up, but it hadn't soured yet. At first I had thought she was having a seizure. She had been sleeping in her chair, and never did wake up. Later I was able to feed her a good lunch, so I hoped she would be all right.

Mary and Joe Spencer came to visit us after evening worship at Rivermont Church. They often did this, and it was always a joy to see them.

On April 23rd Mother's first cousin, Shirley Rhodes Anderson from Milford, Connecticut came for a visit. We had not seen each other since 1950!

On April 29th Lorene stayed longer than usual with Barbara so I could take Shirley to Monticello and to lunch at Michie Tavern. She enjoyed it very much. Shirley went back home the next day.

Sunday, May 12th was Mother's Day. I preached at Pisgah. Barbara had been very restless the night before, so I had not gotten much sleep. That Sunday morning she was like a rag doll, but I was able to feed her a pretty good breakfast. When I took her to the bathroom I could hardly get her back to the den. In fact she slumped to her knees in the hall. For a long time I had found the best way to walk her was for me to grip her arms while I walked backwards. That way, if Barbara did go down, I could ease her down. If I were holding her hands, her wrists might break when she fell. When she was like that probably I should have used her wheelchair. Lorene was able to feed Barbara a good lunch of pizza after which Barbara slept in her chair a long time.

On May 24th Barbara and I went to Kathy and Powell's after lunch. Kathy had a great supper.

The next day I took the whole crew out to brunch at a Golden Corral. Then Barbara and I left for home. Barbara had a bowel movement in her pants early in the trip. There was nothing to do but keep going. There was no way I could think of for us to stop where I could clean her up. So I had a lot to do when we got home. Since I had put a diaper on her over the little pad she wore all the time, it was all contained, in other words, did not run all over the car. But I knew this would be our last out-of-town trip together. It had just gotten too hard to manage. And by that time Barbara did not know where she was anyway.

Lorene and Sherri stayed with Barbara at home while I went to the Banner of Truth Conference with John Mabray. All went well.

By mid-June Barbara was drooling so badly most of the time I had to put a big bib with plastic backing on it to keep her blouse from getting and staying soaked. I knew that would not be good for the skin on her chest either. So from then on I did not put a necklace on her. No point in having it around her neck if a bib kept it hidden.

On June 21st I received a very nice note from Mrs. Grubbs (widow of the pastor who had married Barbara and me to each other). The note was actually written by Mrs. Grubbs' daughter, Carlone, with whom Mrs. Grubbs lived. She would be 91 the following week, and was thinking about and concerned for Barbara and asked Carlone to write for her. I was quite touched by her thoughtfulness.

On July 13th Mary Beth got to our house from Tennessee about 7:30 PM. She handed me a baby picture frame. I was puzzled until she said, "This is for a picture of our new baby when it comes!" They had just found out a few days before and were overjoyed. I was so happy about it! The baby was expected in March. If it were a girl they planned to name her "Addie Ruth" – after two of her great grandmothers: (Alan's mother) Syble's mother and my mother. If they had a boy they did not know what they would name him.

On July 19th Mary Beth and I took Barbara to the Medical Care Center for respite care while we went to the Sykes family reunion in Lebanon, Virginia. They did not seem ready for her or prepared to meet her special needs as they had done so well in previous visits. Mary Beth wept as we left the nursing home. I told her I would take Barbara back home right then and not go to the reunion. But she said, "No, I think this is the right thing to do, but it is so hard!"

I got back to Lynchburg from the reunion earlier than I had planned, and went and picked up Barbara from the Medical Care Center. She was fine, but very sleepy.

The next morning Barbara was so sleepy I was unable to feed her breakfast. I did get a glass of orange juice down her by giving it to her in her child's "medicine spoon."

Lorene was able to get a little food down Barbara. I hoped it was simply that she was very sleepy. It was like she was in a stupor. I put her to bed and it was only 7:00 PM.

In early August Barbara's sleep seemed all messed up. She slept soundly in her chair in the daytime. And she was awake much of the night. We were trying to adjust her medicine, but had not gotten it right. I was pretty tired.

Sherri said she could stay with Barbara the last weekend in October, so I could plan to go to my 50th high school reunion on Long Island, New York.

On August 10th Barbara was like a rag doll. I could hardly manage her. I was able to give her a bath, but it was very hard.

Barbara did not sleep at all the night of August 13th. She jabbered all night long! She did not seem at all distressed, but I noticed in the morning she had bruised her right shoulder on the bed rail. I had changed her twice, and put her in a better position in the bed. I hoped and prayed I could get her back on a better sleep schedule.

Scott ordered stronger pills for Barbara, to try to get her to sleep more soundly at night. I was about worn out.

By September 1st Barbara had slept well the previous two nights. I was so grateful!

On September 10th Powell called. When I answered the phone he said he was glad to know I was not dead! Ben Trawick, a minister in his presbytery who knew me from when he was a member of my presbytery, had called Powell to express sympathy concerning my death! It turned out Powell had called his presbytery office to request prayer for Kathy's upcoming gallbladder surgery and someone else had called in about the death of another man's father. The person who took the messages got them confused and it came out in their presbytery newsletter that Powell's father had died!

Barbara had a bowel movement on my feet. I had just gotten her pants down, and it came pouring out. More fun! I burst out laughing.

Barbara started sleeping better most of the time. For a while Barbara had not been able to stand up from her chair on her own. She could still use her hands on the hand rests of the chair to shift her weight, but never stood up on her own after that. It was really safer that way, but a further deterioration. She never complained.

On Sunday September 15th I worshiped at Rivermont Presbyterian. I had not been there since Easter because I had preached all the other Sundays except when I had gone to the family reunion in July. It was the first Sunday I had been to Rivermont without taking Barbara with me. Lorene was able to stay with her, and we both thought Barbara was more comfortable at home by then.

On September 17th Barbara had diarrhea twice while I was taking care of her (and had done it twice earlier with Lorene). The second time in the evening she was like a rag doll… I could not get her on the toilet seat… she was on her knees on the floor with her back to the toilet with bowel movement all over her and me and the floor. Her arm was draped over the edge of the bathtub. I thought I might at least get started with the clean up in that position. But she started shaking and crying. She had not cried for years, not since she had been frustrated when she could not do what she wanted to do in the earlier stages of Alzheimer's. I said, "Darlin', are you scared?" She replied, "Yes, I scared. Cry." I told her she didn't need to be scared, that I was with her and taking care of her. I stroked her. Then I got behind her, put my arms under her armpits and lifted her to the toilet seat and started cleaning her up. She was fine then. It took me quite a while to take care of her and myself and the bathroom, but it turned out all right. I felt so badly that she had gotten scared and cried.

Keeping her comfortable and safe was what I always tried to do. One good thing: once the reason for her discomfort was removed, she had no memory of it. So everything was just like nothing bad had happened. (I am typing this November 21, 2007. So far, Barbara has not cried since that day, September 17, 2002.)

On September 27th as I got Barbara up I sang to her as usual. Then I asked (as I usually did), "How are you today?" She smiled and said, just as plain as day, "Fine!" A little later I asked her again. She smiled, a big smile, and said, "OK." I tried to get her to do it more, but there was no response.

On Sunday, September 29th I took Barbara to church at Rivermont. We sat next to Wayne and Brenda Kasperski. He had become paralyzed a while before as a result of neck surgery gone wrong. So he was in his wheelchair where the back pew had been, and Barbara was in her wheelchair. The church had taken out the back pew to accommodate worshipers in wheelchairs. One tends not to appreciate such things until one has a need for them.

We got about twenty minutes into the service and Barbara had a bowel movement. I had a diaper on her over her pad, so none of it leaked out, but I could smell it. Nothing to do but take her back home and put her in the shower. I was so sorry we had to leave before the sermon, but it could not be helped.

On October 10th the agency called to say Faye was sick. I told them not to bother to send a substitute. It was more trouble to me than it was worth to orient a new person to be with Barbara for just one time. I would stay with Barbara myself all that day.

The night of October 12th Barbara did not sleep well. She woke up about three o'clock in the morning and stayed awake. Once, while I was stroking her, I said playfully, "Whatcha doin'?" "Not much," she replied. I broke up with laughter and she had a huge smile on her face. I felt so pleased when she responded like that which was very rare by then.

On October 16th I took Barbara to the dentist for cleaning at noon, and then by the doctor's office for our flu shots. The nurse came out to the car and gave both Barbara and me our shots so I would not have to do the hard work of getting Barbara inside. Scott had arranged it, and it was very kind of them.

On October 24th Sherri stayed with Barbara so I could fly to my 50th high school reunion. My brother Ern met me at the Islip, Long Island, New York airport. I got back home three days later.

On November 6th I did a "trial run" on baking a turkey, so I would know how to do one for Thanksgiving. I did it by Barbara's method of high oven temperature (450 degrees) and wrapped in foil. It turned out OK, although we had to bake it longer. Mary Beth figured out that the reason we had to extend the time was the turkey had not been fully thawed. So now I felt confident. I thought I would buy the Thanksgiving turkey on the Friday before Thanksgiving and let it thaw thoroughly until I baked it on Wednesday. (I found out later I could buy a fresh turkey which I did.)

Powell arrived. He, Mary Beth and I went to the Briar Patch in Amherst for lunch and then went to a shop Mary Beth and Pam had visited earlier in the week, to pick up a couple of Christmas presents.

Then we drove to Morris' Orchard and bought apples, cider and an apple cake. Such a beautiful day! This had been one of the "highlight" days of my life! Such joy! The only sadness was that Barbara could not enjoy it with us.

November 10th was Barbara's 69th birthday. I sang "Happy Birthday" to her. She smiled.

Mary Beth called from Tennessee on the 14th. They said it would be a girl! So "Addie Ruth" would be her name – for two of her great grandmothers. Mary Beth had said when she had been at our house the previous week, "Grandmother was such an important part of my life! It's sad to know my children will have no memory of her, except what I tell them." Yes, it seemed sad, but I reflected that this was the universal human experience as the generations rise and fall.

On December 5th Barbara was both restless and like a rag doll. I did not remember her having this combination before.

I was supposed to take Barbara to have her teeth cleaned, but I postponed it because of the bad weather. At that point it was hard enough getting her into the car without battling the rain too. I could not push her wheelchair and hold an umbrella at the same time.

On December 14th I had a nosebleed. Barbara had three bowel movements.

The next day, a Sunday, I took Barbara to Rivermont Presbyterian. David Etheridge preached. It was a good service. We sat next to Tom Hatmaker. His little son (two years old) slept in Tom's arms the whole time, a great illustration of the sermon.

On Christmas Eve Shirl and Cliff Thomas brought our Christmas dinner from them, Liz Broyles and Pat Hylton. The Stinesprings also came by with more food. We would have a fantastic dinner!

My sister Sarah was visiting from South Carolina and went to the 7:00 PM Christmas Eve Service at Rivermont. I had Barbara in bed and asleep so I went to the 11:00 PM Service while Sarah stayed at home with Barbara.

We had our Christmas dinner the day after Christmas. To what others brought in I added a corn pudding and plum pudding. We ate in the dining room. Faye looked after Barbara. Kathy and Powell did most of the cleaning up from dinner. Mary Beth's feet were swelling so she tried to keep them up. She had worked very hard all morning getting ready for the meal. Laddie's daughter Lauren (almost two) was so cute!

In our Christmas letter I wrote:

Barbara continues to decline with Alzheimer's Disease. She is quite helpless now. But I am very grateful to the Lord that I can care for her at home. And I love doing it! I am blessed by some wonderful people who give me part-time help with Barbara. That way I have been able to preach most Sundays at various churches this year. And I still play racquetball about three times a week.

Chapter Fourteen: 2003

On Sunday, January 5th I took Barbara to Rivermont Presbyterian. The church was packed. Barbara was like a rag doll.

The following Saturday Barbara had a huge bowel movement accident. I had to change all she had on except her bra, and most of what I had on. It was even all over my watch!

On January 15th Meg and Rodney Laughon came over and brought supper with them. It was so good to visit with them, and, of course, the meal was excellent.

On January 17th I got a call saying Faye would be late because of the snow. I cancelled my regular racquetball game with my friend and lawyer, Dan Sweeney. Tulane Patterson, another friend who was head of the agency *Generation Solutions, Inc.* brought Faye later in his four wheel drive vehicle. He asked me if I could go play racquetball with him. (By that time it was too late to play with Dan.) So I did and we had a good time. Then Tulane asked if I could have lunch with him and Claudia and their girls (who were out of school because of the weather). We ate together at the Cavalier.

On February 5th I took Barbara to have her teeth cleaned. Raine also filled two very small cavities for which he did not think Barbara would need anesthetic. She did fine. Raine gave me a small baby toothbrush to slip over my finger and told me to get toddler toothpaste that tastes good and can be swallowed. I had not been able to brush Barbara's teeth because she could no longer swish and spit; she simply gagged. I hoped this would work and it did! I had also started using baby shampoo to wash Barbara's face. That worked well too.

On February 8th I wrote in my journal: "Barbara has been 'winning' her bathroom games. I've had lots of washing and drying to do!"

Sunday, February 16th most churches were closed because of the snow. Rivermont was having only the 11:00 AM service. I could not take Barbara out in that.

On February 22nd Starke Sydnor called early and said his brother Raine (our dear friend and dentist) had had a massive stroke the day before, and it looked very bad. Raine had not regained consciousness. Before this he had been fine. It had happened at his office. Earlier that same day he had passed his annual physical examination with flying colors. We never know.

I was not able to "hit it right" with Barbara that day. I sat her on the toilet, we waited a long time, she did not do anything, and then would do it after I brought her back to her chair. I had to change her pants and the pads she was sitting on four times and the day was not over.

On February 25th Powell called. Rachel Kathleen was born to Kathy and Powell's daughter, Christie, and her husband, Jim, a little before 5:00 AM. Both baby and mother were doing well. How I wished Barbara could take in the fact that she had a great-grandchild!

I spent some time with Raine in the hospital. When I had prayer with him he opened one eye. Who knows if he could hear me? I thought he did.

On February 27th Starke called to tell me Raine had died about 7:00 AM. Faye came so I was able to go over to the Sydnors'. I felt so sorry for Raine's wife Mary Jane.

Faye was able to come March 1st so I could go to Raine's burial at 10:00 AM in Spring Hill Cemetery and then to the Memorial Service at Rivermont. The church was packed. The choir sang. John

Mabray started his sermon: "We were not ready for this… BUT RAINE WAS!" Powerful!

On March 5th Addie Ruth was born at 7:59 PM CST to our Mary Beth and her husband Alan. Everything went well. When Addie Ruth started coming she came quickly. I had been getting updates throughout the day, but received word of the baby's birth about 10:30 PM our time. Barbara would be unaware of Addie Ruth too. How she would have loved these little girls!

While turning Barbara around I wrenched my left knee. It hurt, but not too badly. My knee was really sore the next day. It was difficult to walk. I was afraid I had done some serious damage. The day after that my knee was worse. I decided I needed to go to the doctor.

I saw Cap Eschenroeder, my orthopedic physician, about my knee. He said, "I know exactly how you did this. When you transfer a helpless person from one chair to another, the natural thing to do is to pivot with your knee. And you can injure yourself like that. Instead, take several short, quick steps." The x-ray showed nothing broken, but the meniscus might be torn. He put me in a knee brace and wanted to see me in a couple of weeks. He said it might just get well… and then again, it might not. If it did, I would not need to keep my next appointment with him. If it did not, we would do an MRI. If that showed a tear we would have to decide whether or not to do surgery. It really did hurt that day! By March 19th my left knee was well, so I cancelled my second appointment with Cap.

Both Barbara and I had our annual physicals. OK, OK. Scott was pleased to note I had lost a little weight.

On March 31st the Home Health person came. She thought it would be good to have a physical therapist come and show us (Lorene, Faye and me) how to give Barbara some helpful exercises. This might keep her limbs from "freezing up" because of lack of use.

A couple of days later the physical therapist did come. She thought Barbara was quite limber, which rather surprised her since Barbara had not been getting exercise. She showed me some exercises she thought would be helpful.

On April 16th I took Barbara to have her teeth cleaned. Bo Sorenson, Raine's younger colleague, and Teresa Cheverton (Bo's dental assistant) did very well.

On Easter Day I took Barbara to Rivermont Church. The sermon was powerful, the music wonderful and the church was packed. Barbara hummed quite a bit during the service, but not when the music was going on! I had put a large disposable diaper on Barbara. When we got home I found she had had a small bowel movement.

On April 21st Mary Beth called. They were in Kingsport, Tennessee because of the death of the father of Alan's best friend. (Kingsport is about halfway between Cookeville, Tennessee, where Mary Beth and Alan lived, and Lynchburg, Virginia. The total distance between Cookeville and Lynchburg is about 425 miles.) Although they had not planned this when they had left home, Alan suggested that he borrow one of his parents' cars to go back home to work, and that Mary Beth and Addie Ruth come on to Lynchburg in their car that night! So they were going to come. What a happy surprise!

I really enjoyed holding Addie Ruth. We were bonding! Barbara would have loved her little granddaughter so!

The following Saturday everybody came home for a picnic lunch! I got the food. Laddie grilled the hamburgers. Even though it was pouring rain, he managed by pulling the grill under the overhang of the roof. So we had 16 people, including the babies. Most everyone had left by 2:00 PM. I think it was a fine event, and we got plenty of pictures.

Barbara did not sleep well the night before, so I was exhausted even though the children would not let me do anything while they were here.

Mary Beth told me she and her brothers were worried about me. They had observed how much harder it was to care for their mother than it had been. Mary Beth had tried to take Barbara to the bathroom and Barbara had almost sat on the floor. Mary Beth and Addie Ruth left April 28th.

In the middle of the night when I was working with Barbara on the toilet in the new bathroom, the bolt that holds the toilet seat sheared off. Glen Murphy came over the next day and replaced the plastic seat with a much heavier one held on with metal bolts.

May 27th through May 29th Lorene and Sherri split the shifts to stay with Barbara in our house while I attended the Banner of Truth Conference with John Mabray. All worked fine.

Charlotte, Barbara's sister, arrived by plane from Kansas. She had a good trip.

Our larger family gathered at our house Saturday, June 7th. It poured rain all day. There was quite a crowd, but it worked out fine.

The following Monday Charlotte and I had lunch at Milano's. Charlotte helped me with some of her and Barbara's childhood experiences I was trying to write down for our children.

On Friday, June 13th Faye came early so I could get Charlotte to the airport on time. Charlotte cried as she kissed Barbara "goodbye." When we got in the car she said through her tears, "It's just so hard to leave her!" Barbara had enjoyed the visit. Charlotte had been able to get Barbara to laugh several times. Charlotte loved coming in to watch me put Barbara to bed, and see her smile contentedly. I could always count on a sweet smile as I tucked her in and sang, "Jesus, Loves Me," and also when I got her up in the morning.

On June 14th I wrote in my journal: "Barbara is like a rag doll today. And she has had five bowel movements in her pants. I'm afraid I've pulled my back out. She simply cannot stand up today. I've prayed for special strength from the Lord. I want so much to see Barbara through this."

In late-June Powell and Kathy's son Chad – almost 15 by then – came and spent a few days with us. I had a wonderful time with him. I think he enjoyed it too. He and I visited some of the local places of interest: Thomas Jefferson's Poplar Forest (Mr. Jefferson's summer retreat home), the National D-Day Memorial, and the Confederate Section of the Old City Cemetery. Chad taught me some things about my computer. He certainly knew a lot about it. Barbara did not realize Chad was here. I felt sad when I thought about the fact that, because of Barbara's illness, we had not been able to have him come and spend time with us when he was little. Barbara had always loved children so. I'm sure she would have "spoiled her grandson rotten!"

On July 6th Barbara was having some big involuntary jerks; I was afraid they might lead into a grand mal seizure, so I gave her an extra Ativan. That seemed to have stopped the jerks, but it made her very sleepy.

On Sunday, July 20th I was deeply moved as I baptized little Addie Ruth at the First Presbyterian Church, Bristol, Tennessee. I missed Barbara so! The family had a catered brunch together in a private room at the King College Student Center.

On July 22nd Barbara was like a rag doll. I found myself hating to take her to the bathroom because it was so hard when she could not support herself at all.

August 2nd Barbara had three bowel movements in her pants. I had planned to wash and dry towels and washcloths in addition to the regular wash, but did not have the time or the energy. I thought I had thrown my back out pulling and holding Barbara up.

The following day I took Barbara to Rivermont Church. She did fine.

Bert Murphy suggested I get the kind of belt people use to protect their lower back when they are lifting weights because my back had been bothering me a lot. I decided to try it.

On August 9th I wrote in my journal: "Wow! Barbara has been a leaky faucet today! I've had to change her completely six times. I can't imagine how she could have that much urine in her."

Friday, August 15th was Faye Hughey's last day with us. She was going to Nursing School to get her LPN. She had been great for us the past two years. I would miss her. I hoped they would be able to send a good replacement!

Mary Beth wanted me to go to go to Kansas with her and Addie Ruth. "I want to do this for Mama," she said. We talked about either the first or third weekend in October. I called Charlotte, and the third weekend worked best for her.

Well, the replacement for Faye the agency sent did not work out at all. I hated to do it, but I called and asked them not to send her back again. I had enough to deal with without, in addition, having the helper argue with me. I felt exhausted!

Suzie and Donna came over from the agency and showed me some better ways to handle Barbara, and suggested I get a wheel shower chair with a hole in the seat so her bottom could be washed without getting her to stand. They also showed me how to get Barbara up without putting so much strain on my back, and suggested "pull-up" absorbent panties which could be done in one quick motion, unlike the "saddles" with straps she had been wearing for a long time. They also suggested I remove the absorbent mats in front of the shower because we might trip over them.

I thought Barbara had gone down a lot in the past month. Before then she sometimes was like a rag doll, but usually could stand while I work on her. Now she seemed always to be limp. She simply could not support her weight on her own legs. I hoped I could keep this up.

I started putting Barbara to bed around 7:00 PM most nights. She had been sound asleep by then in her chair anyway. If she did not seem sleepy, of course, I did not do this.

On August 26th at my request a salesman came to sell me a roll-in shower chair for Barbara. He also tried to sell me a hospital bed, but I did not think I needed one for Barbara at that time. I did not have any trouble getting her in and out of bed. (Lorene agreed with me that we did not need a hospital bed at that time.)

My younger brother Ern died suddenly August 27th near his home on Long Island, New York. I was really sorry I could not go, but there was not time to make arrangements to be away from Barbara for a few days.

Near the end of August I found when I tried to sing to Barbara I couldn't. It seemed like laryngitis of only the upper register of my voice. I could not sing in church either, except two octaves lower. I could tell it when I spoke, but I did not think others could notice it.

On September 4th I wrote in my journal: "Our 48th wedding anniversary. This is beyond Barbara's comprehension. But I thank the Lord for every year he has given us together, including these last years since Barbara has been sick. Although there has been much sadness and difficulty, in some ways these have been the best years of my life. I love taking care of Barbara."

I had made some changes in the way I took care of Barbara. I had realized that I needed to care for her "smarter." Otherwise, I was going to give out. Until then I had tried to "walk" her in the house from room to room. I had walked backwards and held on to her arms. I had felt that little exercise was good for her. But I began to realize that if I gave out she would not be able to be at home with me. So I started using the wheelchair all the time to get her from room to room and, therefore, from then on, always took her to the new bathroom. (I had been taking her to the bathroom off the hall because it was a much closer walk from the den.) There was a lot more room for me to work with her in the new bathroom. I started pulling her up to the table to eat in the wheelchair; she sat higher in the wheelchair and it was easier to get her there. Also, I stopped using panties over the pads she wore – less to pull up and less to wash.

On September 13th I bathed Barbara in her new shower chair. It worked very well. As I started to bathe her I stood her up so she could get back further on the seat I said, "Darlin', you need to get further back on the seat." She replied, "Well, I'm tryin' to." I hugged her and told her how precious she was. It had been a very long time since she had said that much, and she spoke clearly.

In mid-September I saw Graham Gilmer (our ear, nose and throat physician) about my laryngitis. He thought it was acid reflux and gave me some pills. He did not see any growths for which I was thankful.

On September 26th Scott Wade, our physician and friend, came over for a social visit. While he was here Barbara had a huge diarrhea mess – it went through to the pad she was sitting on. (She had already had a normal bowel movement earlier that morning.) When I stood her up to put her in the wheelchair the mess rolled down her leg and got all over the carpet. Scott insisted on helping me clean Barbara up, and also the carpet. I begged him not to, but he said he had come to help me, and wanted to.

Scott told me he thought I ought to be thinking about putting Barbara in a nursing home. But I replied that although I might need to do that in the future, right then I felt I was taking much better care of her than the best nursing home would, and I was committed to doing that as long as the Lord gave me the strength to do it. He complimented me on the great care Barbara was getting and how good she looked. Again I apologized for his having gotten in the middle of our mess, but he said he was glad to have seen us like this. "I usually see you when things are not like this," Scott said, "but I know you have to deal with this sort of thing frequently."

Ralph Motz brought the little wooden ramp he had made to help us wheel Barbara's shower chair into the shower. It worked very well.

I picked up Barbara's newly made flannel nightgowns at Aunt Weeda's Closet in Madison Heights. They made some that tied in the back from material I had brought them. This style was much easier to get on Barbara.

In mid-October Barbara stayed at the Medical Care Center while I flew to Kansas. I met Mary Beth and Addie Ruth in Wichita. We rented a car and had a nice drive to Bunker Hill where Barbara's sister Charlotte and her husband Everett lived.

Charlotte, Mary Beth, Addie Ruth and I drove to Bennington (north of Salina) where Barbara's family, the Powells, had lived for three years (1944-47).   Then we drove to Salina and took pictures of the houses the Powells had lived in and the schools the girls had attended. We visited Barbara's parents' graves, and I took pictures of their gravestone. We also stopped in the park where I had proposed to Barbara. Addie Ruth was so good! That was a great day. I only wished Barbara could have enjoyed it with us.

The next day we went back to Salina where Barbara had grown up. We took more pictures. We stopped at Glendale (about 20 miles west of Salina), where Barbara had first taught (1954-1955). (In those days several states, including Kansas, allowed people to teach after two years of college on a temporary certificate. Barbara would receive her degree from Oglethorpe University in Atlanta in 1959.) The year Barbara had taught at Glendale she had lived with her parents in Salina. She had had a combination of grades one through four. As we looked at the old two-room schoolhouse, then abandoned, I felt very emotional. I thought of my darling – a twenty-year-old, fresh-faced, eager, capable young woman – going out there every day for that year, working in that very building, finding she had a real gift for teaching, loving it and the children, and looking forward to our marriage the following year. During that period she had written to me (I was doing my third year at Wheaton) of the wonderful youngsters in her classroom, and that she was anticipating us having some "precious little ones" of our own someday. As I gazed at that dilapidated structure which was falling down, where generations of children had been taught "reading, writing and 'rithmatic," I thought it was a visible illustration of our brief, earthly life. I reflected on Barbara's current situation, where her "body of this earthly tabernacle" was just about abandoned too. I was not ashamed to shed some tears. Then we went to the Greenwood Cemetery in Newton, Kansas where I took pictures of the gravestones of some of Barbara's larger family, including both sets of her grandparents. This had been quite a pilgrimage. I was so glad I had come.

When I got back to Lynchburg I went from the airport to the Medical Care Center. Lorene was already there and had Barbara all packed up and ready to go home.

On November 5th Wanda cleaned up Barbara after a big bowel movement accident. She was very understanding and sweet about it. I realized anew that I was extraordinarily blessed in the wonderful people who helped me.

November 10th was Barbara's 70th birthday. It was hard to realize my bride was 70!

Frank Gough sent one of his workers over to install a screen door on the porch that held itself open and then closed with a gentle push. It would be a great help when I took Barbara in and out in the wheelchair. I had seen one similar to it in Kansas.

Sunday, November 16th I took Barbara to Rivermont Church. She was very restless so we left immediately after the sermon. I was especially sorry to miss the last hymn, "Jesus Comes with Clouds Descending" which was one of my favorites. But, since my throat was no better, I could not have sung it anyway. Barbara was very wet when we got home, but had only started to have a bowel movement. (Although I did not make any decision about it that day, I believe that was the last time I attempted to take Barbara to church. It simply had become too difficult for me when there was apparently no benefit for her.)

Christianity Today came. It contained an announcement that Muriel McQuilkin had died September 20th. Her husband, Robertson McQuilkin, had been my mentor in showing me how to be faithful to a wife with Alzheimer's Disease. I would feel forever indebted to him.

Frank Gough planned to take me to the hospital and home again December 2nd when I would have further tests done on my throat. He was such a good friend.

Thanksgiving Day I baked the turkey. It turned out very well. We had a large crowd for the family dinner at our house.

The following day I found water leaking in the basement, and I could not figure where it was coming from. I thought I would call Frank Gough the next day to get his advice. I was stunned the following morning to get word of Frank's sudden death from a heart attack the night before. He was only 49 years old and had been in excellent health. I felt so sad! He and I had been speaking of death and the Christian's assurance that "to depart and be with Christ is far better" (Philippians 1:23b) only the previous week, because of the unknowns concerning *my* throat. Neither of us dreamed *he* would die soon. (Later I discovered the water in the basement was coming from a hose which had worked its way out of the drain of the humidifier on the furnace.)

Because of Frank's death I postponed the tests on my throat a week so I could go to his funeral which was the very day he had planned to take me to the hospital. Max Guggenheimer would take me for my tests the following week and Bill Gayle would bring me home.

On December 10th Harold Riley came by so I could show him how to use the scanner. When I asked Barbara to say "hello" to Harold, she did! She did seem more alert. Perhaps the new medicine was doing her some good.

The sewer backed up in the basement when the washing machine was draining. I called Roto-Rooter. Their man cleaned the line and said it was the wet wipes that were clogging it. We would have to stop putting them into the toilet (although the package said you could). I put a plastic wastebasket next to the toilet in which to put the used wipes.

Greg Alty said my hospital tests had proved I did not have throat cancer, lung cancer or stomach cancer. He was almost certain the whole problem was acid reflux which we could control with a heavier dose of medicine.

Liz Broyles brought some food for Christmas dinner. Then Shirl and Cliff Thomas brought more. We were going to have a feast!

We had a blessed Christmas Day. There had been powerful services at church the night before.

At the end of that year we were blessed with a visit from our old friends, Ellie and Jim Gustafson who lived in Massachusetts. We had a great time of fellowship.

In our Christmas letter I wrote:

Barbara continues to decline with Alzheimer's Disease. Starting this past summer I began moving her from room to room in her wheelchair. Until then, I had thought that my bearing most of her weight while she "walked" would be at least some exercise for her. But my back started to give way, so we had to make some changes. We also got a "wheel-into-the-shower" chair that makes bathing her safer for both of us and more effective for her. So I thank the Lord we are doing fine. I continue to be grateful for two wonderful women who help with Barbara part-time.

Chapter Fifteen: 2004

Greg Alty thought he had my acid under control, but that general reflux was causing my continued hoarseness. Perhaps I would have to live with it. A person my age should expect diminishments that do not improve. I would miss being able to sing (especially hymns at church), but this would be a very small thing compared with the problems many have to deal with. And, if this were the worst thing with which I were dealing, I would be in high cotton indeed!

Joe O'Brien called (he had been an elder in our church in Augusta, Georgia who was now a retired physician living in northern Virginia.) He invited me to go to a Bach concert with him and his wife Edith. As always, he asked how Barbara was doing, I told him that just that morning I had made an appointment with the dermatologist because of a persistent sore on her ear – the one she always slept on because she would sleep in bed in just that one position. He said it sounded like a pressure sore to him. He advised me to get the pressure off that ear and to use some cortisone cream on it. So I went by medical supply places to get a special pillow and also a nursing home, but found nothing. So I bought what was sold as a cushion to sit on (egg crate), cut it in half and slipped it into a pillow case. We would see if this helped.

Barbara slept fine on the new egg crate pillow. Lorene brought a satin pillowcase to put on it. In a few days Barbara's ear seemed to be getting better. I was so glad!

On January 22nd I felt frustrated when the agency called and said our caregiver had quit! But the person they sent in her place seemed very good. She noticed Mother's portrait on the wall and said, "That's Ruth!" She had known Mother (and Dad too) at Westminster Canterbury.

On January 28th we kept Barbara's appointment with David Wilson, the dermatologist. Her ear was already all healed (following

Joe's advice). Dr. Wilson did look at a sore on her back (probably a boil) and a spot on each leg which he said were nothing to worry about – many people with light complexions got them with aging.

On March 1st I called the agency to see if they could get Faye Hughey to stay with Barbara the following Sunday. (Lorene could not.) If Faye could come I would be able to worship at Rivermont Church. (Faye could not take care of Barbara that day either, so I stayed home. For years I had told Confirmation classes that I could think of only two reasons why a believer in Christ should not be present at public worship on the Lord's Day: if he or she were sick or if it was his or her responsibility to care for someone else who was sick.)

Scott called. Because Barbara's "little seizures" were worse, he wanted me to stop the Memantine altogether immediately.

On March 22nd Barbara and I got our annual physicals. She got her ears cleaned out. Except for Barbara's *big problem* she was fine – excellent blood pressure and cholesterol. My blood pressure was up so Scott doubled my medicine. And he wanted to check my pressure again the following week.

March 30th I went to Scott's office for blood pressure check. It was still very high, so he doubled the daily dose of Altace and wanted me to come back the following week for another check.

On April 6th I got my blood pressure checked again. It was still too high. So Scott wanted me to add another new medicine.

On April 19th I took Barbara to get her teeth cleaned. She was quite listless, which made her easy to handle in the dentist's chair, but hard to get to and from the car. Bo Sorenson helped me do that. He found four tiny cavities which he planned to fill the following week.

On April 26th I took Barbara to have the four fillings done. Bo said he thought she would do fine without anesthetic because the cavities were near the surface. She did not flinch.

Sunday, May 2nd Lorene stayed with Barbara while I worshiped at Rivermont. I felt for the first time since the previous summer that my singing voice was coming back. I was very glad about that.

By May 6th my blood pressure was 120/80. Scott was pleased, and so was I.

On May 17th two ladies from the agency came by and wondered if it would be all right with me for Tracy to keep taped diapers on Barbara and change her on the bed. Tracy was afraid she was going to drop Barbara getting her on and off the toilet. I told them that would be fine with me. By that time some days I too had trouble keeping her standing for even a moment. But other days we seemed to do all right with it.

On May 24th Lori Widmeyer stayed with Barbara an hour so I could do some errands before my trip to the Banner of Truth Conference the next day. Lorene Payne would stay with Barbara at our house the whole time we were gone. That all worked out well.

On Sunday, May 30th I preached at Diamond Hill Presbyterian. They sent one of the bouquets home "for Barbara." They did not realize she was long past being able to notice flowers, but, of course, I appreciated their thoughtfulness.

June 14th was the forty-fifth anniversary of my ordination to the gospel ministry. I thanked the Lord for calling me to and equipping me for that task. I had loved being a pastor: the preaching and teaching and pastoral work. The only thing I found tedious about it were the administrative chores which, in the later years of my public ministry, were accomplished mainly by excellent co-pastors and an outstanding staff.

On June 15th Lorene came early so Mary Beth, Addie Ruth and I could go to Springdale Water Gardens near Greenville, Virginia (between Lexington and Staunton). We bought some goldfish, tadpoles and water plants for our new pond. Addie Ruth had the time of her life playing in the water running down the fountains.

On July 10th Barbara (for the first time) pitched forward out of her chair onto the floor. I thanked the Lord she did not seem to have gotten hurt. I got her up and back into her chair. I guessed I would have to use the restraining belt from then on to keep her from falling.

July 17th Lorene got here at 7:00 AM and Barbara's sister Charlotte (who had arrived from Kansas) and I left almost immediately for Lebanon, Virginia where we were having the Sykes Family Annual Reunion.

The next morning we worshiped at First Presbyterian, Bristol, Tennessee. Then we drove through the King College campus so Charlotte could see where Mary Beth had gone to college. Charlotte and I got back to Lynchburg in mid-afternoon. All had gone well at home while we had been away.

On July 24th I got Barbara into the car and we took Charlotte to the Lynchburg airport. We did not wait for her plane to leave because it was just too hard to get Barbara in and out of the building, and I could not leave her in the car alone.

I preached at Pisgah Church August 8th. Before the end of the sermon my nose started bleeding! I had to hold my nose for the rest of the service, which I shortened. Pam and Richard Ruble were there and drove me home. My nose did not stop bleeding until about the time we arrived at our house. I had never had this happen before while I was preaching. I had no idea what had triggered it.

August 12th was my 70th birthday! By God's grace I had reached my "three score years and ten." I had become an old man! All our children called. When I talked with my sister Virginia she told me the reason they had sent a bonsai plant: "I used to think this was a weird hobby. But then I realized it was making something beautiful in the small space you have. So I thought of you. Your space has become greatly diminished in recent years. But you have chosen to make it beautiful." What a thoughtful sister!

The following Sunday, August 14th I went to Powell and Kathy's to celebrate my birthday. As usual, Kathy pulled out all the stops with the great dinner she fixed. Powell preached a fine sermon. Lorene stayed with Barbara while I was gone.

On August 25th for the first time Barbara fell off the toilet! She was only bruised, but it scared me to death. I had a time getting her up off the floor, but I did. From then on I would have to stay right in front of her – knee to knee – when she was on the toilet.

On September 11th Shirl and Cliff Thomas brought lunch over and ate here with us. It was great to see them.

The night of September 16th I had a horrible nightmare about Barbara. I dreamed Barbara and I were at the top of a very high fire escape. I was holding onto her with one hand and onto the rail with the other. She twisted out of my hand and fell and fell and fell. I felt as if I still had hold of her and could soften the impact, but when she hit the ground I knew she was dead. I woke up panting and sweating, and could not go back to sleep.

On Sunday, September 19th Faye Hughey came and stayed with Barbara while I went to Rivermont Church. It was wonderful to see Faye. (I had not seen her since she had stopped working for us a little more than a year before.) Her nursing school program was going well.

On September 28th when I came in from grocery shopping Lorene told me she had felt a hardness in Barbara's left breast when she had been bathing her. I could feel it too, but I did not know what to compare it to. I would ask Scott to check it when he came to the prayer group at our house a couple of days later.

Scott examined Barbara and said there was indeed a mass there. Scott called Greg who said he would stop by and do a biopsy at our house the next day.

On October 1st Greg came at 1:30 PM. We put Barbara on her bed and he did the biopsy. Right away he said he was confident it was cancer. I asked him how he could tell before the pathology report. He answered, "If it is benign it is like pushing a needle into an orange; if not it is like pushing a needle into a carrot." Barbara had not jumped when he had stuck the needle in. Greg took the tissue to the pathology lab. He called and said the pathologist agreed with his initial observation. But, of course, the results of the pathology reports would not be ready until the middle or end of the next week.

I felt so sad! I had imagined a lot of "end of life" scenarios, but never that! There was no breast cancer, so far as anyone knew, in Barbara's family. They had had heart trouble, heart attacks, and strokes. I told Greg the main thing I wanted was to keep Barbara comfortable. I called all the children and Charlotte. Powell said, "Well, Dad, I feel like in many ways we lost Mama years ago. I'm sure I would feel differently about this news if she were otherwise well."

I knew this was irrational, but deep down, I felt I ought to have been able to protect Barbara from this. "I take care of her. And I let this monster through the gate." I knew that did not make sense, but that was how I felt.

In a few days I talked with Greg. This was a kind of cancer (the pathology report showed) that ought to respond well to a pill a day.

Greg called. Dwight Oldham, an oncologist who is a member of Rivermont Church, suggested a new drug. He offered samples (about six weeks' supply), so Greg went and got them and brought them to me. Barbara had her first pill of Aromasin (25 mg) that evening.

On October 12th I worked in the yard for a while, planting bulbs that had come in the mail. But I ran out of energy and thought, "I don't have to finish this!" So I gave the rest of the bulbs to Lorene. I felt exhausted.

Greg and I played racquetball. He told me the pill Barbara was taking was chemotherapy, but a mild form that did not cause hair loss or vomiting. Even if it were initially effective (and Greg thought it would be), it would stop working in about five years. But Greg felt it would last as long as Barbara would need it. He said if Barbara were otherwise well they would do surgery too. But he wanted to avoid surgery with her if at all possible. "Of course, if this does not stop the tumor's growth, we'll have to do surgery. We can't allow it to burst through the breast wall. That would be a smelly mess and most difficult for you to take care of."

Mary Jane Sydnor came over one evening and sat with Barbara (who was already asleep in bed) so I could go to the church and get my picture taken for the "Pastor Emeritus" spot in the church Pictorial Directory. Bobbie and Dwight Oldham and their son John were just behind me in the line. I had an opportunity to talk with Dwight about Barbara. He said the new medicine might take from three to six months before we would know if it were working for Barbara. Greg had said it would take a while, but I had not realized it might be that long.

On November 1st I made the steamed puddings for Thanksgiving and Christmas using Mother's recipe. They had been traditional in Mother's family for the holidays, she had continued having them in her and Dad's family, and Barbara and I had enjoyed carrying on the custom.

I put Barbara in the car and did some errands. She had diarrhea, so I had quite a mess to clean up when we got home.

On November 5th Mary Beth, Addie Ruth and I went to Morris' Orchard and bought some apples. We got some fine pictures of Addie Ruth and a pile of pumpkins they had there. Then we took Addie Ruth by the beauty shop and Lorene Payne gave her a first haircut.

For months Mary Beth and Alan had been making plans to adopt a baby girl from China. When they had heard of the terrifying plight of many infant girls there, they said, "We can't do much about most of them, but we can rescue one!"

Later in November Mary Beth called from Tennessee. They had heard from China! Their little girl was born January 18, 2004.

On November 22nd I found out Tracy, one of our helpers, could get here at noon on Mondays (she had a class in the morning) and stay until 3:00 PM. I had been taking care of Barbara by myself on Mondays. Because I thought I needed the additional help, I asked Tracy to begin coming for those three hours on Mondays.

My nose started bleeding. I finally got it stopped, but it started again. I wondered what I was going to do. It was hard to take care of Barbara with a bloody nose! I got blood all over her and myself. It would stop when I lay quietly, but when I got up to take care of Barbara (bending over, pulling her up) it would start all over again.

I talked with Greg about my nose bleed problem and he advised me to see Graham Gilmer. Dr. Gilmer worked me in at 1:00 PM that same day. He cauterized my nose, hoping that would cure it, which it did.

On November 24th I played racquetball with Greg. Then he came over to the house and examined Barbara. Although her tumor had not gotten smaller, it had not grown any. He thought that was good.

My sister Sarah arrived mid-afternoon. She made the cornucopia for Thanksgiving and it looked very nice.

On Thanksgiving Day Tracy came at 9:30 AM to stay with Barbara. Sarah and I went to church and then had a simple lunch at a restaurant.

We had our Thanksgiving Dinner at home the following day. Laddie brought the turkey and dressing and made the gravy.

I called David Wilson about the breaking out in Barbara's scalp. He prescribed a new medicine and changed her shampoo.

Mary Beth and Alan would be leaving for China early January 2005, so they would be with Maggie in China on her first birthday. That was really exciting.

On December 18th I got started on making a DVD of Barbara's life. I knew this would mean a lot to our children and to me too.

We had a quiet Christmas Day – just Barbara, my sister Sarah and me.

A couple of days later our granddaughter Lauren (almost four years old) wanted to see the goldfish. It was very cold outside. Lauren said she thought it would be nice if we fixed the fish some hot chocolate! Then she said she thought they would like for us to get sweaters for them!

On December 30th a possible new helper Sharon came during Tracy's first hour to learn the ropes with Barbara. She planned to work at our house with Barbara on Thursdays starting the following week because Tracy could no longer come on Thursdays. Sharon came with good experience and worked at the hospital on weekends.

Our Christmas letter for that year contained the following:

I am thankful I continue to be able to take care of Barbara at home, and, with some part-time helpers here, play racquetball about three times a week, walk six miles once a week, and preach most Sundays. Although Barbara is quite unaware now (she has had Alzheimer's for years), she still smiles when I tuck her into bed at night, tell her I love her and Jesus loves her, then kiss her and sing to her, "Jesus loves me, this I know, for the Bible tells me so." Needless to say, that makes my day! She is the delight of my life. I'm so glad I get to look after her. On October 1st we discovered Barbara also has breast cancer. She takes a mild chemotherapy pill we hope will shrink the tumor. In her general condition we want to avoid surgery if at all possible.

Chapter Sixteen: 2005

I was continuing to work on Barbara's life DVD and I was loving it.

On January 10th Mary Beth called. They were about ready to leave for China! They had already taken Addie Ruth to their friends' with whom she would be staying while they were away ("that was the hardest part," Mary Beth said). They did not think they would try to get any sleep that night since the taxi would come by for them at 3:00 AM.

A couple of days later I went to see Cap Eschenroeder about my sore heel which had been bothering me for several weeks. He said it was Plantar Faciitis; I would get well, but slowly. He wanted me to put gel caps in my shoes that would support my heels, to take a low dose of anti-inflammatory medicine and to see a physical therapist. And he asked me to come again in six weeks.

January 13th Latisha worked here for the first time. She seemed all right. I hoped so. Sharon was afraid she might drop Barbara so decided not to work for us. It did take a lot of physical strength to handle Barbara by then.

On the 15th I received an emailed picture of Mary Beth and Alan on the Great Wall of China! Wonderful! They were not with Maggie yet.

Two days later I received emailed pictures of Mary Beth, Alan and Maggie! Maggie was a beautiful child.

Mary Beth telephoned from China! She sounded like she was just next door. She said, "Today is Maggie's first birthday." I replied I had thought that was tomorrow. "It is already tomorrow here." They were 13 hours ahead of us. I heard Maggie babbling. Mary Beth said

Maggie was warming up to them, and was by then welcoming their touch. What an unexpected thrill to talk with her on the phone! How I wished Barbara could know about this. She would have been so pleased.

On the 19th Greg came over and examined Barbara. The tumor was still not growing, which was a sign that the medicine was working. She had been on it for about three months.

On January 26th Mary Beth called. They were safely home from China in Cookeville, Tennessee! They were very tired, but very happy!

I went to heel therapy. I thought it was helping. My sister Virginia told me she had had the same problem about twelve years before, and said it was very important to do the exercises.

A week later I had my last heel therapy. My heel was much better and the therapist said if I kept doing the exercises there was no reason why it should not get completely well.

Pam and Richard Ruble came over with the gowns Pam had fixed for Barbara. It was so kind of Pam to do this!

I began to notice a roughness on Barbara's chin. I called David Wilson, our dermatologist. He said saliva has digestive juices and when one drooled constantly (as Barbara did) the skin itself began to get digested. He said to buy zinc oxide on the "baby aisle" at the drug store. If that did not help after a week's use, he would prescribe something stronger. (It did take care of the problem.)

I was very surprised one morning when Tracy came instead of Latisha. She said she was working that day and Latisha the next; they had traded days. Latisha would stay with Barbara the two more hours than usual until Lorene got to our house at 5:00 PM the next day. I was not very happy about that, but there was nothing I could do about it. The reason for my uneasiness was that the next day I was planning to fly to Tennessee to be with our Mary Beth and her family. Tracy and I had agreed to her staying longer that day so that I could do that. In fact, catching my plane depended on it.

The next day when Latisha arrived she told me she could not stay beyond 3:00 PM! I felt fit to be tied! I was to fly to Mary Beth and Alan's later that day for Addie Ruth's birthday the following day and Maggie's baptism on Sunday. I had had my plane reservations for weeks. I had made all the necessary arrangements for Barbara to be covered at home. Latisha said there was no one to pick up her children from school. After many phone calls to the agency (they told her she would be fired if she left), she called her mother to pick up the children. I do not know why she did not do that in the first place. I left at 3:00 PM for the airport, but was very uneasy leaving Barbara – even for a couple of extra hours – with someone who had not wanted to stay with her. When Lorene came at 5:00 PM everything was fine.

March 5th was Addie Ruth's 2nd birthday. It was fun to be there for that, and, of course, to meet Maggie for the first time. My niece Deb Sykes had come from Maine for the events of the weekend. Alan and Mary Beth took us to see the house they were buying – a pretty Cape Cod style. After the children went to bed we watched my uncompleted DVD about Barbara. Mary Beth loved it.

On Sunday, March 6th Deb had caught whatever stomach virus had gone through Mary Beth and Alan's little family the previous week. She had been up most of the night.

Jon Bell, the pastor of their church, was very welcoming to me. I was so pleased to have been invited to participate in the leadership of Maggie's baptism. Deb was there for it although she had to leave the service twice because of illness. The family went to brunch together afterwards.

Then Syble and George (Alan's parents), on their way home to Kingsport, Tennessee, took Deb and me to the airport at Knoxville and we flew out on different flights. Everything was fine when I got back home. Lorene left about 9:30 PM.

The next day I was very sick to my stomach. Mary Beth called that afternoon and asked if I were sick. She told me Syble and George had been sick as dogs the night before – Alan had called a cousin of his in Kingsport and asked her to go over and help them.

Wow! I had not been that sick since I had returned from a trip to Haiti in 1989. I mainly rested while Lorene was with Barbara. After Lorene left I had a hard time taking care of Barbara. But, of course, one does what needs to be done whether one feels like it or not. I thought of sick mothers with young children.

I prayed Barbara would not catch the bug from me! Of necessity, I was "in her face" during much of my care of her. It would be difficult if she were, as she used to say, "running at both ends!" I was very grateful that Barbara did evade this illness.

Lorene suggested that I consider getting a new chair for Barbara. Lorene was afraid Barbara was going to pitch forward out of her rocker when she was restless.

I bought an electrically powered two-position "lift" chair for Barbara. She seemed very comfortable in it. Because it raised her to an almost standing position, it also made transfer from that chair to the wheel chair much easier on my back.

On March 16th Greg came by the house and examined Barbara. The tumor was not shrinking, but neither was it getting larger. He was going to consult with Dwight (the oncologist) and get back to me.

Tammy called from the agency. Tracy would be leaving us, but would train a new worker, Barbara Richerson, on Friday. If I felt Barbara Richerson could do the job, which Tammy assured me she could, we would also replace Latisha with her.

On March 17th Greg called. He had consulted with both Dwight and Scott. They were all three in agreement that since there was no growth in the tumor we should avoid surgery and continue as we were. They felt Barbara would be at very high risk of getting pneumonia after the surgery because she could not "cough it up." "Of course," Greg said, "if the tumor starts to grow, we may have to do surgery anyway. But Barbara very likely would not survive. I don't want to kill her!" Naturally, I thought they had made a wise decision.

I had the feeling Barbara might not be with me much longer. And that made me very sad. She was much sleepier all the time. And for the first time that week she did not seem sure what to do with her straw (to suck up liquid). I had to help her drink by holding her head back and tipping the glass to her lips.

On March 18th the new Home Health Caregiver Barbara Richerson came by for a "get acquainted" visit. I liked her very much. She was quite tall and strong looking. She was very cheerful. She seemed genuinely interested in my Barbara. There was an air of "can do" about her that gave me confidence. I had a keen sense that she would work out fine with us.

I had had a hacking cough and night sweats for two weeks. It continued to hang on. I got Scott to listen to my lungs. They sounded clear to him.

On March 24th Barbara Richerson came to work for us for the first time. She talked to my Barbara a lot, and seemed to enjoy being here.

The next day I bought a vest for my Barbara to see if we could hold her up better to eat. I also got a neck brace, but I returned it, because, although it held her head up, the chin cup was so deep we could not feed her while she was wearing it.

Barbara Richerson knocked on my study door. She said she had bathed my Barbara, fed her lunch and now "Miss Barbara" was asleep in her chair. Barbara Richerson wondered if I would like her to dust and vacuum. I told her she did not need to do that. She said she liked to keep busy and would really enjoy doing it. She said if I would show her where the things were she would clean the bathroom. I could hardly believe my ears! So she did make the bathroom sparkle where she had bathed my Barbara.

On March 26th I watched the DVDs I had made of my Barbara's life. I discovered a few minor things I wanted to correct or do again, but, overall, I was very pleased, and I thought our children would be too.

I had been thinking about what would happen to Barbara immediately (before our children could get here) if something should happen to me, either my death or other incapacitation. I would need to get this worked out in a legal document with Dan Sweeney.

On April 13th Scott suggested he would examine Barbara at home from then on because it had become so difficult for me to get her to his office. So I had my annual physical without Barbara for the first time in a number of years. Scott was very concerned that, since the previous year's examination, my PSA had jumped from 1.7 to 11.5! He made an appointment for the next week with David Leftke, a urologist. Scott said my prostate felt normal to him.

In mid-April Joe Ernsberger brought me a CD of the Rivermont Church choir doing the hymns I needed to complete Barbara's DVD. I really appreciated Wes Bettcher and the choir doing that for me. So I finished it up and was very pleased with it.

It had become much harder (physically) to care for Barbara. She was not eating as well as she had and she bent her head down so low I had to push her head up with a lot of pressure to get food into her mouth. And her legs were apt to give way more often – she simply "let go" and would fall to the floor if I were not holding on to her for dear life. I hoped I could hold out.

On April 20th I saw the urologist. My prostate felt normal to him. He ran another blood test to test my PSA. He said it was either a lab error or an infection that was a result of my recent illness (which he thought). The results of the test would not come back for a week or so. If the reading came back way down, it had been a lab error. If it was on the way down, it had been an infection. If it was still up or higher, he would need to do an ultrasound and biopsy. Since I had never had those kinds of symptoms until I had gotten sick the month before he was inclined to think it was that same infection that had not yet gone away.

On April 27th I walked about six miles on the Blackwater Creek trail with John Mabray. I had no discomfort at all in my right heel, for which I was very thankful.

The next day I talked with the urologist's nurse. She said my PSA was down to 7.5, so the doctor thought the jump in my PSA had been caused by an infection of the prostate which was clearing up.

A possible new helper (in addition to the people we already had) for my Barbara from the agency interviewed. She decided she did not have the physical strength to handle Barbara.

On April 30th Barbara was so hard to handle! I felt exhausted and wondered how long I could keep it up. I still wanted to as much as ever, but she was so "ragdollish." I needed much more strength. I wondered if it were almost time to get her a hospital bed and keep her in bed most of the time. A couple of days later I called and ordered a hospital bed for Barbara.

My First Monday Discussion Group in May met as usual in my home study. They said they hoped I would not be upset with them, but out of genuine concern for me, they had talked about it among themselves and thought I should seriously consider putting Barbara in a nursing home quite soon. They were afraid I would give out if I did not do this. I assured them they could say anything to me without making me angry at them. After all, we had been meeting together almost thirty years! I certainly did not want to keep Barbara at home mainly out of my unreasonable stubbornness. But I did think I needed to figure out how I could be smarter about caring for her. We were definitely at another place where some changes needed to be made in the way I handled her, or I would not hold up much longer. Perhaps it was time to start using the Hoyer Lift regularly; I would need to be instructed again in how to use it.

On May 9th Statham Gilliam and Ron Carter came by to talk with me about the hospital bed. Ron thought when I use the new bed and the wheelchair together with the lift it would be much easier if I took my bed out of there and slept across the hall. "You need plenty of room to maneuver," he said. I expressed concern about hearing Barbara in the night. He suggested I get a baby monitor. He also gave me a lesson in how to use the Hoyer Lift. I hated to move out of our bedroom! But I guessed I would just have to accept that as another inevitable diminishment along this road.

On May 11th Scott came by the house and examined Barbara for her annual physical. Except for her *big problem* and cancer she was fine. Scott thought when I got the hospital bed I ought to leave her in bed more so I would have less "hauling" of her to do. I would need to learn to change her in bed. The women who helped me could teach me that.

On May 18th Greg came by and checked Barbara. He thought her breast tumor was getting smaller. He also lanced a boil on Barbara's bottom.

Tuesday, May 24th through Thursday, May 26th Lorene stayed with Barbara until Barbara Richerson came Thursday while John Mabray and I went to the Banner of Truth Conference. All went well.

On June 1st they brought the hospital bed for Barbara, together with a computerized air bubble mattress cover that changed the pressure on Barbara's skin every two minutes. This meant we no longer needed to have her sleep on the "egg crate" except for her pillow. They also took down our twin beds and set them up in the basement. We had reached another milestone in Barbara's illness. I felt sad about moving out of our bedroom, but we really did need the space for the special equipment we would be using for Barbara from then on.

On June 13th I took Barbara to get her teeth cleaned. Although she fell out of the wheelchair as we were getting her up the steps, she did not hurt herself, and did very well.

One afternoon Lorene left early. She was in great pain in her shoulder from a fall she had had (not at our house) a couple of days before. She said it had caused her almost to drop Barbara. If Lorene could not work for us anymore, I might be forced to make some other arrangements sooner than I had imagined. It was not long before Lorene was feeling much better. I was so glad!

On July 16th I went to the Sykes Reunion in Lebanon, Virginia. Lorene stayed with Barbara.

At the reunion Mary Beth told me she and her brothers wanted to have a small family celebration of Barbara's and my 50th wedding anniversary Labor Day weekend. They had invited my sister Sarah too. How nice! I had not expected we would do anything special because of Barbara's condition.

By July 29th Barbara Richerson was using the Hoyer Lift with my Barbara most of the time. She noticed when she bathed Barbara that the skin under her breasts was peeling. We decided to leave her bra off, at least for a while. I put some Cortisone cream on her skin. (We never did put her bra on again.)

By that time I was getting Barbara as near as possible to the chair I was transferring her to, so I walked her much less. It seemed to work better for both of us: from her bed to her wheelchair, from her wheelchair to the toilet and back again and then from her wheelchair to the chair she sat in during the day.

Ron Carter had told me (when he and Statham Gilliam had brought the hospital bed) to let gravity work for me: "When you are moving Mrs. Sykes from the bed to her wheelchair, have the bed higher than the chair. And when you are moving her from the chair to the bed have the bed lower. You'll find it takes a lot of the strain off you." He was right!

On Saturday, August 20th about 1:00 PM when I got Barbara up from her chair to feed her lunch, her legs collapsed. She landed on the floor – not hard, I eased her down – and I could not get her up! (Before when this had happened, I had been able to get her up because she could brace her feet for me. She had had some sense of what I was trying to do. But by this time she could not help me at all.) I tried and tried in vain to get her up until I was trembling. I called twelve different people. No one was home. I called the EMT. They were there only Monday through Friday. I called the church to see if anyone was there – no one was. (I deliberately had not called friends who had had heart problems or back trouble.) Barbara did not know she was on the floor so was not at all distressed. At 3:00 PM I was praying about what to do. I heard the mailman putting the mail in our box by the front door. I rushed to the door and asked him to help me, which he did. Together we had Barbara up in no time.

On August 23rd Barbara went to the floor as I was getting her out of bed. I had hold of her, so she was not hurt. But, again, I could not get her up! I tried and tried until I was shaking and sweating profusely. In the midst of that our friend and lawyer, Dan Sweeney, called about something else, and, when he heard about our emergency, came from his office downtown to help me. Dan and I got Barbara off the floor. I simply had to get better at transferring Barbara! I would try to get whatever I was transferring her to very close to what I was transferring her from. I also needed to get a better grip on her. I needed not to try to hold her by her arms any longer, but to take hold of her body. And I knew it was imperative that I do all this thoughtfully, slowly and deliberately. I also realized I needed to re-learn how to use the Hoyer Lift, so I could get Barbara off the floor by myself with that.

On September 3rd my sister Sarah from South Carolina and all our children, their spouses and their children gathered at our house to celebrate our 50th wedding anniversary. They brought in a picnic lunch for the middle of the day. They also provided a beautiful anniversary cake. Barbara Richerson helped with my Barbara and took a group picture of the rest of us. The boys and their families went back home in late afternoon.

September 4th was our actual anniversary. Mary Beth and Alan, Addie Ruth and Maggie, Sarah and I worshiped at Rivermont Church. The gorgeous flowers under the cross were "to the glory of God and in honor of the 50th Wedding Anniversary (September 4, 1955) of Barbara and Lowell Sykes by their children."

The following week I asked Dan to go ahead and draw up papers concerning Barbara's care if something should incapacitate me.

On September 19th Greg came over and examined Barbara. He thought the tumor was smaller. Her right hand was swollen, so he checked under her arm, but did not feel any swelling of the lymph glands.

In early October I decided to revise Barbara's life DVDs to include more of our college years on disk one and to include our 50th wedding anniversary on disk two.

Barbara started pushing herself up as if her bottom were sore. I checked carefully and could not find any sores or red places. When Barbara did this she grimaced, so I thought she was either in pain or had pretty severe discomfort. Lorene thought it might be a hemorrhoid. Greg Alty came and examined Barbara. He could not find anything that would be painful to her. But she was still trying to do something.

On October 11th Barbara had a bowel movement in bed. This was very unusual for her.

On October 18th Barbara suddenly fell off the toilet! I was sitting right in front of her (practically knee to knee) so I grabbed her before she hit the floor, but we both went down. At first I thought she was bleeding, but I discovered I had cut my own arm in the fall – did not know how or on what. Barbara did not seem to be hurt. I got her off the floor with the Hoyer Lift.

The next day Barbara had a mark on her head and one on her shoulder from the fall. But she seemed fine and the marks were minor. She did not sleep well that night.

I came across this quote from Katherine Anne Porter: We must "salvage our fragments of happiness out of life's inevitable sufferings." Realistic!

I picked up a new sleeping medicine for Barbara at Scott's office. But then I could not use it because it was timed in release layers and could not be crushed. And Barbara had not been able to swallow uncrushed pills for years.

On November 8th Barbara was so droopy I used her shower chair over the toilet. I was afraid she would fall off the side of the regular toilet seat.

November 10th was Barbara's 72nd birthday. She got some gifts and lots of cards. But, although I sang, "Happy Birthday" all throughout the day, there was no response.

The new bibs I had ordered for Barbara came. They were very attractive and did the job well.

For a while I had asked Wanda not to attempt to get Barbara from her chair to the bathroom. I would take care of her when I got back about 10 AM from playing racquetball with Greg on Wednesday mornings. But Barbara was so sleepy when I got her up at 7:00 AM she simply could not eat her breakfast. So in mid-November I told Wanda I would leave Barbara in bed on Wednesday mornings (she was fast asleep then anyway). And when I got back I would get her up, wash her, dress her and feed her breakfast, and there would still be time for Wanda to change the bed. Wanda thought this was a good idea.

In lifting things from my old journals about Barbara's illness, I came across the time that she sang "Love Lifted Me" many years ago. I sang it to her again. She could no longer sing it with me, but she did smile – a radiant smile! What a blessing – a shaft of light! Those beautiful smiles were fewer and farther between.

On Thanksgiving Day Barbara Richerson stayed with my Barbara while I went to Rivermont Church. I was greatly moved by the Thanksgiving hymns.

A couple of days later Barbara had violent "small" jerks in the morning. She even slammed her face into the table once while I was feeding her. I had to give her an extra Ativan.

On December 1ˢᵗ the agitator of our washing machine broke. Since our machine was nine years old, they no longer made parts for it. So I ordered a new one. They said they would bring it and install it the next day. With all the laundry Barbara produced, I could not be without a washing machine very long!

We received the Gustafsons' Christmas letter. They ended it with, "We do hold all things lightly…, understanding our constant peril in this increasingly dangerous world. The God we serve is able to save us, but if disaster strikes, we know the way home, and we put our trust in him for all eternity." So true. And eloquently put!

On Sunday, December 4ᵗʰ I worshiped at Rivermont. During the Distribution of the Lord's Supper the choir sang: "Every valley shall be exalted, and every mountain made low; And the crooked made straight, and the rough places plain. And the glory of the Lord shall be revealed; And all flesh shall see it together; for the mouth of the Lord hath spoken it!" (Isaiah 40:4,5). And it seemed to me that I heard this as a direct Word of the Lord to me.

I read in "Christianity Today" (December 2005) "Into the Wonder," an excerpt from the book The Narnian: the Life and Imagination of C. S. Lewis by Alan Jacobs who wrote:

He (Lewis) lived with his brother and an elderly woman named Mrs. Moore, whom he often referred to as his mother – though she was not. Both of them were unwell and dependent upon him… Lewis had written to an American friend that he was "tied to an invalid," which is what Mrs. Moore had become, confined to bed by arthritis and varicose veins. For her part, Mrs. Moore proclaimed that Lewis was 'as good as an extra maid in the house,' and she certainly used him as a maid. She seems also to have become obsessive and quarrelsome in her latter years, worried always about her dog and constantly at odds with the domestic help. Lewis hired two maids to help with cleaning and nursing when he had to be at Magdalen (College) *where he maintained a grueling schedule of lectures, tutorials, and correspondence. But for a time, one of the maids became mentally unstable, and he occasionally had to return home to sort out conflicts the women had with each other and with Mrs. Moore. He (Lewis) was determined to answer every correspondent, and his brother Warnie normally assisted him, primarily by typing dictated or drafted letters and keeping the files organized. But at the beginning of March 1949, Warnie was in Oxford's Acland Hospital, having drunk himself into insensibility... In early April he (Lewis) wrote to a friend who had reproached him not for not replying promptly to a letter, "Dog's stools and human vomit have made my day today: one of those days when you feel at 11 A. M. that it really must be 3 P. M." Two months later, he collapsed at his home and had to be taken to the hospital. He was diagnosed with strep throat, but his deeper complaint was simply exhaustion.*

When I read again the above facts I had known for years, I realized the difficulties I faced were small in comparison. But this did underscore the importance of the advice Scott Wade had given me as my retirement neared about the necessity of taking care of myself if I wanted to see Barbara through this. I had tried to heed Scott's wise and good advice.

On December 6th there was black ice on the driveway I did not see as I went out for the newspaper. In a flash I went down and landed on my left hand and behind. I hurt my wrist, but not seriously I hoped. And I was able to get up and walk back to the house with no trouble. Since Barbara had become disabled I had been very aware that if something happened that put me out of action, there would be no one at our house who could telephone for help. Therefore, whenever I knew there was ice on the ground and I had to step outside I carried my cell phone, just in case. Also, I never climbed up to change a light bulb unless it was just before one of our helpers was scheduled to arrive.

One night I had Barbara sleep on one of the new thin pads I had gotten for her. She urinated so much it stopped absorbing and made a puddle. When I got her up it poured on the carpet! So I would not use that kind for sleeping on again.

On December 22nd Barbara Richerson was telling me my Barbara had a loud explosion of gas on the toilet. When she said to me, "It went BOOM!," my Barbara laughed which was very rare at that point.

I discovered a good use for the thin pads. Since they were thin enough to still get the benefit of the egg crate pillow, I started putting them on Barbara's pillow. They absorbed the drool. Then, when I got Barbara up I put the damp little pad in the wheelchair over the larger pad, and did not have to wash the larger pad for the one short ride to the bathroom before I changed her.

On Sunday, December 25, Christmas Day, we decided to open gifts after lunch. I preached at Pisgah Church and all my houseguests went to Pisgah too. Lorene stayed with Barbara. Lorene left to visit her parents as soon as we got back from church. I think my larger family enjoyed the dinner at our house.

We opened gifts. Several were given and received. I said, "You children have spent far too much money on us." Powell replied, "That's what Grandmother used to say." I retorted, "Yes, but *she* meant it!" Everybody cracked up with laughter. Powell said he thought maybe I did have some of Granddaddy's genes after all (my dad was a great joker, but I can rarely say anything funny).

Kathy had found an old video tape Chad had made during Christmas of 1997. From that tape she burned each of us a DVD. It showed Barbara greeting them as they had come in, not knowing how to open her presents, but having some appreciation for them when they were opened for her, and being able to hold them up for the camera. I had no memory of this existing! Then, back in 1997, they went over to visit Mother and Sarah, and Chad continued to let his new camera roll! So far as I knew, this was the last home video of both Barbara and Mother. Priceless!

In our Christmas letter I wrote to our family and friends:

I am thankful I am able to continue to care for Barbara at home. Because she cannot bear much if any of her own weight on her legs now, I have gotten a hospital bed and a "lift chair" for her that take some of the strain off my back. We already had a Hoyer Lift, and I am using it for her more frequently. Again I express my gratitude for two wonderful ladies who help me part-time. This allows me to do some studying, preach in a small country church twice a month, get a little exercise and do errands. I have also enjoyed creating a two-DVD life of Barbara for our children from old snapshots, photographs, and home movies. Magnificent memories! As I have worked on this project I have realized more and more that I may have been doing it mainly for me. Anyway, I have received a great blessing handling, sorting, arranging and putting together these materials.

CHAPTER SEVENTEEN: 2006

Pam and Richard Ruble came by for a visit. Pam was planning to fix some nightgowns for Barbara, as she had done before. Pam would buy them, cut them up the back, bind them, and sew ties on them. Fixed this way they were much easier for me to get on Barbara than the conventional kind.

(I want to record here that after Barbara became ill, and before she got completely disabled, Pam was her constant friend. Pam took Barbara places, did things for her, called her every day, came by to see her and arranged for others to help. I do not know what I would have done without her. Of course, Pam is still Barbara's friend. But, at this stage of Barbara's disease there is little even a close friend can do for her.)

On January 3rd Barbara began having hard, small seizure jerks before I got her out of bed. They continued as I started feeding her breakfast. I was afraid she might slam her face into the table, so I placed a pillow right in front of her. A couple of minutes later I was so glad the protection was there! She jerked hard right down onto it, but was not hurt because of the cushioning effect. I gave her an extra Ativan which stopped the seizures in about ten minutes. I hated to give the Ativan in the daytime because it made her so sleepy and therefore, harder to handle. But that was better than either her getting hurt or it leading to a big seizure.

January 7th was a very difficult day. Barbara had been so limp. And, although we spent long periods of time in the bathroom, I had not been able to "guess" right, so we had lots of accidents away from the toilet. A couple of times I was certain we were both headed for the floor, but, thank the Lord, we did not go down. I felt exhausted that evening.

A couple of days later after breakfast Barbara had a bowel movement in the toilet. A little after that while sitting in her chair she started moving her feet and legs. I took her back to the bathroom. While I was turning her to sit her on the toilet she had an explosion of diarrhea: on the floor, the wall, my feet and legs, her feet and legs. It took me more than a little while to get it cleaned up. After Barbara Richerson came my Barbara had another bowel movement in the toilet and another one in the toilet after Barbara Richerson left. Her functions were functioning!

On February 3rd Ellie and Jim Gustafson arrived. It was always great to see them! The next day Ellie said, "I keep thinking of Barbara's words back when she still had them (in the earlier stages of Barbara's illness), 'I just hunch over a cup of coffee and say, 'Jesus is Lord!'" Ellie continued, "A thing I need to remember every day. And it is good to remember, too, that somewhere daffodils do bloom in February!" (Our early daffodils were very pretty just then.) Right after breakfast the Gustafsons continued on their journey back home to Massachusetts (where daffodils do not bloom in February).

A few days later, while I was washing Barbara's face with a warm cloth before I got her out of bed, she had a huge smile. It made my day!

On February 20th Barbara Richerson suggested I might want to get a lift for my Barbara that would pull her up from a seated position into a standing position and hold her there as long as was necessary in order for us to dress and clean her. Barbara Richerson had started using one of these with another patient who was a very large man. She said she was able to clean him and pull up his pants without having to try to hold him up which she had no longer been able to do. It sounded very good. I had not known such a lift existed. I asked her to bring me information about it, so I would be able to check it out and order it if it seemed appropriate. A couple of days later she brought the specifics. It looked like just the thing. I ordered it for my Barbara.

On March 13th as I was transferring Barbara from the toilet to her wheelchair, she and I both about went to the floor. But I was able to pull us out of it. I felt a great need for that new lift which had not yet arrived.

On March 26th when I was giving Barbara her afternoon meds in applesauce, I said, "Does that taste good?" She replied, "Yeah," just as plain as day. She had not spoken at all for quite some time.

On March 28th the new lift was delivered. I was feeling a great need for it. Barbara Richerson was out of town for a few days, so my Barbara was going to have to put up with me full-time!

I was so thankful for the lift. I had been at home alone with Barbara all day and, by using this device, my back was fine. The Hoyer company made this lift too, but it was quite different from the "sling lift" that had been around for quite a while.

On April 12th Scott came by and gave Barbara her annual physical examination. He said we could give her a second Ativan if one did not stop the jerking.

Barbara Richerson told me she had been offered a job with Hospice which paid more. She had not decided what to do. "I would hate to leave Miss Barbara," she said. Of course, she would need to do what would be best for her, but I would really miss her if she did leave. I remembered what a difficult time I had had getting the right person before she came.

On April 26th I took Barbara to the dentist for her teeth to be cleaned. She did fine. Just after we got back home she had a big bowel movement in the toilet. I was so glad that had not happened at the dentist's office.

On April 30th Barbara started small (but strong) jerks before I got her up. I had to give her a pill and put a pillow on the breakfast table in front of her. Several times she slammed her face into the pillow (so was not hurt).

Early in May I went to my 50th college reunion at Wheaton College in Illinois. (Barbara was well cared for at our house the whole time by Lorene Payne and Barbara Richerson). It was good to see old friends back at Wheaton. Most of us looked at least our age (old!), a few looked quite decrepit, and a handful looked younger than they actually were. Some looked much the same, though older. Others did not seem to look anything like they had appeared fifty years before. I wondered if the others could see any traces of my "young face" in my "old face." Our nametags carried our college senior pictures, so we were able to establish the connections even if there had been great changes. Over 80 of our classmates already had died. This whole trip was bittersweet for me. I missed Barbara terribly; she would have enjoyed it so if she had not been ill. Although she had already started to show Alzheimer's symptoms in 1991, when we had gone then to our 35th college reunion (her first time back since we had left Wheaton in 1956), she had been thrilled to walk again on the familiar campus and see some dear old friends. Being at our 50th without Barbara forced me to think again on the brevity of this earthly life. All of us had been young back in our college days, just starting on the journey of our adult lives. Now we were getting toward the end. The old house which had been divided into apartments where Barbara and I had lived our first year of married life (my senior year) had been torn down; new buildings had been built in that spot – a visible illustration of what I was feeling. The 50th reunion trip also filled me with gratitude to God for having allowed me to go to Wheaton and for all the good things that had happened to me there, not the least of which had been the Lord's bringing Barbara into my life.

On May 15th Lorene told me Barbara had said plainly, "I feel good." Lorene had tried to get her to do it again, but there was no response.

June 8th I drove to Burlington, North Carolina for Chad's (Kathy and Powell's son) graduation from high school. (Barbara Richerson and Lorene Payne were taking care of my Barbara at home.)

I felt extremely proud of my grandson as he marched with his classmates down the aisle. (He had maintained straight A's all through school, much better than my record.) Again, I felt very sad that Barbara could not be with me. She would have enjoyed it so much. (Her Alzheimer's symptoms had started about the time Chad was born, but she was able to enjoy him when he was an infant and tiny boy. I remembered the delight I had had in baptizing him when he was about five weeks old. We had taken family pictures after that church service, and they show no one expressing more joy on his or her face than Barbara. [*Chad* is his nickname; he was named after his father who was named for Barbara's father, *Charles Powell*.] We have pictures of an enchanted Barbara feeding Chad in his highchair a few months later. We also have some pictures of Barbara playing with two-year-old Chad in a big box that had contained a stove. They were both having such a good time!) Barbara would have been so grateful that Chad, as he had become old enough to understand, had become a committed Christian who was seriously trusting and following Jesus. The morning after the graduation Powell and Chad took me to see the Community College where Chad would attend in the fall. At noon Kathy had a nice lunch for the larger family who had come for Chad's commencement.

When Barbara Richerson came on June 19th she was crying. The large man she had used that lift with successfully had died.

I got a new phone for Barbara's bedroom on the 21st. A second phone worked off of it by radio. I put that second one in Barbara's bathroom.

On the 27th I discovered a better way of getting Barbara up in the morning: I took the pad she was wearing off before I got her out of bed. That way it did not squeeze out and drip on the floor by the side of the bed. Much better!

On July 25th Greg came by and examined Barbara. He thought her tumor was a little smaller.

On August 1st we had a court hearing to give one of our children authority to take responsibility for Barbara's care in case something should happen to me. The judge's parents had been life-long members of Rivermont Church and I had had their funerals years before, so the whole thing was more like a friendly chat than a formal court proceeding, but it did accomplish the purpose.

Dave Norman visited for a few days, including my birthday. When he went back home (Rome, Georgia) he emailed me: "It was good to see you in your daily environment and how well and lovingly you handle trying times. I am amazed at the 'organized peace' with which you handle everything. It was good to see you are taking good care of yourself too."

In early September Lorene suggested I might want to put a small absorbent pad around Barbara's neck at night, so the drool would not soak her neck and shoulder. Good idea!

In the middle of the month Linda Paulson, the new parish nurse at the church, came to visit us. She was very nice and made a few helpful suggestions.

Barbara became much more difficult to feed because she bowed her head so low; her chin was almost on her chest. I did not know if that hindered her swallowing, or if it was independently failing. Whatever the reason, it took much longer to feed her than it had previously.

I started putting just one earring on Barbara. She bent her head so low the other way, that the earring on that ear was regularly working its way loose and falling either to the floor or down in the chair beside her. We could not usually see the bottom of that ear anyway because of the tilt of Barbara's head.

On September 23rd Barbara had another grand mal seizure. She vomited twice. She remained in that deep, post-seizure sleep. I had a time getting her into bed. I hoped she would rest well.

Sunday, September 24th I could not get Barbara awake in the morning. I did get her up and changed and washed her, but she continued in the kind of sleep that normally came after a seizure, but had never lasted anywhere near that long before. I could not get her to swallow anything. I did get a little juice into her mouth with a syringe, but it simply ran out the corner of her mouth and dribbled down her chin. I put her back to bed.

Lorene came and I went to preach at Pisgah Church. It was their Homecoming, and I was supposed to stay for the "dinner on the grounds," but did not because I felt I needed to get home to see about Barbara. When I got back to our house I found there had been no change in Barbara. I called Scott at home, but no one was there. Then I called Greg at his house. He said he would come right over. I told him I hated to call him away from his family on a Sunday afternoon. But he replied, "I really think I need to come."

Greg arrived in a few minutes. He examined Barbara and thought she had inhaled some vomit and had pneumonia. She did have fever. Greg went to the drug store and came back with antibiotics. He gave her two shots. He had expected that to hurt her, but she did not wince or flinch. She was really "out of it." He said most people would put her in the hospital, but he would try to help me keep her at home. I told him I did not want him to use any heroic measures, but neither did I want to have her neglected.

About 9 PM Greg showed up on our doorstep (on his way home from church). Was I glad to see him! I told him there had not been any change in Barbara that I could observe. He had hoped she would be showing some signs of improvement by then in response to the injections he had given her in the afternoon. He examined her, and agreed that she was no better. "We really need to get her to the hospital," he said. From a couple of things he said, I gathered he had thought I would object, but I did not. By that time I was feeling rather desperate. I called an ambulance. Greg went to the hospital with us and helped us negotiate the emergency room. The charge nurse there said Barbara had taught her in second grade! I went back home and got Barbara's computerized "bubble" mattress cover for them to put on her bed in the hospital because none was available at the hospital that night. I did not want her skin to begin breaking down.

The next morning Barbara was resting comfortably in the hospital. She was getting I-V fluid and her medicine that way. They wondered if she might have had a stroke. Powell drove up from North Carolina. It was very good to have him there.

On Tuesday morning Scott called, and we had a long conversation. He doubted Barbara would be able to be at home again. Dr. de Marchena, the neurologist, came by. He said the EEG and CAT scan did not show anything that would have triggered this episode (such as a stroke). He said he had never had a patient live so long with Alzheimer's Disease, and he had never seen such an atrophied brain. He was surprised Barbara was alive at all. He noted she was very well-nourished and her skin was flawless. He did not believe she could ever come out of this unconscious state. He thought the seizure the previous Saturday had pushed her to this lower level which she had been very near anyway. He said I would need to make some decisions (not that day, necessarily, but before long) about continuing I-V fluids and a feeding tube. I told him I knew right then I would want those things for her, if they were temporary measures to get her back to where I could feed her, but I would not want to prolong her time in a coma if she was going to stay that way for the rest of her earthly life. When he said she would never regain consciousness and get to where she could swallow again, I started sobbing. I was shocked at myself. I had thought all that was behind me. I had known for years that unless something else took Barbara first, that was the way it would end. But it jolted me. I told the doctor I would make my decision within a couple of days, but right at that point I thought I would want to continue the fluids, but withhold a feeding tube.

As Dr. de Marchena was leaving, Gina and Laddie arrived from Richmond. I was so glad to see them! I wept as I told them what the doctor had just told me. We called Mary Beth, Powell and Barbara's sister Charlotte.

(A little later, on reflection, I realized my initial reaction to the news that Barbara was dying was immediate and emotional, not thoughtful or prayerful. That afternoon I prayed, "O Lord, I thank you for letting me have Barbara with me this long. I bow to your sovereign will. If you want to take her home now, 'it is well with my soul,' but if you choose to leave her here a little longer I will be very glad. Not my will, but yours be done; through Jesus Christ our Lord who himself prayed this prayer concerning himself; Amen.")

I talked with Greg. He explained to me why a decision to continue fluids but no feeding tube could be a cruel one. "To continue fluids while withholding food would make Barbara starve to death, and could take a long time because she is unusually well-nourished for someone who has been so sick so long." He asked me to consider discontinuing the fluids and not adding a feeding tube. That would cause much less discomfort to Barbara. Paul Mudrick, another Rivermont Church physician friend, came by and agreed with what Greg had said. He assured me Barbara could be given morphine and Ativan by injection and have no discomfort at all. Death would be expected in a few days.

I shared this with our children. All of them said if I went with Greg's suggestion, they would fully support me. Powell reminded me that Francis Schaeffer had written that Christians had an obligation to sustain life, but were not required to prolong the process of death. I decided I would talk this over with Scott the next day, and, if he agreed with Greg and Paul, I would act according to that advice. I felt very sad about this, but believed it was the best thing to do under the very difficult circumstances, and it was what I would have wanted done to me in a similar situation.

On Wednesday, September 27th in the morning as I drove back to the hospital, I telephoned my friend and lawyer, Dan Sweeney. I told him Barbara was dying, touched on some of the things I had done to prepare, and wondered if there were things I had forgotten.

When I walked into Barbara's room, she seemed somewhat alert (for her at that stage). I offered her a little water in a syringe. She responded to it eagerly and seemed to swallow it well. Then she sipped some from a straw and swallowed it. Scott came by a few minutes later. I told him what I had done and asked him if I could try a little pureed food. He was amazed at this change. He said he would order a "swallow test" to make sure that what Barbara was swallowing was going into her digestive system, not her lungs. Barbara still had a shadow on one of her lungs and a temperature of about 102 degrees.

The swallow test was done, and all seemed normal about the flow. I fed Barbara a little pureed food. She opened her mouth like a begging little bird. Amazing! From death's door to this! I was so thankful.

Mary Beth and her family arrived from Tennessee. They had thought they were coming to a funeral, and now they were so pleased that it did not look that way.

Greg Alty came by. He was happy about Barbara's reversal. The night before Dr. de Marchena had told him Barbara could not possibly pull out of this.

A few spoke of Barbara's improvement as "a miracle." I did not think so. It would have been a miracle if Barbara had recovered from Alzheimer's Disease. But all this little change for the better showed was that doctors, as trained, experienced and intelligent as they are, do not know everything! One of the doctors himself reminded me of that obvious truth. (But then, of course, neither do preachers – or any other human beings – know everything. Only God knows all.)

A few days later Scott told me he did not think I ought to take Barbara home when he dismissed her from the hospital. He felt it would simply be too difficult for me to take care of her – that I would be putting both her and myself at risk. I said, "Let me make a deal with you: I want at least to try it at home. If I feel that I am putting either Barbara or myself or both of us in any danger, I will readily acknowledge it, and we will put her in a nursing facility." He agreed that we could try it.

With a nurse and also Barbara Richerson present in case I should need help, by myself I transferred Barbara from her bed to a chair we had pulled up close. It was really hard to do. She was so limp. But I had done it!

On September 30th an x-ray showed Barbara had a little pneumonia in the other lung! I wondered if her body were trying to shut down. But, when I fed her supper, she ate every bite eagerly.

The next morning I fed Barbara her breakfast. She responded very well. I watched the hospital staff bathe Barbara in bed, so I could do that at home. They even changed the bottom sheet without her leaving the bed. That also was a skill I needed to develop.

I got an idea for when Barbara went home from the hospital: I could put the Hoyer lift sling in her chair, so I could get her out of the chair with the lift instead of pulling her up as I had been doing before this episode.

On October 2nd Scott dismissed Barbara from the hospital. We took her home by ambulance. I followed in the car. I ran to the house, got it opened, and the ambulance workers carried her in. I asked them to put her in her chair in the den. In a short while Barbara Richerson came at her regular time and Greg Alty stopped by to see how we were doing. While they were both there, I told them I would like to try to get Barbara back to the bathroom by myself, but be able to call on them if I should get into trouble attempting to do it. They readily agreed. So they followed Barbara and me back to the bathroom. I was able to do it without their help! I was very pleased. Perhaps I would be able to care for Barbara at home as I so much wanted to do.

Later that day Greg said to me, "You know, when Barbara was diagnosed with cancer two years ago, none of us (meaning the physicians) dreamed she would be living two years later. I know the ultimate reason for her extended life is the Lord's will; he has not been ready to take her to heaven yet. But, I think the main human reason is the devoted love and excellent care she has received. The hospital staff was amazed at the condition of her body. They usually don't see that in someone who has had such a long and severe illness."

Before Barbara had left the hospital our Mary Beth had suggested that I would not need to dress Barbara every day as I had done all the previous years. She said, "I think it is wonderful the way you have kept Mama looking so pretty all the time. But now, I think you need to simplify." I thought she was probably right. I wanted always to take excellent care of Barbara, but now, perhaps, it made sense to eliminate some of the unnecessary frills. It would be just as healthy, safe and comfortable for Barbara, and much easier for me and those who helped me, to keep her in a nightgown most days. Lorene continued to wash, dry, set, comb and style Barbara's hair each week. So Barbara usually looked well-groomed.

That first weekend Barbara was home from the hospital Laddie came and stayed with us to help me in any way he could with Barbara. He loves his mother!

My "Monday through Friday" schedule with Barbara by that time looked like this: I would awaken her about 8:30 AM if she had not wakened earlier. Then I would change and wash her, put a fresh gown on her, carry the things that had gotten wet overnight to the washing machine where I let them soak, take Barbara to the den, put her in her chair, feed her breakfast (which by then took about an hour), return her to the bathroom and sit her on the toilet for a while (sometimes we got results, other times we didn't), then get her back to her chair in the den, and she was ready for our helper to come. In the late afternoon, after feeding Barbara her supper, I made sure she was clean and dry, and put her to bed around 7:00 PM. On Saturdays and some Sundays when I did not preach I took care of Barbara myself. On the Sundays I preached I would get up very early, spend some time in prayer and going over my sermon, and then would get Barbara up, changed, fed and ready for Lorene who would arrive in time for me to get to the church on time.

Linda Paulson suggested a transfer board might help me with Barbara. I bought one, but never found it useful in our particular situation.

I acknowledged to myself that Barbara was by then much harder to care for than she had been before the hospitalization. But I was very grateful to the Lord for giving me the strength necessary to do it. I loved taking care of her.

We continued to feed Barbara pureed food. She ate it well. I no longer fed her grapes and oranges and a cinnamon roll for breakfast because they had told me at the hospital those things might choke her. So her regular breakfast became a mashed banana, a cup of light yogurt, a bowl of oatmeal and apple juice.

I found it was best for me to feed Barbara in her lounge chair in the den by tipping it back all the way. That way, her mouth was easier to reach. By that time we were propping her up in her chair with pillows at her sides. Barbara Richerson fed my Barbara that way too. Lorene preferred to continue feeding Barbara in her wheel chair at the table. Of course, the only thing that mattered to me was that she got the nourishment she needed to sustain her.

In mid-October Barbara's right leg and ankle started swelling. It looked like phlebitis to me. Scott did not think dragging Barbara back to the hospital for tests would be necessary. So he treated Barbara as if she did have phlebitis, and that regimen proved effective.

I picked up our flu shots at Scott's office and our daughter-in-law Kathy, a nurse, who was visiting gave us the injections. I was taught how to give Barbara's "blood thinning" medicine by shots into her abdomen until they were able to get her "pro time" right. (The "pro time" has to do with the clotting quality of the blood. Phlebitis is caused by a blood clot in the leg. Therefore, the medicine is given to lessen the blood's ability to clot. However, care must be taken not to give too much medicine or it will cause internal bleeding, so it has to be carefully monitored regularly.) When the blood was properly regulated by the injections, the proper balance would be sustained by pills for at least six months. The Home Health nurse, Angie White, came by periodically to take blood samples for that purpose. She was so cheerful and helpful and kind.

On October 23rd a large blister came up on Barbara's arm for a reason none of us knew. It broke and bled quite a bit. When Angie came to get Barbara's "pro time," she put a bandage on it.

The next day I cancelled Barbara's appointment to have her teeth cleaned. I could no longer get her in and out of the car, and, because she was on blood thinner, Scott did not think it would be wise at that time anyway. I did not know how we could check and clean her teeth from then on.

October 27th Angie came by to check Barbara's wound and it was much better.

November 10th was Barbara's 73rd birthday. Of course, she was completely unaware of it. But I sang "Happy Birthday" several times anyway.

Laura from Home Health came and "dismissed" Barbara from Medicare Home Health, which she had been accepted into in order to have Angie White come and check "pro times." Lots of paperwork! If Barbara needed them again all the forms would have to be done over.

On November 16th I spoke to a group of pastors at a luncheon on "Caring for a Loved One at Home." It seemed to be well received. Angie White was there and remarked on "the love and peace" she had sensed in our home.

On November 21st Barbara had another "small jerk" seizure. This was the first one she had had since that big seizure in September.

On the day after Thanksgiving, November 26th, I took our larger family to a restaurant for our Thanksgiving dinner. I thought (and the family agreed with me) it was too much by then to try to do at home.

On December 6th I had lunch with Andre Whitehead. He had a public service television program and planned to do one on Alzheimer's Disease. He wondered if he might use our story in it. I told him if it would be helpful to others I would agree. He asked if Barbara at that point knew who I was. I replied, "She doesn't know who *I* am; but I know who *she* is." Later, he told me he had decided to use "I Know Who She Is" as the title of "our" portion of the program.

We had started feeding Barbara more regular food. Although we no longer had to puree it, we used soft foods such as chopped meat, roasted chicken, mashed potatoes, sweet potatoes, casseroles, bananas, and cooked cereal. It worked very well.

On December 11th my first Monday discussion group had our annual supper together. Ed Lovern picked me up to take me to the meal. He loaned me a book the author had given him: <u>Help for Alzheimer's Caregivers, Families, and Friends</u> by Jean Robinson. I found this book to be the most practical thing on the subject I had read. I wished I had had this or something like it twenty years before when

Barbara and I had started our saga. I emailed Mrs. Robinson to compliment her on the book and she replied warmly.

On December 13th I decided to use the Hoyer Lift regularly to get Barbara from her wheelchair to the chair she sat in all day in the den. It required more procedural steps and therefore took longer, but it was much safer and less strenuous. My right arm had begun to hurt most of the time.

At that point Barbara could no longer sustain any support of herself on her legs. She weighed almost as much as I did, so I could not lift or carry her. Because our house was not built with handicap accessible widths, I could not get Barbara down our hall to the bathroom in the lift. But I found that by using the stand-up lift in the bathroom, then putting her in her wheelchair with the sling from the other lift already in the wheelchair, I could take her back down the hall in the wheelchair, then lift her out of it with the other lift and put her in her handicap chair in the den with the sling remaining under her. Then, I could reverse it when we went the other way. And it worked quite well. Another advantage of having Barbara in the standing lift in the lowered position when she was seated on the toilet was that she could not possibly fall off. And that was no small thing. Although this process took a lot more time, it was by far the safest for both of us and therefore the most sensible thing to do.

On December 20th Andre Whitehead came by for a first interview with both Lorene and me. He hoped to have the program ready by the following April.

On December 27th I had a real scare with Barbara. I did not know how she had done it, but when I had her in her standing lift she somehow got her feet off its platform. And I could not get her up or down. She started breathing funny and turned very pale. I was frightened and called 911. They sent three men. We got her down onto the bed. Soon her color returned and she seemed fine. I started tying her legs to the lift, so she could not do a repeat of that morning.

Later I figured out a safer way to place her feet on the platform without tying her legs to it.

In our Christmas letter I said about Barbara:

Early in 2006 we got a new lift for Barbara that pulls her into and supports her in a standing position so I can work on her without danger or discomfort to either of us. What a great help! We almost lost Barbara in September. She did not swallow or respond for four days and nights. The doctor said she could not pull out of it, but she did! And by God's grace we are managing quite well here at home.

CHAPTER EIGHTEEN: 2007

On January 6th Barbara was quite unresponsive. She would not chew, but would swallow baby food and the like. I wondered how much longer she would be with me.

The next day Barbara could chew, but very slowly. It took a long time to feed her, but I was glad she was eating at all.

Barbara's arms and legs were "freezing up," even though we were continuing to do her exercises.

On January 9th I made an appointment with my orthopedic doctor, Cap Eschenroeder. My right wrist was sore and getting worse. It seemed to hurt most when I was working with Barbara.

On January 11th I stopped by Scott's office to get an DNR (Do Not Resuscitate) order. The doctors told me I needed to have it in an easily accessible place at home and inform those who helped me where it was kept. If Barbara's heart should stop, we did not think it would be appropriate to use "heroic measures" to get it going again. Unless ambulance drivers were given such a written order, they would have no choice but to use every means they could to restart it.

On January 15th Lorene got and fixed three flannel nightgowns for Barbara. They were very nice.

On Sunday, January 21st I wrote in my journal: "I had a bad dream last night that woke me up with my heart racing. I dreamed Barbara and I were with a group of people. For some reason Barbara and the group (except me) got on an escalator. She was laughing, but no one knew how to look after her properly and, although I could see them, I could not get to them. Barbara fell over backwards and rolled – head over heels – all the way to the bottom. I started to rush over to where she was, but woke up sweating. Terrifying! Of course, it has been years since she could have gotten on an escalator, but it seemed very real and horrible to me."

For some time I had been missing having a dog. I had always had one when I was a boy. When I was in my early years of high school I had thought seriously about becoming a veterinarian. Barbara and I had regularly had one or two dogs until I had been obliged to give our last one away for Barbara's safety in 1999 because she kept tripping over him and falling. But now, she had not walked in several years. So having a dog again could not carry the same risks we had back then. I had always admired from afar Border Collies, but had never had one. As I read about them I discovered they were exceptionally high-energy dogs. If they were kept in the house and not exercised vigorously every day, they were almost certain to use that energy destructively. So, I knew that was not the breed for me in our circumstances at home.

I found on the Internet a breed I had never heard of, but it seemed to be just what I needed: a Silken Windhound. They are medium sized sight hounds, long-haired dogs which shed very little, if at all. Although they can bark, they rarely do. They are affectionate towards people and not aggressive towards other animals. In fact, they are so friendly they are not recommended as guard dogs. Similar to other sight hounds, they can run like the wind, but are content to snooze much of the time. I telephoned Francie Stull in Austin, Texas (now in Bowling Green, Kentucky), the developer of the breed. She answered further questions for me. I told her our situation which made it necessary for me to get a young adult, housebroken dog. She happened to have a handsome two-year-old dog she thought would be just the thing. I thought about it, and within a couple of hours called her back and told her I would take him. She said her husband Chuck would ship him by plane as soon as he could.

On a Sunday morning one wheel of Barbara's standing lift froze in the "locked" position. Statham Gilliam came and fixed it temporarily with some tape and a paper clip! It would take a few days for the replacement part to come in.

On February 8th our son Powell met me in Hillsboro, North Carolina and we went to the Raleigh-Durham airport to get my new dog, Rocky, from the plane. What a fine-looking fellow he was! The dog and I had a good trip home.

I saw Cap Eschenroeder about my wrist. He said the pain was caused by osteoarthritis. He prescribed some anti-inflammatory medicine (for a limited period) and also a custom made brace for me to wear when I was working with Barbara.

Linda Paulson came by. She wanted me to consider being the facilitator of a new group she planned to start at the church for caregivers. I told her I would if it would be all right with the present pastors and it was.

By March 11th I had used Re-lev-it (an herbal medicine) with good effect for a few weeks. That, together with the brace, had helped my wrist become almost pain-free.

April 17th was the last day for Barbara's "blood thinner." It seemed to have done its job well. There had been no swelling in her leg for a long time.

The next day I noted that both Lorene and Barbara Richerson had said they thought my Barbara's breast tumor was getting larger. Greg checked her. He said, it did feel like it was getting larger, but it really was not. Her medicine suppressed estrogen, so some of her natural breast tissue had shrunk. This made the tumor feel bigger, but actually it remained the same size. I was glad to hear this.

In May Barbara started going to sleep when I would put her to bed, then would wake up anywhere from 2 to 4 AM. Sometimes she sounded as if she were moaning lightly with every breath. I wished I knew what was going on. Scott came by and examined Barbara. He could find no obvious reason why she should be experiencing discomfort or what might be causing the moaning and look of distress on her face. Of course, in a case like this, a physician is pretty much limited to what a doctor can do for a baby: he could not ask where it hurt, but had to go by what he could see, hear, feel and measure with lab tests. He prescribed a morphine-based medicine I could give her when she seemed to be in pain.

In the middle of the month it seemed like Barbara might be on her way out of this world. But then she got a lot better. It turned out I only gave her the new prescription twice. It did the job each time, but then she did not display those symptoms anymore. Her legs were becoming more twisted (especially the right one), and that right leg started trembling a lot.

I noticed that the skin near the center of Barbara's bottom was looking strange, so I started putting Cortisone cream on it and also started using an "egg crate" cushion in the chair in which she spent most of the day. Within a few days her skin was back to normal, but I continued to use the cushion.

Andre Whitehead came by and interviewed Mary Beth (who was visiting from Tennessee) and me separately about Barbara. He had gotten behind in his schedule for producing the program on Alzheimer's, mainly because of the Virginia Tech massacre and Jerry Falwell's death.

On July 14th Barbara fell out of her wheelchair! I cried, but she did not. I examined her carefully and she did not seem to be hurt at all – not even any bruises. I got her off the floor with the Hoyer lift.

On the 18th I took Barbara to have her teeth cleaned by way of a medical transport van where I rolled her wheelchair onto a lift attached to the van.   This was necessary because, since her hospitalization the previous September, I had not been able to get her in and out of the car.   The medical transport worked all right for

Barbara, but it was very difficult for me. I had to stand behind her and put my arms around her chest to make sure she did not fall out of her wheelchair. When we went around curves I had trouble keeping my balance, but I did not fall. Bo Sorenson, our dentist, told me that because it had become so difficult for me to get Barbara to his office, from then on, he and his dental assistant Teresa Cheverton would come to our house. He said they had already talked about it together and planned to schedule Barbara as the last appointment of the day and come by on their way home. How very kind of them!

By early August I had had my dog six months. He had been so good for me! I had never had so gentle a dog. He was a fine companion. The long walks we took together were good for both of us. And sometimes he made me laugh. Shortly after he began living with us, our Mary Beth, with her little girls, visited for a few days. She and her husband had a couple of pretty rambunctious dogs. She said to me, "Daddy, Rocky is so good it is almost like not having a dog!"

On August 13th I thought I could detect that Barbara's breast tumor was getting bigger. Of course, I was not sure: it could be getting larger, but, on the other hand, it could still be the natural breast tissue shrinking. Greg came by to check her. He agreed with me that the tumor was larger. He consulted with Dwight Oldham, the oncologist, and they decided to change her medicine from Aromasin (which she had been given since the discovery of the tumor almost three years before) to Tamoxifen.

At the end of August and beginning of September I had four straight days without any help – my usual helpers were away, and I did not want to go through the uncertainty and anxiety of having unknown substitutes. Barbara and I did just fine. Of course, we were normally without help all day Saturday. But most other days of the week our helpers came in the middle of the day. That meant Barbara and I were usually at the house by ourselves from mid-afternoon to the following mid-morning. And it worked out very well. When my helpers were here with Barbara I was able to run errands, get some exercise playing racquetball and walking the dog, have lunch with friends, work in my garden and do some studying and writing and other projects.

Barbara started having her involuntary "small jerks" about 4:30 AM. I would give her one Ativan with applesauce, and in about forty-five minutes the jerking would stop. Then it would start again about mid-day, and I would give her another pill with the same result. I hoped these would not lead to a big seizure. I remembered what that had led to almost a year before.

September 4, 2007 was our 52nd wedding anniversary. Little did I think at the end of September of the previous year that my bride would still be with me a year later. And I was grateful.

Barbara's very early morning "small jerks" continued. On September 11th I realized she had missed very few nights having them. For example, about 3:30 AM that day she had started, and, even with the medicine, it had taken almost an hour to settle her down. And then it started again at breakfast. Perhaps I should add another pill to her regular schedule just as I put her to bed, and see if that would help with the middle of the night routine. I felt exhausted.

That night Barbara did sleep through the night. By breakfast time she was jerking again, so I gave her another Ativan. In about an hour they stopped.

Greg Alty came by for a visit. I told him what I was doing with the Ativan. He suggested I talk with Scott about it. He thought Scott might think it was time to try another anticonvulsive drug. The last time we had had to stop the anti-seizure medicines because they had made Barbara so extremely drowsy, but now she was always very lethargic anyway. Scott talked with Miles Wallace, the neurologist, who recommended a newer drug (Keppra) which did not usually have some of the negative side effects that the others had had. I was to give her one in the morning and another in the evening. If seizures continued to break through, I could double the dose.

By the end of the following week Barbara had not had a single involuntary "jerk." She did seem a little more in a haze, but not so much so that she could not eat. It seemed to me like a pretty good trade-off.

As Barbara Richerson was leaving our house September 21st, she told me about another patient who called out to her all the time, "Barbara, Barbara! Help! Help! I need you! Barbara, Barbara!" My Barbara started laughing out loud. Her body shook with laughter. We were amazed. Barbara Richerson did it again, and my Barbara laughed again. A little shaft of light pierced the darkness for a few seconds that day.

The weekend of September 22-23, I was very aware that just a year before was when Barbara had gotten so sick the doctors had told me she could not regain consciousness. As a consequence I had prepaid the funeral expenses both at the funeral home and the cemetery. So a year later I knew I had much for which to be thankful to the Lord. Whereas I had not been able to stay at Pisgah Church for their Homecoming "dinner on the grounds," the previous year because of Barbara's emergency, for Homecoming 2007, I did stay. And Barbara was fine with Lorene when I got back home.

I emailed Greg Alty, reminding him that it had been a year since he had come over that Sunday afternoon, had treated Barbara, and then later that evening had helped me get Barbara to the hospital. I said, "Who would have dreamed then that she would still be with me a year later?" He replied:

Lowell, Your loving care of Barbara is so far beyond the experience of any physician taking care of her or any physician caring for someone with her disease, that there is no basis for an informed prediction of her longevity. In other words her longevity is a testament to your love for her. Such love is not often witnessed, and we are all blessed by your example. Greg

On October 2nd Greg and I hiked with Rocky on some trails connected with Peaks View Park. When we got back Greg said it had been a couple of months since Barbara had been on the Tamoxifen. He thought he needed to check her tumor. He did and found that it had grown considerably. Lorene was working that day at our house and said she thought the tumor had expanded a lot in just the past week. Greg said he would consult with Scott Wade (internist), Dwight Oldham (oncologist), and Paul Mudrick (anesthesiologist) about what we ought to do next. Greg observed that with the tumor growing that fast, we probably did not have much time before it would break through the breast wall. He thought perhaps they could use a "local" anesthetic to do surgery. "Three years ago, I never dreamed that Barbara would still be alive. If I had known that then, I would have done surgery then."

Greg called back later. He said Dwight had recommended we change the drug to Megestrol Acetate. However, he was not optimistic about its effectiveness. He said that if one of this family of drugs fails, the likelihood of another working is minimal.

I emailed our children: *Yesterday afternoon Greg came by and examined Mama's breast tumor. It has grown rapidly. Apparently the new medicine she has been on the last two months has not been effective. We are trying a new drug today (which I have yet to pick up from the drugstore), but the doctors are not very optimistic about its working for her. Surgery may be necessary. The oncologist, surgeon, internist, and anesthesiologist are in consultation concerning recommendations for the next step. Just wanted to keep you up to date. I love you all, Dad*

They emailed back and telephoned. They were, as usual, lovingly supportive.

The following night Greg called. He said he wanted us to get head and chest scans of Barbara to make sure the tumor had not spread to her lungs or brain. (The reason for these tests was that if a brain or lung tumor were going to kill her soon anyway, there would be no point in putting her through surgery on her breast.) Greg would call the radiologist's office the next day and arrange it. I guessed I would get her to the radiologist by medical transport. Then, we would schedule surgery pretty soon after that. Greg said, "Of course, with Barbara, this is very high risk. But we can't allow the tumor to break through the breast wall."

I emailed our children:

Greg Alty just called. He has consulted with the other physicians. They think Mama ought to have surgery. But, before that, they want to have her head and chest scanned to see if the tumor has spread to her brain or lungs. I'm not sure when we will be able to schedule either. I will have to get her to the radiologist's office for the scans. Will probably take her by medical transport. Greg does not think it is in either her brain or lungs, but wants to make sure. He had felt yesterday that if she did need surgery, she might be able to have a local anesthetic. But Paul Mudrick believes that would not be wise with her, because for that to be effective, the patient needs to be able to be cooperative. They all realize surgery is especially dangerous for her, but the alternative is not something we can accept. I love you all, Dad

The following afternoon, October 4th I received a phone call from Scott Wade's nurse. They wanted to do the scan and x-ray at the hospital right away. She would send a non-emergency ambulance. I emailed the children:

We are taking Mama to the hospital in a few minutes by ambulance (no emergency) to have her scans done. This has all come about faster than I had expected it. This is all I know. Will keep you posted. Love, Dad

Greg called to inform me of the new plan and was amazed to learn that it was already underway.

The CAT scan and the x- ray showed that Barbara did not have cancer in either her brain or her lungs. Therefore surgery to remove the breast tumor was scheduled for October 11th. Later that evening I emailed a number of friends:

A few days ago we discovered that the pill Barbara was taking to control her breast cancer is no longer working. Today I took her to the radiology department at the hospital to have a CAT scan and an X-ray. These showed that there is no cancer in either her brain or lungs. So surgery to remove the breast tumor is scheduled for next Thursday, October 11th. This is quite high risk for her, but the alternative, to let the tumor break through the breast wall, is not acceptable. I would ask you to pray that the Lord would keep her free of much pain. Beyond that, "Thy will be done," is always appropriate. As most of you know, I have been very blessed in that I have had Barbara much longer than the physicians had thought would be possible. If the Lord should see fit to take her soon, "it is well with my soul," but if the Lord should leave her with me for a while yet, that would be "well with my soul" too. Whatever the outcome, I am full of gratitude to our gracious Savior. Thank you for your prayers. Lowell

I received many gracious and loving responses.

Greg Alty had given up his hospital privileges a couple of years before so he could spend more time with his family, and, from time to time, fill in temporarily for surgeons in Christian mission hospitals. Therefore, he was not in a position to do the surgery on Barbara. He arranged for another surgeon he thought highly of, Robert Bass, to operate on Barbara October 11th. The plan was for her to be taken to the hospital by non-emergency ambulance the afternoon of the day before, have Dr. Bass examine her that evening, and do the surgery Thursday at 12:30 PM.

On Sunday, October 7th Mary Beth, Addie Ruth and Maggie, visiting from Tennessee, worshiped with me at Rivermont Presbyterian. For the Offertory Anthem the choir sang, "For I know the plans I have for you: plans of welfare, not of evil; Plans of hope and a future. I will bring you out of bondage to the land I have prepared. I will bring you out of bondage, I will bring you home to me" (based on Jeremiah 29:11-14). I "claimed" that promise for Barbara.

Wednesday morning the ambulance for transporting Barbara to the hospital had been dispatched to our house. We were waiting. Then the doctor's office telephoned and said the surgeon was out of town and his flight had been cancelled, so the surgery could not be done until Friday. I made some quick telephone calls so people could rearrange schedules.

We got Barbara to the hospital by ambulance Thursday. Rob Bass came by and examined Barbara. Our friend Paul Mudrick who would be in charge of giving Barbara's anesthetic came very early Friday morning to check her.

Barbara's surgery started at noon on Friday, October 12th and lasted about forty minutes. Laddie, Powell and Mary Beth waited with me during that time. When the operation was over, Rob Bass came and told us the surgery had gone very well. Then Paul Mudrick came and said none of the things they had feared had come to pass. They thought Barbara would have a good recovery from the surgery. My children and I thanked the Lord for this very positive report. I fed Barbara her supper, and she ate it all. I spent that night at the hospital by Barbara's bed. She seemed to be doing well.

Greg Alty came by the hospital Sunday afternoon, examined Barbara's incision which he thought looked very good and changed the bandage. He recommended we take Barbara home from the hospital as soon as possible. "The routine you and your helpers have for Barbara at your house is much better for her than what can be done here. You have her out of bed throughout the day and take her back and forth to the bathroom. That regular activity is much better for her skin and circulation than leaving her in bed all the time."

Scott Wade dismissed Barbara from the hospital Monday morning. We returned home, and nothing seemed much different from when we had left, except Barbara's left breast was gone, and, with it, the cancerous tumor. I felt very grateful to the Lord. Angie White, the Home Health nurse, would be coming every other day for a while to check and change Barbara's bandage. I was glad about that because Angie always brought, in addition to her professional competence, a ray of sunshine.

One of my friends said, "Barbara continues to amaze me! She is like the 'Energizer Bunny.' She keeps going and going and going…"

On Wednesday, as Lorene was feeding Barbara her lunch, Barbara burst out laughing a few times. We wondered what was going on in her mind. Might she have been mocking death?

Joe O'Brien, a friend who is a retired physician, telephoned to inquire about Barbara. When I told him she had not experienced any congestion at all following her surgery, nor had any developed since, he said, "I've never heard of that happening before!"

A couple of weeks later Bob Dendy, Superintendent of the Presbyterian Home in Lynchburg, called. (His father and I had been in seminary together.) Bob expressed sympathy because his father, visiting in Georgia a few days before, had heard Barbara had died. The father was in the process of writing me a letter of condolence when he had talked with his son. Bob was glad to know the rumor of Barbara's death was quite premature! He said, "I'll have to call Dad and prevent him from sending you an inappropriate note."

Greg Alty came by the house to check Barbara's incision. He said it was healing nicely – it was dry with no drainage. We would no longer need to keep a bandage over it. It had been exactly two weeks and five days since Barbara's surgery. So our care for her at home would revert to what it had been before her operation. I felt very blessed.

The autumn leaves were especially beautiful in central Virginia just then. That had always been Barbara's favorite season of the year. She had loved the brilliant colors and the crisp air. What a wonderful display of God's artistry! Of course, it had been a very long time since Barbara had been able to notice.

Other than her failing brain which had taken away from her much awareness of anything at all, her speech, her ability to walk or stand, her capacity to turn herself in bed or shift her position in a chair, her capability of sitting up without being propped up, control of her bodily functions, Barbara was in quite good health. Her blood pressure and pulse and oxygen levels were excellent. Although she ate (when we fed her) slowly, she consumed all we offered her, so she had maintained her weight. She had no breaks or sores on her skin except one very small "burn" from the tape on her recent bandage (and we were treating that).

November 10th was Barbara's 74th birthday. I was grateful for all the years the Lord had given us together, and wondered whether, during the following year (until her next birthday) by God's grace he would leave her home with me, or by his grace allow something to happen that would make Barbara's continued homecare impossible, or by his grace take her all the way Home. There was no way for me to know these things, and, of course, that was just as well. But I did understand that whatever came to pass, it would "work together for our good" (Romans 8:28), that *good* being, conforming us more nearly to the likeness of Jesus (Romans 8:29b), according to God's promise. Therefore, I could sing, "It Is Well with My Soul:"

When peace, like a river, attendeth my way,
When sorrows like sea billows roll –
Whatever my lot, Thou hast taught me to say,
It is well, it is well with my soul.

Though Satan should buffet, though trials should come,
Let this blest assurance control,
That Christ has regarded my helpless estate,
And has shed his own blood for my soul.

My sin – O the bliss of this glorious thought –
My sin, not in part, but the whole,
Is nailed to the cross, and I bear it no more:
Praise the Lord, praise the Lord, O my soul!

And, Lord, haste the day when my faith shall be sight,
The clouds be rolled back as a scroll:
The trump shall resound and the Lord shall descend,
"Even so" – it is well with my soul.

(Horatio G. Spafford)

In our 2007 Christmas letter I wrote among other things:

Some of you will remember that in September of last year (2006) the doctors had told me Barbara's death was imminent. Did she fool them! Now, over a year later, no one is offering any speculations on what kind of longevity we might expect for her. I am so glad the Lord continues to enable me to take care of Barbara at home. With a couple of wonderful part-time helpers, I am able to do some studying, preaching and writing, and get a little exercise.

So, at the end of 2007 we raise our "Ebenezer" (which means a memorial "stone of help," 1 Samuel 7:12). "Hither by God's help, we've come." And whatever the future has of wonder, sorrow, disappointment, grief, danger or surprise, it belongs to our Redeemer, Jesus Christ, who has won the victory for his people over sin and death and hell itself, and is sitting at the right hand of the Majesty on High. Therefore, come what may, we will be all right!

On Christmas Day, 1939, during World War II, King George VI of Britain made a radio broadcast to his people. Those were dark days for them – and we know now that they were to get much darker before victory finally came. As Britain looked toward a new year – uncertain and afraid – her king spoke: "And I said to the man who stood at the gate of the year: 'Give me a light that I may tread safely into the unknown.' And he replied: 'Go out into the darkness and put your hand into the hand of God. That shall be to you better than light and safer than a known way.' So I went forth, and finding the Hand of God, trod gladly into the night. And he led me towards the hills and the breaking of day in the lone East" (from Minnie Louise Haskins' "God Knows" in The Desert before the First World War*).*

CHAPTER NINETEEN: WHY CARE FOR BARBARA AT HOME?

People sometimes ask me, "Why do you continue to care for Barbara at home? Why not put her in a nursing home? At this point she would not know the difference, and it would make life much easier for you." Although I have touched on this earlier, I want to give a more complete answer here.

I thank the Lord for nursing homes. They fulfill a critical and necessary role in thousands of lives. I have visited in many nursing homes in the course of my public ministry and my larger family experience, and I acknowledge that this is the best alternative in countless situations. (What else can a family do if the one who would be the caregiver must be away from home at work or is himself or herself either too frail or sick to take on or sustain the task?) I know there are a lot of dedicated, loving and skilled people on the nursing home staffs who labor very hard (it is tough work!), and most of the time get little appreciation for their efforts in either kind words or adequate salaries. My hat is off to them!

But most nursing homes, including the better ones, are understaffed and therefore their employees are overworked. Too many patients are assigned to each caregiver. So it takes even the most conscientious of the "hands on helpers" far too long to make their rounds. (It is usually not their fault.) Therefore the patients, even if they are able to call for help, are apt to get a greatly delayed response if they get one at all. The end result is that the humanity of the patients gets demeaned.

Also, very needy people in nursing homes tend to become malnourished. (It takes me or one of my helpers about an hour to feed Barbara each of her three meals a day. The best nursing home in the world could not afford to keep enough help to spend that much time with each patient who might need it.) A malnourished, bedridden patient will probably develop skin sores which do not heal. And that condition brings on all sorts of serious problems that may hasten death.

Lorene Payne who helps me with Barbara has worked in nursing homes. She said to me once, "If you had put Barbara in a nursing home, she would have died years ago."

For these reasons, if a family can afford it, they provide around-the-clock private duty nurses for their loved one who is in a nursing home. But, even if I were to consider it, which at this time I would not, frankly, taking on the costs of a nursing home plus private duty nurses for an indefinite period would be beyond my means.

At our house Barbara is always the focus of attention. She is loved. She is hugged and kissed a lot. She is spoken to with patience, tenderness, affection and respect. She never sits or lies in a mess for any length of time. She is never scolded or ignored. She is certainly never struck! She gets plenty to eat and drink. If she seems reluctant to take her food or liquid, she is always gently encouraged. Her every move and sound is noted and responded to if needed. I pray with her regularly. So far, I am convinced Barbara receives much better care from me and my helpers than she would get in the best nursing home I could find.

The most important reason I take care of Barbara at home is I feel called by God to do it. I would be like Jonah running from God's call if I should turn away. So long as the Lord gives me the health and strength to do this I plan to continue. Of course, if God were to diminish significantly or withdraw my vigor, he would by his Providence be showing me that he had changed my call. If such a time comes I pray I will make the adjustments graciously. I realize I may reach a point when I can no longer handle Barbara, either because of her increased needs or of my own diminishing ability. I hope not, but I have never said, "never." Only the Lord knows if sufficient strength will be given to me until the end.

There is also the important fact that before God and hundreds of witnesses I made a solemn vow to Barbara, now more than fifty years ago, in the University Methodist Church, Salina, Kansas, "to have and to hold from this day forward, for better for worse, for richer for poorer, in sickness and in health, to love and to cherish, till death us do part." I take this very seriously.

Over the many years of my public ministry, at weddings I never tired of reminding people about to be married that one could not promise or vow how he or she would *feel* five minutes from then, let alone fifty years into the future. The vow to love "till death us do part" was a promise to *act* in a loving way: "Love is patient and kind; love does not envy or boast; it is not arrogant or rude. It does not insist on its own way; it is not irritable or resentful; it does not rejoice at wrongdoing, but rejoices with the truth. Love bears all things, believes all things, hopes all things, endures all things. Love never ends" (I Corinthians 13:4-8a). All of these biblical facets of love are actions, not feelings. And if one acted in a loving way, the feelings could be expected to come right along to match the actions. Obviously, there is nothing in the vows about "getting my own needs met." My job as a husband is to seek to meet my wife's needs. That is at least something of what the Bible means when it says that husbands are to "love their wives as Christ loved the church and gave himself up for her" (Ephesians 5:25).

Robertson McQuilkin tells of a letter written to a national columnist: "I ended the relationship because it wasn't meeting my needs." The counselor's response, McQuilkin says, was predictable: "What were your needs that didn't get met by her in the relationship? Do you still have these same needs? What would she have to do to fill these needs? Could she do it? Needs for communication, understanding, affirmation, common interests, sexual fulfillment – the list goes on. If your needs are not met, split. He offered no alternatives." McQuilkin comments, "There is an eerie irrelevance to every one of those criteria for me." Also from Barbara and me Alzheimer's has stolen all these so called "necessities" and others as well. But Barbara is more precious to me than ever. I could never think of abandoning her. Indeed, it seems the very enormity of her need draws me irresistibly to remain by her side as I vowed long ago I would.

Then too, it is a matter of justice: Barbara took care of me and most of the details of our family's life over our early and middle years to free me for my public ministry. It is only fair that I take care of her now in her time of desperate need.

I hope by my care of Barbara I am setting a good example for God's people. A few years ago the mother of a teenager at Rivermont Church confided to me, "What you are doing is not going unnoticed. My daughter said to me the other day, 'Mom, how do you know before you marry somebody, that if you get sick he'll take care of you like Pastor Sykes takes care of Mrs. Sykes?'." The mother went on to tell me this opened up a very significant conversation about Christian marriage, commitment, faithfulness, keeping of vows with God's help, and the cost of real love. Someone else said to me at the time of my retirement from Rivermont Presbyterian, "As I have sat under your preaching for the past twenty-five years both my mind and heart have been richly fed. But I must say, that what you are doing now is the most important sermon of your life." (And, speaking of sermons, I am more than a little embarrassed when I hear that some pastors are using my care of Barbara as a positive illustration to their congregations. I know so many other people are quietly carrying loads much heavier than mine. And doing what I love so much to do does not seem all that remarkable to me.) To be sure, I am not taking care of Barbara in order to get noticed. But I am glad that apparently through what I am doing a few people are catching a glimpse of something of what love and faithfulness in a Christian marriage might look like.

And, last, but not least, I love Barbara. Of course, I believe caring for her is my duty, but it is not a responsibility I fulfill reluctantly. I enjoy taking care of her. She is my "sweet girl," my "darlin' baby." I am so glad I get to take care of her! I find great satisfaction in keeping her safe, clean, comfortable and loved. It is my distinct privilege to serve her. Of course, I do not by this mean to imply it is all fun. It is increasingly difficult, often frustrating, sometimes baffling, recurrently messy, occasionally frightening, intermittently dangerous, and frequently lonely (as is any grief). But, by God's grace, it is always rewarding.   At this stage of our lives I would not want to be doing anything else.

CHAPTER TWENTY: FOR THE RECORD...

As I approach the close of this account, there are a few things I wish to record that I do not think have received adequate attention so far. (They are not given in their order of importance.)

Some of my readers may wonder why (before I retired) I waited so long to have a companion at home with Barbara. Frankly, as I read my own narrative, I am surprised at that myself. On the one hand, I now regret that I did not make an "executive decision" and insist, even against Barbara's repeatedly expressed wishes. On the other hand, I have known similar cases where the sick person resents the "intrusion" into her or his space and keeps firing the people who have been employed to help. It seems difficult, perhaps impossible, to get this exactly right.

When I came near the time I was to retire from public ministry in order to take care of Barbara, my friend Scott Wade who is also my (and Barbara's) physician gave me some important and good advice: "Be sure to take care of yourself. It is very easy, when you love the person you are caring for as I know you love Barbara, to lose yourself in that increasingly demanding, all-consuming job. But then your own health is apt to give way, and you will be of no use to her. So, eat right, hold your weight down, continue playing racquetball, maintain your friendships, reading and other interests. Do some projects that are unrelated to taking care of Barbara." I have tried to heed his wise counsel. And I would urge others who are in similar situations to consider it seriously.

I note my thanks to the Lord that, although I have written in these pages of a little negative behavior from Barbara, in her this has never lasted long. People with Alzheimer's often get stuck in fear and suspicion of and/or hostility towards those who are trying to help them. Even if the caregiver understands this is a part of the disease, it is still very hard to be trying one's best to help and regularly get falsely accused, yelled at or physically attacked. For the most part Barbara has been very sweet during this trial – another gift. Her tendency has been to become more like a little girl, rather than to get mean. Her ugly words and defensive behavior have been so minimal it would have been easy not to record them at all. But, since I have wanted to give as complete a picture as possible, I have not omitted them. To tell the truth, if Barbara had not been sick, I expect she would have said many more negative things to me than she has during her entire illness!

Another thing, if Barbara suddenly had become as disabled as she is now, I am not sure I could have taken care of her at home. I believe I would have felt overwhelmed with what would have seemed like an impossibly difficult task. But the fact is, all this has come on gradually. So I have had an opportunity to learn from others or figure out myself, a little at a time, what has been needed. And, so far, by God's grace, taking care of Barbara at home has been possible.

I think it is important, when a person is going down the Alzheimer's trail, for the caregiver to do for the patient what she or he can no longer do, but not try to take over tasks the sick one can still accomplish. Obviously, that is sometimes difficult to discern. However well meant, the one giving the care will make mistakes along these lines. Sometimes, to offer assistance with a task in a gentle way, for example, "Let me help you with that, Darlin'," or "Would you like for us to do this together?" gets good results. What never works is confronting or arguing or criticizing. Let it go! The person with Alzheimer's does not need to be "straightened out." It helps tremendously if she or he is happy and content. The situation is stressful enough without the caregiver making it more so by trying to get the sick person to acknowledge "the facts" or "the truth."

At this point Barbara does not smile as frequently as she did before her hospitalization in 2006, but I can almost always count on a smile from her when I wash her face with a warm cloth (especially when I get to her "chinny-chin-chin" and speak of it) before I get her out of bed in the morning, when I brush her teeth, when I give her crushed pills in applesauce or liquid medicine and say to her, "You ate (or drank) the wh – O – O – O – le thing!," and when I tuck her into bed at night, tell her I love her and Jesus loves her and sing to her,

"Jesus Loves Me, This I Know, for the Bible Tells Me So." Occasionally she smiles when I say, "You are a fine woman! Pretty too!" So, although Barbara is no longer very responsive, she sometimes can and does react to thoughtful attention. Intermittently she still smiles when I hug and kiss her. She seems to find special pleasure when I take her cheeks in my hands and talk to her. Sometimes I simply hold her face, on other occasions I stroke her cheeks.

Barbara has always liked music. She had a very pretty voice. Before she got sick, we sometimes sang together. As Alzheimer's Disease increasingly robbed her of most things that matter, she continued to respond to music and would sometimes hum along. She did this at church as long as she could. Although she is unable now to hum a tune, occasionally she does hum off key as music is playing. Because music has seemed to soothe her restlessness I have usually had either hymns or "easy listening" songs playing in the background.

And, throughout the course of this illness, I have sung with, for and to Barbara. For years when I have wakened her in the morning I have sung a silly song I made up, "Good morning, good morning, good morning to you; Good morning, Miss Barbara, and how do you do? This is my sweet Barbara, her name's Barbara Jean; She is my sweet darlin', she is my queen." Another fun song I made up and sing to the tune of the theme of "The Beverley Hillbillies:" "This is my sweet girl and her name is Barbara Jean, and I want you to know she is every bit a queen; And something else you need to know is she is very clean! And she's so sweet, she's never, never mean! This is my sweet girl, Barbara Jean."

I think it is important for a caregiver to cultivate a sense of humor. It is better to laugh at some of the preposterous situations you have to manage than to cry!

Also, try to let the enormity of the *big problem* you are dealing with every day, give you a sense of perspective about everything else. There is so much that can threaten to upset us! But make an effort to measure all such things by saying to yourself, "If this were the biggest problem facing me, I would be just fine!"

Although Alzheimer's is a dreadful disease, it seems to me, so far as the impaired person is concerned, there is a "mercy" in it. That is the fact that, except for a comparatively brief period in the early stage when the sick person does realize abilities are slipping away and gets frustrated because of it, the ailing one's brain soon becomes so foggy that he or she cannot step back and look at all the diminishments. By the time the symptoms get severe the patient is unaware of them. Certainly, the caregiver bears the awareness and the accompanying grief.

By now most people in our culture are familiar with the "stages of grief" first defined by Dr. Elizabeth Kubler-Ross, in her book <u>On Death and Dying</u> (1969): Denial, Anger, Bargaining, Depression, Acceptance. This familiar pattern can usually be noted when a person experiences any significant loss. Of course, this includes when you love someone who has Alzheimer's Disease. But this illness goes on and on and on..., and so does the grief it produces. As with any grief, there is a loneliness about it. You know that even the people who are closest to you, who care the most, even those who have had a similar experience, cannot possibly know just how your own life has been and continues to be turned upside down. You come to realize that the depth of your grief is your own in a way that it cannot be anyone else's. If you are a Christian you can sing from your heart the old African American spiritual:

Nobody knows the trouble I've seen,
Nobody knows, but Jesus.

And you are grateful that you can turn to Jesus in prayer. Jesus knows; Jesus understands; Jesus cares "for we do not have a high priest (Jesus) who is unable to sympathize with our weaknesses, but one who in every respect has been tempted (or tested) as we are, yet without sin. Let us then with confidence draw near to the throne of grace, that we may receive mercy and find grace to help in time of need" (Hebrews 4:15, 16).

Occasionally someone tries to probe my feelings about all this. It seems he or she assumes that, given my circumstances, underneath my calm exterior I must be seething with resentment. I am asked questions like, "Don't you get angry with Barbara – at least from time to time? Do you ever wish she would die?" I did get angry with her before I knew what was wrong. Back then, it sometimes seemed that she was being stubbornly unreasonable, and I would feel defensive and set out to "bring her around," with some harsh words of my own. But when the truth became known to me, I felt very ashamed for having spoken sharply to her, even out of my ignorance. And truly, since her diagnosis, I cannot remember being angry with her at all. She could not help what was happening to her. I felt it was much worse for her than it was for me. So, although I have felt grief, frustration, and sorrow for her (and myself, not because of what I do for Barbara, but because I have lost her – almost – as she has gradually faded before my eyes), I don't think I have felt any hostility towards her. I thank the Lord that he has filled my heart with compassion for my dear, helpless wife – this is a gift from God. I know it has been made easier for me to have had a keen sense of God's call to this task. And the Lord has accompanied that call by giving me a love for it. I really do delight in taking care of my Barbara. Perhaps this is the primary reason I have never resented "doing" for her. The psalmist said, "I delight to do your will, O God; your law is within my heart" (Psalm 40:8). It seems to me this is the joyful obedience of a loved child, not the sullen, resentful submission of a cringing slave. Because serving Barbara and her special needs is now God's primary call to me, Barbara is in no way "interfering" with my life. She *is* my "life's work" during this season of our marriage. Indeed, anything that would get in the way of my helping her would be meddling with my call, and need to be eliminated or curtailed.

I have never wished that Barbara would die. If she does go before I do, I know I shall miss her terribly. After all, for many years now taking care of her has been the primary focus of my life. (When she was in the hospital recently and I would come home for brief periods I found myself constantly listening for her, starting to go check on her and then I would realize, "She is not here." And I would become conscious of how much I pined for her.) I have wondered what in the world I will do if I outlive her and still am blessed with good health. I have not been one to look forward to "doing nothing." Well, for one thing, I will visit my children and grandchildren. (I give them fair warning!) For another, because I have learned a lot about caring for a totally helpless person over these years, I have thought, when Barbara no longer needs me, I might offer my services as a volunteer to help other utterly dependent people. But of course, Barbara may outlive me!

I do not mean to imply that any feelings of anger on the part of a caregiver are wrong or show a lack of faith. If someone is yelling at you, accusing you falsely, lashing out at you, misunderstanding you, demanding what you cannot possibly give, even if he or she cannot help it, it is very hard to take. Don't add to your burden that of guilt for very natural feelings. Accept the negative emotions for what they are, do the loving thing, and get on with your day.

I have been asked many times, "Don't you wonder why God has allowed this to happen? Aren't you angry with God?" Although I do not think it wrong to ask God "Why?," (after all, God did not reprove Job for his relentless questioning – even anger – and Job had a pretty robust faith), I have not wondered and I am not angry with God. Indeed, me angry with God? Because I am a sinner, God has every reason justly to be angry with me. But he is not! In Christ God loves me, receives me, forgives me, adopts me into his family and sustains me. And I am eternally grateful for such grace.

After a lifetime of pastoral work, dealing with people in all kinds of crises, I have discovered that God rarely answers our "Why?" about the painful particulars of our lives. We live in a fallen world where awful things happen. Rather than ask, "Why me?," I think it is more appropriate to put it this way, "Why not me?" God does not need to explain our agonizing experiences to us at the present time. If we know God, we recognize there is an ultimate purpose, but we don't necessarily understand what it is now. Our responsibility is to "trust and obey," with the assurance that, if we need to by then, "we'll understand it better by and by." The cross of Jesus Christ is the evidence of infinite weight that God loves us. All the pain and agony, sorrow and grief that can be piled up as negative evidence, cannot hold a candle to the blazing light of the cross.

I hope my readers will have noticed that several times in my account, when I have gotten near the end of my rope and wondered how I would be able to continue, a fresh idea (either from someone else or that I have thought of myself), or a different procedure, or a new device has enabled me to carry on. I do not for a minute think these "helps" came about or to my attention by chance. I believe they are evidences of the Providence of God. And I am grateful to God, the Father of lights with whom there is no variation or shadow due to change, from whom comes every good and perfect gift (James 1:17). Of course, by saying this, I do not mean to imply that I am certain that solutions for my care of Barbara at home will be provided until the end of our journey along this road. Only God knows that. In the meantime, we walk one day at a time.

The other morning a news broadcast was playing in the background as I was feeding Barbara. Because my focus was on her, I really had not been listening. But, all of a sudden I heard someone say, "My joy is back; my peace is back." Since that sounded like a Christian testimony I started paying attention. But it was only a commercial for a product which promised hair restoration! As one who has inherited male-pattern baldness from both sides of my family, I know that more hair on my head would bring me neither joy nor peace. But I do know where true joy and peace are to be found – in Jesus Christ my Lord. Another promotion, from a life insurance company, assured me that with the right financial planning – with them, of course – they could "assure your future" for "the future belongs to you." Then came the assertion, from an airline, "Where you go in life is up to you." I laughed out loud in scorn. What arrogance! If people believe these lies they get hooked by a false god who at best will disappoint them, and, if followed to the end, will utterly dash them on the rocks. A terminal disease might help bring them back to reality before it is too late. In that sense the illness becomes, as C. S. Lewis pointed out "a severe mercy."

Death is out there stalking all of us. And he will get us – sooner or later – in the end. It will be disastrous to place our ultimate confidence in ourselves or other earthly things. Only God is worthy of such trust. Jesus said, "I am the way, and the truth, and the life. No one comes to the Father except through me" (John 14:6). "I am the resurrection and the life. Whoever believes in me, though he die, yet shall he live, and everyone who lives and believes in me shall never die" (John 11:25, 26). Our Lord Jesus, by his own death and resurrection, has pulled the stinger out of death! Thus, we can taunt death: "O death, where is your victory? O death, where is your sting?" And we shout, "Thanks be to God who gives us the victory through our Lord Jesus Christ" (I Corinthians 15:55b, 57).

CONCLUSION

It may seem presumptuous to write a "conclusion" before the conclusion. After all, Barbara is still living. There will be more to this story. But I have no way of being certain that I will outlive Barbara, or, if I do, that I will be capable of writing the real finish. Both my grandfathers did not know, when they got up the last morning of their earthly lives, that they would not see the sun set on that day or any other day. They died suddenly and unexpectedly of heart attacks – one, when he was 67, the other 79. At the present time I am in the middle of this age range. So I write this premature "ending" now. If I am able, I may write the real earthly conclusion some day. If not, at least this much is preserved.

Not long ago I was talking with an old friend who is my age and continues to have a wide ranging public ministry in many places around the world. He said that he sometimes hesitated to share with me his itinerary, because he was afraid it might make me feel badly that my own sphere had become so restricted. But I assured him that was not the case. "I rejoice in the ministry the Lord continues to give you. And I pray for you regularly. I want very much to know all about it. In no way do I feel "cheated" that my vocation is different from yours at the present time. I am happily content to be fulfilling what I believe is God's call to me now at home." And I meant every word.

In <u>A Testimonial to Grace</u>, Father Avery Dulles wrote, "If I had been asked to choose the course of my life I would not have done as well as the leading of Providence and the direction of superiors have done for me. I can honestly say that there is no one in the world whom I have cause to envy. All of this is not of my own deserving. It is God's gift, and he alone deserves the praise." If I were to delete the phrase about religious superiors (he is, after all, a Jesuit), I could say exactly the same thing.

This is a road I never would have chosen. But since it has been given, my responsibility is to run it well for the glory of God,

Barbara's welfare, the surrounding "great cloud of witnesses" (Hebrews 12:1) and my own fulfillment. For I believe with all my heart that to do God's will is to find our own deepest joy. And I have no doubt that I am finding mine. What more could I ask? In the words of the Apostle Paul, "in all our affliction, I am overflowing with joy" (2 Corinthians 7:4c) So, although I bear a great grief, I am a profoundly contented and happy man.

The Heidelberg Catechism asks those who are living by faith in Jesus Christ: *What is your only comfort, in life and in death?* (Question #1), and answers gloriously: *That I belong – body and soul, in life and in death – not to myself but to my faithful Savior, Jesus Christ, who at the cost of his own blood has fully paid for all my sins and has completely freed me from the dominion of the devil; that he protects me so well that without the will of my Father in heaven not a hair can fall from my head; indeed, that everything must fit his purpose for my salvation. Therefore, by his Holy Spirit, he also assures me of eternal life, and makes me wholeheartedly willing and ready from now on to live for him.*

And, *What do you understand by the providence of God?* (Question #27) *The almighty and ever-present power of God whereby he still upholds, as it were by his own hand, heaven and earth together with all creatures, and rules in such a way that leaves and grass, rain and drought, fruitful and unfruitful years, food and drink, health and sickness, riches and poverty, and everything else, come to us not by chance but by his fatherly hand.* Then, *What advantage comes from acknowledging God's creation and providence?* (Question #28) *We learn that we are to be patient in adversity, grateful in the midst of blessing, and to trust our faithful God and Father for the future, assured that no creature shall separate us from his love, since all creatures are so completely in his hand that without his will they cannot even move.*

The following hymn, based on "Will not the Judge of all the earth do right?" (Genesis 18:25), puts this truth in poetic form:

Whate'er my God ordains is right:
His holy will abideth;
I will be still whate'er he doth,
And follow where guideth.
He is my God;
Though dark my road,
He holds me that I shall not fall:
Wherefore to him I leave it all.

What'er my God ordains is right:
He never will deceive me;
He leads me by the proper path;
I know he will not leave me.
I take, content,
What he hath sent;
His hand can turn my griefs away,
And patiently I wait his day.

Whate'er my God ordains is right:
Though now this cup, in drinking,
May bitter seem to my faint heart,
I take it, all unshrinking.
My God is true;
Each morn anew
Sweet comfort yet shall fill my heart,
And pain and sorrow shall depart.

Whate'er my God ordains is right:
Here shall my stand be taken;
Though sorrow, need, or death be mine,
Yet am I not forsaken.
My Father's care
Is round me there;
He holds me that I shall not fall:
And so to him I leave it all.

(Samuel Rodigast, 1675, Tr. By Catherine Winkworth, 1863)

BRIEF COMMENTS FROM THE FAMILY

"In all things give thanks." "Put Christ first, the rest will be provided according to God's plan." Two lives living these principles with a bounty of understanding, raising the three of us children – what a wonderful place to learn what it is to be a husband and father. I miss you, Mom; I love you, Dad. Thanks for all you have been in my life and all this book can mean to those who read it. Your faith and commitment shine as a lighthouse in the storm, amid the turmoil of life.

– Lowell Beach Sykes, Jr. (Laddie)

Richmond, Virginia

My father has written this book for others who wonder what might happen, given Mom's unusual longevity, and as a witness to the grace of Jesus in his life at a time most people would imagine as one of despair. For me it is a hard read. And yet, it is honest, and a complete fulfillment of the direction to be witnesses of God's grace. I'd rather read about God working his purpose out through neat, tidy circumstances, interesting and surprising plot twists. That's not here. But if we have no hope in the face of death, a hope which must reside in the life to come proclaimed in the resurrection of Jesus, what hope is there?

– C. Powell Sykes, Pastor

Westminster Presbyterian Church

Burlington, North Carolina

"A wife of noble character who can find? She is worth far more than rubies... Her children arise and call her blessed; her husband also, and he praises her" (Proverbs 31: 10, 28). I am truly thankful for my mother and the example she set for me as a loving wife, a supportive mother and a godly woman. I miss her very much. I pray that I can set a similar example for my two young daughters.

– Mary Beth Sykes Marcum

Cookeville, Tennessee

By the time I came into the family, my mother-in-law was already very sick with Alzheimer's Disease, so I have gotten to know her only indirectly, by the values she instilled in her children. Her faith in the Lord and her love for her family were her heart. Given all she has been through, many others would have given up by now. She keeps going, and with her passion for life, she hangs on and lives each day as fully as she can. I'm confident she is ready anytime to hear God call her home, but for now he is allowing her to continue to do his work right here on earth. My mother-in-law is truly an amazing woman!

Gina Sykes, Richmond, Virginia

As I read through this book, I experienced an array of emotions ranging from joy to sadness. I have regretted that my relationship with Barbara was interrupted by this vicious disease. I always appreciated her honest approach. One of the sweetest things that she ever did for me was to attend a Toastmistress meeting where I was giving a speech. I remember that she stayed till it was over and told me afterwards that I had done a good job. That was before I became her daughter-in-law. She was so welcoming to my young daughters, Jodie and Christie. She treated them just as she would have had they been her own biological granddaughters. I look forward to the day when we can take up where we left off, when we can talk and laugh and praise our Lord as we bask in his presence where disease and lost time will no longer exist.

– Kathy Sykes

Burlington, North Carolina

Be still, my soul; the Lord is on your side;
Bear patiently the cross of grief or pain;
Leave to your God to order and provide;
In every change he faithful will remain.
Be still, my soul: your best, your heav'nly Friend
Through thorny ways leads to a joyful end.

Be still, my soul: your God will undertake
To guide the future as he has the past.
Your hope, your confidence let nothing shake;
All now mysterious shall be bright at last.
Be still my soul: the waves and winds still know
His voice who ruled them while he dwelt below.

Be still, my soul: when dearest friends depart,
And all is darkened in the vale of tears,
Then shall you better know his love,
Who comes to soothe your sorrow and your fears.
Be still, my soul: your Jesus can repay
From his own fullness all he takes away.

Be still, my soul: the hour is hast'ning on
When we shall be forever with the Lord,
When disappointment, grief, and fear are gone,
Sorrow forgot, love's purest joys restored.
Be still, my soul: when change and tears are past,
All safe and blessed we shall meet at last.

(Katharina von Schlegel, 1752; Tr. by Jane Borthwick, 1855; modernized, 1990)

SUGGESTIONS FOR FURTHER READING

Davis, Robert. *My Journey into Alzheimer's Disease.* Wheaton, Illinois: Tyndale House Publishers, Inc., 1989.

Mace, Nancy and Rabins, Peter. *The 36-Hour Day*, Rev. ed. Baltimore: The Johns Hopkins University Press, 1981, 1991

McKim, Donald K., editor. *God Never Forgets.* Louisville, Kentucky: Westminster John Knox Press, 1997.

McQuilkin, Robertson. *A Promise Kept.* Wheaton, Illinois: Tyndale House Publishers, Inc., 1998.

Robinson, Jean. *Help for Alzheimer's Caregivers, Families and Friends.* Ormond Beach, Florida: Calm Waters Publishing, 2006. (This is the best "practical help" book I have seen, a "must read." Mrs. Robinson, who at the same time gave home care to her husband and mother, both Alzheimer's victims, lists Alzheimer's warning signs, evaluations and treatments, menu, nutritional analysis, home safety tips, personal care information, activities ideas, challenging behavior coping suggestions, Alzheimer's stages guide, where to turn for help in caring for a loved one with Alzheimer's, physical activity/exercise agendas, medication for Alzheimer's, legal and financial information, and caring for the caregiver's needs.)

Shenk, David. *The Forgetting.* New York: Anchor Books, 2001, 2002.

Strom, Kay Marshall. *A Caregiver's Survival Guide.* Downers Grove, Illinois: InterVarsity Press, 2000.

ABOUT THE AUTHOR

Lowell Beach Sykes has been a Presbyterian minister for almost 50 years. He is a graduate of Wheaton College in Wheaton, Illinois, Columbia Theological Seminary, Decatur, Georgia, and received a Doctor of Ministry from McCormick Theological Seminary in Chicago. He was awarded an honorary Doctor of Divinity from King College, Bristol, Tennessee. Over the course of his public ministry he has served churches in Georgia and Virginia. He retired from his pastorate earlier than he had planned so that he could become the primary caregiver for his wife Barbara in their home in Lynchburg, Virginia. She has had Alzheimer's Disease for about 20 years. They have three grown children, several grandchildren and one great-grandchild. Part of the time Pastor Sykes has a helper at the house with his wife, which enables him to do errands, get some exercise, study, and do a little writing and supply preaching. He might on occasion find opportunities to respond to emails concerning this book: lbsykes@juno.com. In addition he has published two books of sermons, Why I Am a Christian and Other Sermons and Offended by Jesus and Other Sermons also available from Lulu.com.